RYAN CARADONNA
JAKE CAINES

DEBUNKING
THE LEADERSHIP
MYTH

CONSCIOUS
LEADERSHIP

RYAN CARADONNA
JAKE CAINES

DEBUNKING THE LEADERSHIP MYTH

THE STORY OF CONSCIOUS LEADERSHIP

5I'S PUBLISHING

Pennsylvania

DEDICATION

From Ryan:

To the leaders who made a conscious choice to invest in me, transforming me by making me a part of your stories—this book is a result of your impact on my life. To Lindsay, whose constant support and encouragement made this book possible—I am thankful that we get to tell our story together. To Chase, as you begin to write your story—may this book serve as a guide. The significance of your story will be determined by your impact on people.

From Jake:

This book and its intrinsic philosophy are dedicated to the many people that have impacted my leadership journey. To my best friend, Molly, for being an amazing wife and mother and for always ensuring that I "keep it at a conscious level." To my extraordinary daughter, Zoe, for inspiring me in ways that words cannot capture and for the incredible story that you have just begun to write. Thank you all for your consistent and continuous wisdom and for investing in my story at the belief level.

CONTENTS

INTRODUCTION
PLAGIARISM

*"We **know** what we are, but **know** not what we may be."*
   - William Shakespeare

"The reasonable man adapts himself to the world. The unreasonable man persists in trying to adapt the world to himself. Therefore all progress depends on the unreasonable man."
   - George Bernard Shaw

This book is written for leaders who are frustrated with the current state of leadership. It seems that leadership, as currently practiced, doesn't matter. It isn't powerful; it doesn't make a difference, nor does it accomplish anything significant.

Leadership should be characterized by impact. Impact is more than change; it is *transformational* change. Impactful leadership should be able to take a bad situation and make it better. It should be able to transform negative circumstances into positive outcomes.

Today's leadership might not be dead, but it's definitely dormant. It is certainly not impactful; it lacks both the ability and the power to generate transformational change. Occasionally, current leadership will result in change, but the change is rarely meaningful, relevant, or substantial. This leaves you constantly frustrated and disappointed, because this is the exact opposite of what you expect from leadership.

We are all familiar with the legendary stories of leadership: Churchill, Lincoln, Thatcher, Gandhi, and so on. We know these stories because of the impact generated by these leaders. Leadership that generates legendary impact results in legendary stories. But when we examine today's leadership and the tales of current leaders, we quickly discover that they bear no resemblance to these great stories.

Does the leadership you currently experience resemble impact? Probably not. Most likely, it doesn't even come close. Although you could think of several words that could describe today's leadership, "impact" isn't one of them. The leadership you encounter is neither powerful nor significant, neither inspirational nor meaningful.

Current leadership doesn't create transformational change, but it does maintain the status quo. It champions the value of "normal" by constructing systems of control, ensuring that tomorrow does not vary too much from today.

Unfortunately, your experience with leadership has become the status quo, but it doesn't have to remain the status quo. Leadership is about creating transformational change—change that is substantial and significant. As fellow leaders, you can impact the current state of leadership and construct a new standard.

So what should this new standard of leadership look like? Or ask yourself a better and more personal question: How do you want to be described as a leader?

A leader should:
- Generate sustainable impact consistently
- Create transformational, substantial change—in yourself and others
- Perform at levels of excellence
- Work more efficiently and effectively, producing positive results in less time
- Connect with and motivate people through meaningful relationships
- Discover new ideas and breakthrough innovation
- Challenge conventional boundaries and normal solutions
- Develop other leaders

That's a pretty lofty description. But is it unrealistic? Do you think it sounds like fiction? We don't think so. This should be the standard of leadership, and this is how *you* could lead.

So what happened? Can leadership be fixed? Can it once again be capable of generating impact? Can you change the status quo and create a new standard?

We will answer all of those questions—and there is good news! But first, we will start by telling you a story.

The Story

All leaders write a story.

Some stories serve as inspiration, others as a warning. The majority of leaders write stories that have been forgotten. Unremarkably normal, these stories have never been retold. They fade into obscurity not because they were bad but because they were meaningless.

However, throughout history the stories of a few leaders stand out. These are the rare stories full of meaning and impact. They motivate you and excite you because they matter. These stories should provide both insight into the ingredients required for impactful leadership and clues as to what is missing from current leadership.

It is difficult to determine the common thread shared between these stories of leadership. Although all of these stories are impactful, some of them are as different as night and day. Churchill's story of impact is told through war and strategic aggression. Ghandi's story of transformational change is told through non-violence and pacifism.

The commonalities shared between the legendary stories of leadership appear to be more coincidental than causative. So what now? The conventional approach is one of limited extraction and insight. It examines these stories to find which leadership behaviors resulted in success, and it then seeks to apply them in current context.

This results in the compilation of lengthy leadership manuals, each containing checklists of appropriate leadership behaviors. We are told that leaders can generate impact by following these manuals precisely. We are told leaders can create transformational change by understanding what to do. This is a myth, and it is the result of asking the wrong question.

The question, "What commonalities exist between the legendary stories of *leadership?*" yields a set of disparate answers. The stories of Churchill's leadership and Ghandi's leadership are vastly different. Churchill created impact through one particular set of behaviors, while Ghandi created impact through a completely different set of behaviors.

However, the question, "What commonalities exist between the legendary *leaders* who wrote stories of leadership?" yields a much more concise set of answers. As leaders, Churchill and Ghandi shared many character traits. Undoubtedly, their characteristics were not identical; they were different individuals. However, there were many qualities of character that were held by both Churchill and Ghandi.

A leadership story is not legendary because of the *topic*. A leadership story is legendary because of the *author*.

The Myth
"A lie told often enough becomes the truth."
    - Vladimir Lenin

This represents the foundational myth that has permeated the current state of leadership. This myth is one of focus. It has rendered today's leadership incapable of generating impact by adjusting its foundation. The myth shifts leaders' perspective and focal point:
- **The myth:** Leadership is about what you should do.
- **The truth:** Leadership is about who you could be.

The appeal of this myth is subtle; the acceptance of this myth is insidious.

This myth is appealing because, on the surface, it makes sense. Transformational change is created through tangible actions. Churchill and Ghandi were able to generate impact because of what they did. Their actions led to results.

This myth is also appealing because it is relatively easier to obtain and measure than the truth. It is easier to evaluate leadership by its quality of its actions than by the quality of the individual who was responsible for those actions. It is also easier to *do* something than it is to *become* someone.

However, if accepted as truth, this myth will slowly destroy leadership, rendering it incapable of generating impact. This is exactly what we observe regarding current leadership. Why is this myth so destructive? The principle of behavioral obsolescence.

Circumstances change. Actions that lead to success today will contribute to failure tomorrow. The level of impact created by your actions is directly determined by the context in which those actions were performed. A different context requires a different set of actions. Thus, memorizing a complex manual of leadership behaviors and checklists is not only frustrating, it is also fruitless.

Impactful leadership is a result of a leader choosing the appropriate action dictated by each unique situation. These behaviors will change, so it is critical that their source—the leader—be capable of determining the appropriate action for each situation. Unfortunately, by focusing on what leaders do instead of who leaders are, the ultimate result of accepting this myth as truth is the reduced capability of leaders to make these decisions.

Coming to Terms

"I therefore claim to show, not how men think in myths, but how myths operate in men's minds without their being aware of the fact."
- Claude Levi-Strauss

Although this myth is foundational, it isn't the only one to have permeated current leadership. There are other derivative myths which we will expose and debunk during the course of this book. This shifted focus from "who leaders are" to "what leaders do" explains much of the current state of leadership.

This myth explains why today's leadership doesn't work. We could provide you with volumes of evidence to support this broad claim (including metrics regarding bankruptcies, integrity violations, and organizational failures). But despite the quantity and quality of external data, the best evidence is your personal testimony. You could serve as the prosecution's star witness. Through experience, you know that today's leadership lacks the power to generate impact.

Despite its inability to generate impact, this form of leadership has garnered tremendous support. It is tangible, measureable, and easier than the alternative. Unfortunately, it is also temporary and requires constant retraining as changing circumstances require different actions.

Organizations currently spend tens of billions of dollars per year on corporate training, much of which is classified as "leadership" training. "Leadership" has been commercialized, and it is now offered as a panacea for every type of issue or problem. Although the presence of leadership has expanded, the resulting impact has contracted.

This form of leadership takes on many disguises, but fundamentally it is all the same. This myth might present as something new and different, such as "Strategic Leadership," "Value-Driven Leadership," "Leadership on Purpose," or "Solutions-Based Leadership." But it's not really new, nor is it really different.

And the results aren't different, either. They won't matter. It is just the same old thing dressed up as something new. Fundamentally, all of the leadership forms resulting from this myth are the same because they follow the same conventions.

For the sake of simplicity, we have aggregated the various forms of leadership spawned by this myth into a single term:

"Conventional Leadership"

Conventional leadership is a myth. It doesn't work. And it is guilty of plagiarism.

Conventional leadership is founded on the myth that leadership is about "what we should do" instead of "who we could become." However, it has assimilated many other myths into its paradigm over time. Skimming through the stories of legendary leaders, conventional leadership lifted elements that were convenient for its purposes. It then combined those elements with its own fables and fairytales. The result? An imposter, a fraud, a fake, a myth!

Conventional leadership possesses the form, but not the function, of genuine leadership. It looks the part, but it can't play the part. There is one element of the genuine leadership story that is impossible for conventional leadership to consistently plagiarize—*impact*. Despite the increased focus on leadership, there has not been an increase in transformational change. Conventional leadership doesn't work. And the story of conventional leaders, void of impact, will be immediately dismissed and forgotten. This might not bother the majority of conventional "leaders." But it bothers you, just like it bothers us.

But it doesn't have to be that way. Your story doesn't have to be average, typical and normal. It doesn't have to blend in with the pages of history. You can write a different story, one that matters and one that inspires future leaders.

Kindergarten Leadership

How do we know that you want to write a story worth telling? Think back to your childhood. When adults asked you what you wanted to be when you grew up, what was your answer? Astronaut? Firefighter? Secret Agent? Military Commander? President? Professional Athlete? Musician? Dinosaur?

Okay—so that last answer was ridiculous (but we guarantee that you know a child who has answered that question this way). Seriously, what is the common thread linking these answers? They all generate impact—a legendary story—and require a courageous hero or heroine—a legendary leader.

What happens when we grow up, and the responsibilities of adulthood lead us down different paths? What happens to the underlying desire to make an impact? We might have dismissed our dreams of walking on the moon, but we didn't abandon that desire. It doesn't go away. It might go into hiding, but it doesn't disappear.

So what in the world does this have to do with leadership? Leadership is how those childhood desires—to be a legendary leader who writes a legendary story—translate into adulthood. As you fulfill those desires and create impact, you write a story that children in the next generation will want to hear.

Acme Office Supply

Every leader writes a story. We want to introduce you to two characters who, like you, are also writing their leadership stories. They will accompany us throughout this journey. They share parts of your story, and they should be familiar to you. You see them daily, either in the mirror or across the hallway. Most likely, you either resemble or recognize one of them. They share your desires and frustrations, your struggles and potential.

Julie is a Senior Director at Acme Office Supply, a large (fictitious), consumer-goods company. She has spent 12 years in the industry, only recently joining Acme. Her move to Acme was a promotion for her, and she has the opportunity to prove herself.

She was hired to run Acme Office Products, a division that has struggled over the past three years. Revenue is stagnant, expenses are up, and morale is down. She has six direct reports. She has been tasked with turning the division around. If she could do so, it would open other doors for her both within Acme and across the industry. Julie is ambitious and driven. In addition to receiving top marks on her annual appraisals over the past six years, she has also gone back to school and received her MBA.

Todd is one of Julie's direct reports within Acme Office Products. Currently a manager with five direct reports, he is responsible for leading the Marketing/Key Accounts Department. Although Todd has been with Acme for almost six years, he has spent the last 5+ years in sales, and has only recently made the transition to the corporate office.

His transition into the corporate office was accompanied by the departure of Julie's predecessor. Although he has lacked an official manager (reporting into various interim managers), he has delivered high levels of performance over the few months. He has excelled both within the marketing and key account aspects of his role, and has garnered the respect of his colleagues and employees. Senior management has identified Todd as a high-potential individual with a bright future at Acme.

As we follow Julie and Todd's journey at Acme, we will see how they operate within the construct of conventional leadership, either conforming to it or challenging it. Until now, you have probably never considered the term "conventional leadership." But as you follow their stories, you will undoubtedly recognize its features.

Being conscious of conventional leadership's characteristics provides you the opportunity to avoid writing a conventional story. You can write a different kind of story, one that people will remember.

The Story of History

"I walk on untrodden ground. There is scarcely any part of my conduct which may not hereafter be drawn into precedent."
  - George Washington

Thus far, we have been describing the story of conventional leadership by what it can't do. It can't generate impact; it can't generate meaningful change. At this point, let's switch gears and describe it with regard to what it can do. Here is the question: "What can we expect conventional leadership to actually deliver?"

Status quo and normal. Although the term "conventional leadership" is new, the concept is not. It has never been able to generate impact. But it can maintain the status quo.

By definition, "conventional" means that something is ordinary, normal, and accepted by general consent. And when someone comes along and challenges the ordinary, the status quo pushes back. Conventional leadership demands conformity. It is interested in maintaining the status quo, and it will reject anything that could produce a change from that which is normal.

Whereas we have become more aware of the presence of myth of conventional leadership over the past 20 years, it has been around for a long time. Don't believe us? Throughout history, the myth of conventional leadership has been most pronounced when it has served as the backdrop for a true leader. Unable to tolerate anything, or anyone, that challenges the status quo, conventional leadership will resort to any means necessary to maintain normalcy, including murder.

Consider Socrates. His model of leadership included challenging, questioning, and self-awareness. Considered by some to be the father of philosophy, he is still quoted today. He has arguably generated more impact than any other Greek citizen in history. Yet, it was this type of leadership—leadership that was truly non-conventional—that resulted in the citizens of Athens voting to silence him with hemlock.

History repeats itself. Consider the Founding Fathers of America. The documents they created bear no resemblance to conventional leadership. The Declaration of Independence illustrates the height of their self-awareness and competence; they had clarity on both their identity and purpose. The Constitution embodies not only a spirit of challenging (checks and balances of the different branches of the government), but also one that embraces learning from failure (the amendment process).

The real leadership shown by the Founding Fathers, leadership that generated impact and created transformational change, was scorned by the conventional leaders of the day. King George, as well as many of their American "friends" loyal to the crown, labeled these leaders as traitors and charged them with treason.

But the stories of Socrates and the Founding Fathers are the stories we remember. They weren't stories inspired by conventional leadership. Their source wasn't a myth; it was something altogether different.

"X" Marks the Spot

"History will be kind to me, for I intend to write it."
    - Winston Churchill

Although history is full of stories written by conventional leaders, you don't have to mimic their stories. This is your chance to write your story.

Chances are, you are one of the rare individuals who isn't satisfied with the status quo. If you were, you wouldn't have picked up this book. You don't want your story to be typical; you want to generate impact. This book is intended to be your guide down that path. It is designed to be your map. You can always identify a good map; they share certain characteristics: creased, folded, torn, marked up, and stained with coffee. Why? Because that's what happens to a map when you use it, and a good map is a map that is used.

We want this book to be used. Not only will it debunk the myths of conventional leadership, but it will also provide a different leadership framework. Without a solid construct, writing a legendary story of impact will be almost impossible. Don't leave this book on your bookshelf for display; highlight it. Dog-ear it. Annotate it. It was designed to be used as your map.

Like Julie and Todd, your leadership is probably intuitive. You make good decisions because you possess a certain "hunch." You might have been told that you have good business instincts or that you are good with people. Although there is a portion of leadership that is instinctive and intuitive, there is also a critical component of leadership that is intellectual.

There must be a structure, a map, by which you understand and apply leadership. Ted Williams could instinctively and intuitively hit a baseball. Tommy Lasorda intellectually knew how to hit a baseball. This is one of the reasons why Tommy Lasorda was a great coach. Although Ted Williams was one of the greatest baseball players of all time, he was a lousy coach. He lacked a framework for communicating and coaching hitting. Like Tommy Lasorda, we need a construct to understand and communicate leadership. We need a map.

This book will not only illuminate the mythical construct of conventional leadership (and its resulting inadequacies), but it will also provide a map and a structure for a new type of leadership:

"Conscious Leadership"

The Story of Conscious Leadership

Conscious leadership is real leadership, a clean break from conventional leadership. Conscious leadership can create transformational change and generate substantial impact. It is what you hope leadership could be, and what you think leadership should be. It is fundamentally different than conventional leadership, and the difference begins by debunking conventional leadership's foundational myth.

The focus of conscious leadership is not *what* a leader *does* but *who* a leader *is*.

Conventional leadership results in complex manuals and checklists about how leaders should act. Conscious leadership isn't a *manual* that trains leaders on what they should do; it is a *mirror* that transforms leaders into who they could become.

This book will act as a mirror, not a manual, allowing you to realize your potential as a leader, seeing who you can become. Debunking myths and restoring focus, conscious leadership re-establishes leadership as an agent of transformational change.

The story of conscious leadership is about impact. As a leader, your story has the potential to be both impactful and legendary. The description of a leader that we provided at the beginning of the chapter wasn't fiction, it was reality. As a conscious leader, you have the potential to write a story where you:
- Generate sustainable impact consistently
- Create transformational, substantial change—in yourself and others
- Perform at levels of excellence
- Work more efficiently and effectively, producing positive results in less time
- Connect with and motivate people through meaningful relationships
- Discover new ideas and breakthrough innovation
- Challenge conventional boundaries and normal solutions
- Develop other leaders

Throughout this book, we will explore and debunk many other myths of conventional leadership. And you will be empowered to write a more significant story.

Your Story
"Many books require no thought from those who read them, and for a very simple reason; they made no such demand upon those who wrote them."
> - Charles Caleb Colton

There are two paths in front of you. Regardless of where you are today, you need to make a choice about which path you want to follow tomorrow. Because the path you follow will determine the story that you write.

You could choose to believe the myth and follow the path of conventional leadership. You can study its manuals, focusing on what you should do. This path is well-trodden, paved, and wide, sloping gently downward. It is safe. The road is well lit and familiar. Many have strolled on this path before you. You know where this leads—this road takes all travelers to the same destination—normal and status quo.

Or you could choose to follow the other path, the path of conscious leadership. You can study its mirror, focusing on who you could become. This narrow and rocky trail twists and turns, lacking signs and mile-markers. Of those who have started down this trail, many turn around. And while the exact destination of this path is unknown (because it is not conventional), the path of conscious leadership leads to impact. And those who journey down this path write a different story.

This isn't a myth. This is the story of conscious leadership. And this can be your story.

CHAPTER 1
TIRED OF NORMAL

"We are shaping the world faster than we can change ourselves, and we are applying to the present the habits of the past."
     - Winston Churchill

"Don't think you are going to conceal thoughts by concealing evidence that they ever existed."
     - Dwight D. Eisenhower

In the last chapter, we looked at a new term, "conventional leadership." And while the term might be new to you, conventional leadership is anything but new. It has been around for a while, and its only function seems to be maintaining a comfortable level of normalcy, the status quo. And it is riddled with myths. These myths, if not understood and debunked, have the power to stifle your potential for impact.

In light of those statements, you might be wondering, "Well, if conventional leadership is so impotent, then why have things seemed to be working so well for the last twenty years?" That is a fair challenge in light of the fact that over the past two decades, the economy has expanded, and the quality of life has improved on a national and international scale.

So why now, all of a sudden, do we see something wrong with conventional leadership? Why are the commonly accepted "leadership" best-practices now producing sub-par outcomes? Why are we now referring to the standard, normal, conventional principles of "leadership" as myths? What happened?

The answer is both simple and complex—pressure.

Under Pressure

Consider coal. If you apply heat and pressure to coal, one of two things will happen. The coal either crumbles into dust, or it fuses into a diamond. Either the coal transforms into something new, different, and stronger, or it is reduced to a fine powder.

Conventional leadership is under pressure. The environment has changed. Leaders face more intense external pressures today than ever before. And it is evident that it is not fusing and transforming into a diamond. Instead, it is crumbling and cracking. So what are these pressure points that are revealing the myths of conventional leadership? This list is not exhaustive, but here are the four primary pressures exposing the myth of conventional leadership:

- **Increased Size/Scope:** Today, one leader is asked to tackle what was delegated to two or three leaders twenty years ago. The increased size and scope of this responsibility has provided a new level of complexity. Today's leaders are accountable for more than ever before. They are responsible for completing large-scale projects, taking a product to its maturity, developing their people, and doing all of this within budget and a ninety-day plan. Leaders are told to "Do more with less." And conventional leadership can't.

- **Globalization:** It's official. The economy is global. And every company is going global—whether they have to or whether they just want to. So now, today's leader must not only deal with familiar, domestic issues, but they also must consider foreign, international problems. Leaders are expected to learn various cultures and be able to develop business plans that are unique to certain geographies. A vision that is truly strategic must be able to translate into different languages and economies. Competition has become exponentially more difficult to both anticipate and counter as players with strong competitive advantages can arise from anywhere on the globe. Supply chains stretch across oceans, threatening core competencies once thought invincible. The impact of a global economy cannot be summarized in a paragraph, but you get the main point. Twenty years ago, conventional leadership didn't have to deal with this level of complexity. Today, it does.

- **Economic Downturn:** As the global economy has "right-sized," leaders have had to face economic pressures at a whole new level of intensity. Thus, today's leaders are forced to make difficult decisions to solve for problems that didn't previously exist. Over the past 20 years, when the Gross Domestic Product (GDP) and international economy were expanding at record paces, even the most mediocre and average leaders could *appear* to be impactful. But their impact was only a myth, and this myth is being exposed as the markets contract.

- **Pace/Cadence:** The speed of change continues to increase. Never before have leaders been tasked with managing people, process, and performance in such a continual state of flux. The market and environment are changing so quickly that we aren't even always conscious of the change. Before one restructuring is complete, there arrives an impetus for another. Technology has resulted in everything moving at a lightning pace, and leaders have to adapt to a different cadence of thinking. The result is a shortened lifespan for successful behaviors, as a particular behavior will only result in a successful outcome within a certain context. They can't just develop answers to problems; the rate of change means that they must *ask* the right questions to accurately diagnose the problem. A leader must have the ability and the vulnerability to adjust and adapt as the circumstances change. Conventional leadership can't keep up.

Conventional leadership hasn't changed. We aren't developing a new truth; we are discovering an existing one: Conventional leadership has *never* been able to generate meaningful impact on a consistent basis. We just haven't been conscious of this reality until recently, but pressure has a way of surfacing the truth. And the truth is—the status quo of conventional leadership isn't working.

You need a change, a transformation, as radical as that of coal becoming a diamond. You don't need to change what you do; you need to transform who you are. You need to become a conscious leader.

The Foundation

To help us set up the framework, the map, of conscious leadership, let's revisit Julie and Todd:

Julie stepped into her role as the Senior Director of Acme Office Products with great enthusiasm. She was tasked with turning this division around, and she knew that the eyes of senior management were on her. She wanted to make a good first impression. She had set ambitious goals for herself that included increasing the profitability of the division by 10% within her first six months on the job. After three months on the job, she realized that this wouldn't happen. Although revenues were increasing, so was spending, and thus profitability remained stagnant. To Julie's surprise, most of the additional spend was coming from Todd's department, marketing. Julie was shocked. She had heard so many great things about Todd, yet he was the individual who was responsible for her not achieving her profitability goals. Knowing that leadership often requires difficult conversations, she decided to call a face-to-face meeting with Todd to discuss the numbers.

Todd, having been in his position for a few months, had made the most of his time. He had been diligent in his approach, thoroughly studying the office supply market. He had gained a great deal of information about the intricacies of the market and its unique dynamics. One of the insights that he gleaned from his research was the identification of a trend that was powerful enough to revolutionize the market: within the next three years, flip charts would replace computers as the dominant medium for presentations (it had a more personal feel). Knowing the level of impact this trend would have on the business, Todd developed some new ideas and made some innovative decisions. He invested in market research and product development. He also launched a marketing campaign to effectively position Acme's flip charts as the premium product in that class. The cost of these investments was large, but it would yield a tremendous return. However, it wouldn't be fully realized for another 36 months.

With that as a background, we can already anticipate the conversation. At the surface level, this may look like a classic case of misaligned goals. But if you look deeper, you discover that it is more than that. Through this simple example, we can begin to see the structure of conventional leadership.

Conventional leadership manages outcomes by influencing behaviors and controlling actions. This principle makes perfect sense and seems almost intuitive; you to understand it completely. How can we say that with such certainty? Because we have sat through identical seminars and were trained in similar workshops—delivered by conventional leaders.

Here is the abridged version of these seminars: As a leader, you set a compelling vision. Then, you set clear performance objectives for those you lead which would make your vision a reality. Inevitably, you witness poor performance (defined by outcomes not meeting expectations). Through observation, you seek to identify what was done that led to this sub-optimal outcome. You then focus your effort and energy towards changing those behaviors. Why? The thought is that if you can improve the behaviors that caused the sub-par performance, then the outcome will also improve.

Does this sound familiar? This conventional approach is not altogether wrong. In fact, this framework has some components that are valuable. Leaders should create a vision and set clear expectations. Monitoring outcomes is natural, and leaders should be able to identify behaviors that contribute to performance.

Unfortunately, this conventional approach doesn't work. Although it may appear to provide moderate benefit in the short-term, it is a myth. The truth is it doesn't work well, it doesn't work consistently, it doesn't work under pressure, and it doesn't work in the long run.

You might see some partial improvement, but you will rarely see complete transformation. The behavior might change temporarily, but within a couple of weeks or months, it returns right to back to normal. Or the same behavior applied to one situation becomes the default for all situations. The outcome might improve slightly, but not to the degree that you know it should—or could. And so, in an attempt to improve performance, we end up trying to change the same behaviors again and again and again. Why? "Why" is both the question and the answer.

Where do behaviors originate? Behaviors come from beliefs. The source of your behavior is your belief.

What you *do* is a result of *who* you *are*, and *who* you *are* is determined by *what* you *believe*. Your actions are a result of your thoughts. Your beliefs (*why* you are doing something) determine your behaviors (*how* you are doing it).

You can change behaviors indefinitely. However, if the core belief system (which is the source of that behavior) remains unchanged, the behaviors will become ineffective. They will either revert back to their original state, or they will be wrongly applied to a new situation. Beliefs drive behaviors, which influence outcomes. The diagram looks like this:

Belief → Behavior → Outcome

This isn't a myth; this is truth. And this truth is a core and fundamental difference between conventional leadership and conscious leadership.

A Deeper Level

"The world we see that seems so insane is the result of a belief system that is not working. To perceive the world differently, we must be willing to change our belief system, let the past slip away, expand our sense of now, and dissolve the fear in our minds."
  - Gerald G. Jampolsky

The "Belief → Behavior → Outcome" flow chart provides a foundation for understanding the differences between conventional leadership and conscious leadership. It may feel weird to you right now. That's okay. We will challenge that "weird" isn't the right word for this principle, but it's definitely different. Naturally, it may feel uncomfortable right now. Because it's new, you might not completely understand it yet. That's also okay. It might help to look at this model from a different angle:

Belief ➜ Behavior ➜ Outcome
"Why" ➜ "How" ➜ "What"
Who you *are* ➜ What you *do* ➜ What you *produce*

Let's examine each component, starting at the end with outcomes.

Outcome/"What"

Belief ➜ Behavior ➜ **Outcome**
"Why" ➜ "How" ➜ **"What"**
Who you *are* ➜ What you *do* ➜ **What you** *produce*

The end result—the outcome—of this equation is the "what." This might be sales numbers, brand awareness, profitability, or earnings per share. The outcome is "what" you, or your company, is expected to produce. It is your output, your accomplishment, your performance.

Performance is extremely important, both to conventional and conscious leadership. And it should be. What is the result of poor outcomes? What happens when numbers are missed, earnings are low, or expenses are high? Companies go bankrupt, divisions are sold, organizations are acquired, and employees are fired.

Performance is an essential part of leadership. Leadership should be able to consistently generate significant, meaningful outcomes. Don't confuse "consistency" with "continuously." In reality, even conscious leaders will fail occasionally. But if leadership isn't consistently generating positive outcomes, it isn't realizing its potential. It is working neither as it should nor as it could.

Although outcomes are critically important, this isn't the only reason that leaders tend to focus on them so much. An outcome is very easy to observe, and it is often quantifiable. It can frequently be measured, and as a result, it is easy to reward positive outcomes and criticize negative ones.

Both conventional leadership and conscious leadership value the outcome. Yet they both recognize that as a leader, the outcome cannot be your sole focus. Why? It just doesn't make sense. Let's revisit the previous example of Julie and Todd to see what an outcome-based dialogue would look like:

JULIE: Todd, I called this meeting to talk with you about the profitability of the department. It needs to improve. It is not where it needs to be because of what you're spending. You need to spend less.
TODD: I know I'm spending a lot, but it is in preparation for the flip chart initiative. The extra expenditure is for R&D, market analysis, and market preparation. It will generate a huge ROI in the future. The initial estimates are between 150% and 200%.
JULIE: Look, the division's profitability needs to improve now. I need you to spend less.
TODD: But then we won't be in a position to capitalize on the flip chart explosion.
JULIE: Todd, you need to spend less. I am going to hold you accountable for that.
TODD: I thought I'm accountable to launch new products and develop new markets. I can't do that without spending.
JULIE: Todd, you need to reduce your expenditures. This doesn't absolve you from your other job responsibilities. The reality is that our profitability is down right now because of your spending. You have to spend less.

This is silly, right? It's like telling a struggling salesperson, "Sell more," or telling a person in financial distress, "Make more money." We recognize that the outcomes, such as increased profitability or sales quotas, are critically important. It just doesn't always make sense to address them from a causality standpoint. Thinking in terms of cause and effect, outcomes are undoubtedly the effect. What's the cause? What influences outcomes? Behaviors.

Behavior/"How"

Belief ➔ **Behavior** ➔ Outcome

"Why" ➔ **"How"** ➔ "What"

Who you *are* ➔ **What you** *do* ➔ What you *produce*

The word "behave" is officially defined as, "To act in a particular way." Behavior is "how" we produce outcomes. Behavior—what you should do—is the focus and foundation of conventional leadership.

Behaviors are harder to observe and evaluate than outcomes. Why? Most of the time, they aren't directly quantifiable; they are qualifiable. Behaviors are easier to measure than beliefs, harder to measure than outcomes, and simple to describe. Although you could paint a picture of good customer service, it is difficult to tell if your call center representatives are providing it. Even if they are, how good is the service? It is difficult to determine with a high degree of certainty whether your sales team is closing effectively or if your IT department is communicating clearly.

You can easily qualify the behaviors that you observe (e.g., the call center representative didn't adequately sympathize with the caller, the sales representative asked for the order without understanding the customer's delivery needs, or your employees keep asking the same questions about the new software rollout). But these behaviors are difficult to measure and evaluate compared to outcomes. So how do we respond?

We create quantifiable metrics. We develop secondary data in an effort to measure behaviors. These come in a variety of forms: customer satisfaction surveys, call activity data, and defect ratios are all examples. These data are collected and studied for linkages, causality, and associations (some of which are better than others). The goal is to allow leaders to more accurately identify, measure, and evaluate which behaviors are linked to which outcomes.

Leaders rely on this data because the relationship between behaviors and outcomes is constantly changing. The behaviors determined to be causally related to performance today will shift tomorrow. Conventional leaders consider these data to be critically important as they are the primary source of behavior adaptation.

With or without data, however, behaviors drive outcomes. Regardless of the context, "how" we act determines "what" we produce. Both conventional and conscious leadership are aligned on this principle. This is what the dialogue between Julie and Todd would look like with a behavior focus:

JULIE: Todd, I called this meeting with you to discuss the department's profitability and specifically, your spending. Your spending is way up. What are you doing and where are you spending all of that money?

TODD: I know I'm spending more, but it is in preparation for the flip chart initiative. The extra expenditure is for R&D, market analysis, and market preparation. It will generate a huge ROI in the future. The initial estimates are between 150% and 200%.

JULIE: Well, that's in the future. I need you to spend less now. Of those three initiatives, R&D, market analysis, and market preparation, which one is critical? Which one would you prioritize over the others?

TODD: Well, they are all critical. You can't really launch a new initiative without all of them. I can't really cut any of them out.

JULIE: I understand they are important, but it is critical that you spend less. That isn't an option. So you need to prioritize and pick one of them to focus on and stop your spending on the other two.

TODD: Instead of cutting two of them out, what if I just reduced the spending on all three elements? Then I wouldn't lose the value of any of them completely. I could still leverage all of those elements, just to a lesser extent.

JULIE: That would work. It's your call; it doesn't matter to me which choice you make. But you must reduce your spending. So decide how you want to proceed, and then let's discuss that choice next week.

The outcome was still the driving factor. But Julie went a step further. She identified the behaviors (investment in R&D, market analysis, and market preparation) that were responsible for the outcome (increased spending). By focusing on those specific behaviors instead of just the outcome, additional options appeared for Todd that will benefit the business. Todd will adjust his behavior (reduce spending in all three categories by a certain percentage) and the outcome will improve (spending will decrease and short-term profitability will increase).

Although that is a better ending than the outcome-based dialogue, it still isn't good enough. But this is where conventional leadership stops, at the behavior level. It focuses on the "how" and "what" but ignores the "why." This is the point at which conventional leadership cracks and is a critical reason as to why it isn't working in the face of intense pressure.

Conventional leadership tells a myth that behavior change is sufficient to produce better outcomes. It's not. To generate meaningful outcomes consistently, to truly make an impact, change must happen at the belief level.

Belief/"Why"

Belief ➜ Behavior ➜ Outcome
"Why" ➜ "How" ➜ "What"
Who you *are* ➜ What you *do* ➜ What you *produce*

A discussion about beliefs is different. It almost sounds taboo, but it shouldn't be. At some point, the familiar adage, "Talk about anything but religion and politics" became, "Talk about anything but beliefs." Your belief is simply your mindset, your viewpoint, your perspective, your motives, or your attitude. Your belief is the reason *why* you act a certain way, and your beliefs are core to who you are as a person.

A belief is different from a feeling. You have control over your beliefs, while you don't always have that same level of control over your feelings. You can choose what you want to think. You can control your mindset or intentionally change your perspective. You can't always control whether or not you feel angry, upset, jealous, or proud.

Beliefs are very difficult to identify. They are not quantifiable, even with surveys or secondary data. They often stay hidden. The best way to identify a belief is to watch for them to surface in behaviors. Why? Your beliefs drive your behaviors; your motives determine what you do; your thoughts lead your actions. But identification requires awareness.

To identify your beliefs, you must first be aware of their existence, and conventional leadership isn't. It doesn't acknowledge the belief portion of the equation. Although it recognizes that behaviors influence outcomes, conventional leadership can't significantly or substantially change behaviors because it can't change beliefs.

Everyone has beliefs, even conventional leaders. They just might not be conscious of them. But even if a belief is subconscious, it still drives behavior. We even have a word for this. A repeated behavior fueled by a subconscious belief is called a habit.

Habits are hard to break. We learned this lesson as children. This is one of the reasons why addressing the belief portion of the equation is so important. The consequence of ignoring beliefs is having your leadership governed by your habits. No one wants to be known as a habitual leader. This is just another reason why conventional leadership fails.

Whether beliefs are at a conscious or subconscious level, identifying and then changing them is difficult and requires effort. But the effort is worth it. Why? Beliefs are powerful. What you believe determines who you are.

You *become* what you *believe*.

As the environment changes faster, a particular set of behaviors becomes obsolete quicker. As the lifespan of behaviors shortens, the importance of beliefs increases, as they are the origination point for all behaviors. Beliefs allow behaviors to adapt to change, and the success of that adaptation is dependent on the accuracy of the belief.

With a focus on who you are, belief and belief change are essential to conscious leadership. As you will see later, changing beliefs is the only way to consistently generate sustainable, meaningful impact. A conscious leader is aware of not just his own personal beliefs, but also of the beliefs of others. Let's look at this dialogue between Julie and Todd one last time, this time from a belief standpoint:

JULIE: Todd, I called this meeting to discuss our department's profitability and your spending. Your increased spending is hurting our bottom line. Why are you spending so much?

TODD: I know I'm spending more, but it is in preparation for the flip chart initiative. The extra expenditure is for R&D, market analysis, and market preparation. But, this program will be incredibly impactful and will generate a huge ROI in the future. The initial estimates are between 150% and 200%.

JULIE: But I need you to reduce your spending now.

TODD: Okay. But can I ask, "Why"?

JULIE: Because I was tasked to ensure that our department hit certain profitability goals within my first six months. And this extra spending is keeping the department from achieving that goal.

TODD: Why six months? That seems awfully shortsighted.

JULIE: That was the original plan set before senior management. And it is their expectation of me. I don't want to let them down. I need them to respect our department, and recognize and appreciate that we can run a profitable business.

TODD: It seems like we are mortgaging tomorrow to pay for today. And, truthfully, it doesn't even seem like we are getting anything of value today. This program will make a difference, not just for this department, but for the entire company. It will be tremendously impactful, but we have to decide to invest in it today.

JULIE: I hear you, but my hands are tied. This isn't an easy decision, but I do need you to cut spending in the present.

TODD: We can't just kill the investment; it's not the right thing for the company. What if I put together a detailed business plan and forecast? It would lay out all of the program's expenditures and returns over time. It would also show what the department's profitability would look like without this program. Then you can show that to senior management. At worst, they will respect your business and financial acumen. At best, they will let us keep the program.

By asking "Why?" Todd was able to flush out Julie's beliefs. These beliefs were the source of her behaviors that were influencing her outcomes. Her belief was that senior management's opinion of her (or her department) and her short-term profitability was paramount. Thus, she behaved in a way where she looked for ways to reduce immediate expenditures, regardless of the long-term consequences. The outcome was Julie telling Todd to spend less.

By understanding Julie's belief, Todd was able to adjust his behavior and understand her behavior. He learned "why" she was acting the way she was acting. As a result, the outcome was much more powerful. But Todd had to get to the "why."

Note that although Julie is Todd's "leader," Todd was the one who took the interaction to the belief level. As a result, he was able to generate positive impact that wasn't limited only to himself, but also included Julie and the entire department.

Levels and positions do not restrict the impact of a conscious leader.

Express Yourself

"The greatest revolution of our generation is the discovery that human beings, by changing the inner attitudes of their minds, can change the outer aspects of their lives."
  - William James

Hopefully, by now, you are starting to see the power of beliefs. And the better you understand beliefs, the better you understand why conventional leadership doesn't work.

Conscious leadership's belief-centric focus is a very different way of approaching leadership. If you are skeptical, that's okay. Leadership that is focused on beliefs isn't commonplace or normal. But really, you should be skeptical if conscious leadership resembled the myths you have been told about conventional leadership. The fact that it's different means that it actually can produce different results. It has potential to generate impact and create transformational change.

The base foundation of conscious leadership will allow you to create sustainable impact. We recognize that the "Belief ➔ Behavior ➔ Outcome" model is new. To help you understand it better, here are some other expressions of the framework. The following models are all different variations of the same core idea. Chances are, one of them will resonate with you and provide more clarity around the central theme:

Belief ➙ Behavior ➙ Outcome
"Why" ➙ "How" ➙ "What"
Who we *are* ➙ What we *do* ➙ What we *produce*
Be ➙ Do ➙ Have
Thought ➙ Action ➙ Result

Why Not?

If the belief portion of the model is where all of the power required to generate impact is stored, why doesn't conventional leadership address it? Why does conventional leadership focus on behaviors and outcomes instead of beliefs? Here are some of the key reasons:

- **Mediocre Satisfaction:** By focusing on behaviors, a conventional leader can generate mediocre outcomes. The outcomes represent improvement that is incremental and temporary, not impactful and sustainable. But they are better today than they were yesterday. The improvement, mediocre as it may be, is just about average. It's normal. And conventional leadership is satisfied with mediocrity.

- **Degree of Difficulty:** A belief-focused style of leadership requires high levels of effort and energy. As discussed, behaviors are somewhat quantifiable and tangible. They can be observed and, with the help of secondary metrics, measured. Beliefs can't. Identifying and changing beliefs requires focus, discipline, and energy that conventional leadership is not willing to expend.

- **Location and Direction:** If you are going to engage in belief change, you must expend effort and energy to understand others. It requires that you focus on them and engage in dialogue where you listen to them, eliciting their opinions and thoughts. Conventional leadership wants to be the focal point, located at the center. It is not concerned with understanding the opinions of others. Instead, it is focused on pushing its opinions outward.

- **Ignorance:** Conventional leadership doesn't really understand the power, or the potential, of beliefs. A conventional leader isn't aware of his own beliefs and their power in his life, and he certainly isn't aware of them in the lives of others. In some circumstances, ignorance may be bliss. For conventional leadership, ignorance is impotence.

There are many reasons that account for conventional leadership's lack of focus on beliefs. But regardless of the "why" or the "how," the ""what" is the same: conventional leadership can't consistently generate impact largely due to its inability, or unwillingness, to recognize the importance of beliefs.

Consistent, sustainable, significant impact apart from belief change cannot happen. It is a myth.

Normal

"We shall have no better conditions in the future if we are satisfied with all those which we have at present."

- Thomas Edison

So how did we get here? How did these myths of conventional leadership arise? And when did we start accepting them as truth? More importantly, *why* did we start accepting them as truth? There are two primary reasons: Success and complacency.

Leaders haven't always experienced pressures with this degree of intensity. The presence of these intense pressures is currently exposing the myths of conventional leadership. However, over the past 20 years, the absence of these intense pressures allowed conventional leadership to masquerade as something that it isn't.

What happened? We experienced positive outcomes as external circumstances aligned with current leadership behaviors. This success was attributed to conventional leadership, but shouldn't have been. At best, they were loosely associated, and at worst, they were purely coincidental. Conventional leadership was perceived as a *cause of*, rather than the *beneficiary of*, that success. Unfortunately, this myth was accepted as truth.

Belief of this myth perpetuated the rise of another myth, the desirability of the status quo. When success is the starting point, change can only produce negative results. Why should things change when all is going well? The thought process was this: Conventional leadership got us here; now it will keep us here.

As the saying goes, "If it ain't broke, don't fix it." Sadly, it wasn't recognized that conventional leadership was broken until the circumstantial tail winds disappeared. We were no longer in a situation defined by success as the default. Reality set in and debunked both myths. It became apparent that conventional leadership didn't get us here. It also became obvious that conventional leadership couldn't keep us here. And unfortunately, it can't take us back.

Today's reality is much different than yesterday's reality. Because circumstances no longer align with behaviors, we are currently in a situation where success is no longer the default. Favorable tailwinds have become formidable headwinds. And while the new situation has introduced pressures that make success harder to achieve, it has also given us clarity into the true nature of conventional leadership: It can't create success nor maintain success. It can't do anything.

Okay, that's not entirely true. Conventional leadership may not be able to generate sustainable impact or create significant change, but it can maintain normal. However, success isn't normal, and that's why it disappeared when the circumstances became less favorable. Conventional leadership can't sustain success, but it can maintain mediocrity by designing systems that control behavior and foster the status quo.

What is the "vision" of conventional leadership? Average, typical, and mediocre. In a word—*normal*. The "vision" of conventional leadership is *normal* people—behaving in predictable, *normal* ways—executing mundane, *normal* tasks—that result in safe, *normal* outcomes. And if everything is perfectly *normal*, then the status quo will be maintained, and tomorrow will look just like today.

As we said earlier, management is about normalcy, control, stability, and status quo. Leadership is about meaningful change and sustainable impact. Conventional leadership can't produce impact. It isn't visionary leadership; it is nothing more than delegated management!

Yet it is dressed up with all kinds of buzzwords, such as vision, transparency, communication, and revolution. These buzzwords, intentionally or unintentionally, blur the true meaning and intent of leadership. And so, it is no wonder that you are frustrated, disappointed, and disillusioned with the state of "leadership" today.

This is why we are starting over. We aren't trying to repair conventional leadership by providing new manuals defining what leaders should do. Instead, we are establishing a new and different form of leadership—conscious leadership. Conscious leadership is a mirror describing who a leader could be. If it resembles conventional leadership, you should be skeptical that it is just another version of the same old thing. But it won't. It doesn't look like or feel like conventional leadership. Conscious leadership is not typical, average or normal, and it will not generate normal outcomes.

Your Story

The whole idea of normal outcomes is…surprise…based on a myth, a myth that is very offensive. Ironically, the conventional leader's flow chart of normalcy begins with a statement about who you are. Predictably, this statement is a myth. It incorrectly assumes that people—including you—are "normal." These "normal" people interact with each other through normal processes, which results in normal performance.

What's the truth?

There is no such thing as a "normal" person. You aren't normal, and you don't want normal. You want anything but normal. You are tired of normal. You are tired of the myths that normal is built upon.

You don't want normal; you want impact. The people that you lead deserve impact. You can write your story with impact.

CHAPTER 2

BRICK
BY BRICK

"If I would have asked people what they wanted, they would have said, 'Faster horses.'"
  - Henry Ford

"Man's mind, stretched to a new idea, never goes back to its original dimensions."
  - Oliver Wendell Holmes

So far in our journey, we have examined the "Belief ➔ Behavior ➔ Outcome" model. We have asserted that for real, lasting, meaningful change to occur, we must make adjustments at the belief level, not just the behavior level. We have also asserted that one of the foundational flaws of conventional leadership is its inability not just to address the belief portion of that model, but to recognize its existence. We compared this model to a new term, conscious leadership, which acknowledges both the existence and the power of beliefs.

Back to School

Now, we are going to introduce another model that will help frame this leadership discussion. This is a model with which you may already be familiar—the Adult Learning Model. The Adult Learning Model contains four distinct stages:

- Unconscious Incompetence
- Conscious Incompetence
- Conscious Competence
- Unconscious Competence

Corporations spend billions of dollars per year in an attempt to train and develop their people. And as training has gotten more sophisticated, the thought leaders within that field have created this model that compartmentalizes and explains the learning process. As conventional leadership often refers to this model, you might be skeptical that we are in danger of blurring the lines between conventional and conscious leadership. We aren't. As you will see, conscious leadership turns this model upside-down.

The Adult Learning Model's four fundamental phases can be applied both in the short-term (acquiring a new skill set or learning a new job) as well as in the long-term (lifetime leadership development). A breakdown of those four unique stages follows:

- **Stage One—Unconscious Incompetence:** This is the level where you don't know what you don't know. This is everyone's starting point for every new journey. Imagine your first week on a new job with a new company. Not only do you not know the answers, you don't even know the questions. Forget providing strategic counsel to the company's cash-flow situation. You don't know enough about the cash-flow situation to be able to provide insight, and you don't even know where to go to get that information! Consider Julie's first 90 days with Acme. Acme Office Supply is facing intense competition from a new foreign competitor. Not only would Julie not know what to do about the foreign threat, she wouldn't even be conscious of it! She is not aware of her incompetence.

- **Stage Two—Conscious Incompetence:** After stage one, you progress to the level where you know what you don't know. You are starting to acclimate to the new job or the new situation, and the more you learn, the more you realize how much you still need to learn. You still don't know what to do, but you know that you don't know what to do. This is normal, and part of the learning process. For Julie, at this stage, she would have become aware of the foreign competitive threat at Acme Office Supply. However, she still wouldn't know what to do or what to change. She is aware of her incompetence.

- **Stage Three—Conscious Competence:** At this point, you have progressed to the level where you know what you know. You have gotten the "feel" for things, and you can adequately and successfully perform a task, although it requires effort and focus. "Muscle memory" does not yet apply. You have knowledge of the situation, and the ability to impact it, albeit intentionally. Julie, at this stage, would have learned how to do a regular foreign competitive analysis based on market data and then incorporate those findings into her current operating model. When conducting her Strengths, Weaknesses, Opportunities, Threats (S.W.O.T) analysis of her business, she would have leveraged resources and connections to account for foreign competition and developed an appropriate strategy. She is aware of her competence.

This stage, "Conscious Competence," does not represent the summit of the Adult Learning Model for conventional leaders. For them, the pinnacle is stage four, which is next. However, this stage does represent one of the foundational pillars of conscious leadership.

- **Stage Four—Unconscious Competence:** Finally, you've made it; this is the pinnacle of the Adult Learning Model. You are at the level where you don't know what you know. It is the "riding the bike" stage. You have mastery of a certain skill, and thus execution of that skill requires very little to no effort. In fact, the skill is so familiar that you don't even have to think about it. It's a habit. Consider Julie's case. Of course she would use competitive intelligence and other external resources in building her S.W.O.T. analysis! Is there another way? Can you really perform a S.W.O.T. without those familiar tools? Doesn't everybody do this? She would automatically account for foreign players in her business plan, and she would look to foreign markets for danger signs and growth opportunities. And she isn't even aware that she is doing this. She can't imagine otherwise. She is not aware of her competence.

This stage sounds appealing, right? Without effort or thought, you can generate excellent performance. Utilizing muscle memory, you can produce transformational change. Relying on habits, you can create sustainable impact.

Or can you?

Is this stage, "Unconscious Competence," truly the summit of adult learning, a "leader's" paradise? Or is it another conventional myth that needs to be debunked?

Back to School…Again

"It is what we think we already know that often prevents us from learning."
    - Claude Bernard

Let us provide you with another example of this model. You've probably experienced something similar in your own life:

- **Stage One:** Think back to when you were 12 years old. You are riding in the passenger seat of your dad's Ford as he takes you to the ball game. You are excited about the upcoming game, and you don't give a thought to your dad's driving ability. Is he doing a good job or a bad job? Should he have been a little more patient while merging? Is he a little too close to the car in front of him? You don't even think to ask these questions. Why? When it comes to driving, a 12-year-old (in most parts of the country) is at the beginning of the Adult Learning Model. With regard to driving, he doesn't know what he doesn't know, Unconscious Incompetence—stage one.

- **Stage Two:** Fast-forward a few years. You just received your learner's permit. Now you are in the driver's seat and your dad is strapped in the passenger seat. Your knuckles are white as you grip the wheel. You think that all of the other drivers are looking at you. You panic when you hit your first yellow light, and oscillate back and forth between pressing the gas pedal and the brake. You hit the left blinker to alert the other drivers that you are about to turn…right. Almost immediately, in that first drive home from the DMV, you have made the jump to the next level in the Adult Learning Model. Driving is difficult. You know what you don't know, Conscious Incompetence—stage two.

- **Stage Three:** Jump ahead in time another two years. You passed the driving test (admittedly struggling some on the written portion) and have been driving solo for eight months. You no longer signal left when you intend to turn right. You don't hit the gas and brake simultaneously when you see a yellow light. Yet driving requires effort, thought, and intentionality. You are conscious of the cars around you. You notice the turn signals of the other cars. You are paying close attention to the speedometer (we didn't say you stayed within the speed limit, just that you knew how fast you were going). You are now a proficient driver. You are aware of the relationship between your decisions as a driver and the changing environment in which you are driving. You have passed into the next stage of the Adult Learning Model. You know what you know, Conscious Competence—stage three.

- **Stage Four:** Present day. Think about your drive to work this morning, or your drive home this afternoon. Chances are, unless something out of the ordinary happened, you don't even remember it. You were completely zoned out, thinking about something else, listening to the radio, or having a conversation on the phone (hopefully, you were not texting). Out of habit, you change lanes while checking voicemail and drinking a cup of coffee. Driving requires little effort and thought; it is second nature. You aren't aware of all of your actions (the speed limit, the distance prior to turning when you activated your signal), yet you still arrive at your destination safely. You are now in the final stage of the Adult Learning Model. You don't know what you know— Unconscious Competence, stage four.

This model, whether or not it has formally been introduced to you, is pretty intuitive. It makes sense, and if we think about different arenas of our life, it is fairly applicable. Every time we enter a new area, we start all over again. Just because you are a stage four at driving doesn't mean that you are a stage four at setting up a wireless network for your house. Just because you made money flipping houses in 2006 doesn't mean that you are an expert at the current real estate market. The Adult Learning Model represents a cycle through which we all progress as we acquire new skills or apply our current skills in new settings.

One Step Back, Two Steps Forward...

So what does this have to do with leadership, both conventional and conscious? More than you might think. For starters, the Adult Learning Model exposes another myth of conventional leadership:

Myth: The ultimate goal of learning is stage four (Unconscious Competence).
Truth: The ultimate goal of learning is stage three (Conscious Competence).

This may not be intuitive at first. Thinking back to the driving example, you are most likely a much better driver now than you were at age 16. That's true, but you would admit that there were at least some other factors that might have contributed to your poor driving at the age of 16. This is a fair challenge, but we think that after further exploration, you will see the dangers of stage four. Let us explain.

A leader who operates at the Unconscious Competence level (stage four) will repeat his previous actions and behaviors. Why? He reasons that because these actions led to success in the past, they will certainly lead to success in the present and future. But this isn't always true. In fact, it is rarely true.

You were not aware of your drive home from work today (you might remember the phone conversation, but you probably don't remember the actual drive). You don't remember your decisions, the dynamic environment, or the relationship between them. So it is with the stage four leader. He is not aware of all of his decisions. He is not aware of the dynamic environment in which those decisions are made. And he is definitely not aware of the interaction and relationship between his decisions and the environment.

He continues to employ the same strategies and repeat the same behaviors that worked in the past, never realizing that his environment has changed. Unfortunately, the conventional leader operating at this level will continue to export his ideas from yesterday into today. He will never pause to reflect on the truth that the very core of what made him successful yesterday might not lead to success today, and could be the cause of his failure tomorrow.

If It Ain't Broke...It Will Be

"People can have the Model T in any color—so long as it's black."
- Henry Ford

Think about Henry Ford and the Model T automobile. When it was first introduced in 1908, the car was wildly successful. Henry, operating out of Conscious Competence, realized that people didn't really want faster horses. They wanted inexpensive transportation. So with the advent of his assembly line, the Model T dominated the automotive landscape. With Henry initially pricing the automobile at $825 in 1908 (eventually lowered to $360 in 1916), he eventually produced and sold over 15 million Model Ts (a record that stood for over 40 years).

By the mid-1920s, however, sales of the Model T began to decline. Competitor firms began to also produce inexpensive cars. However, unlike Henry, they also offered the customer various product upgrades and payment plans. Henry refused to budge on his initial version of the Model T. Why? He believed that the factors critical to success yesterday were the same factors critical to success today. He wasn't aware of the changing environment or his interaction with the environment. In other words, he was now operating on the level of Unconscious Competence.

He had effortless and thoughtless performance, muscle memory, and habits—but no impact. Unfortunately, the same criteria that led to the success of the Model T in 1908 led to its decline 20 years later. And Henry didn't even know this was happening until it was too late.

This story from history, not legend, provides lessons for today's leaders. In 1908, when Henry Ford was operating at the level of Conscious Competence, he was able to generate some new ideas and powerful innovation. His insights into what customers really wanted lead to an outcome that was more than just a new form of transportation; he created a global impact on production methods.

Yet the same man who challenged conventional production theory on a global scale became irrelevant to the American automobile industry only 20 years later. What happened? Henry progressed into stage four of the Adult Learning Model, Unconscious Competence. He was no longer aware of his decisions, the changing environment, or the interaction between them. He believed that he could rely on the habits and experiences that created impact yesterday to create impact today. But they can't. And so he failed.

He failed to create impact towards the end of his career not because of a lack of ability or aptitude, but because he believed a myth. Specifically, he believed that the same behaviors that produced success in 1908 would continue to produce success 20 years later. However, the circumstances changed, and his original successful behaviors were now rendered obsolete. And if you believe that myth, regardless of your intelligence, charisma, or strategic prowess, you will also fail. That is why this myth of conventional leadership needs to be debunked.

Hawaiian-shirt Friday

Unconscious Competence isn't the goal; it's the problem. And just as it was Henry Ford's downfall, it can strip away our ability to create impact as well. Let's revisit Julie and Todd at Acme Office Supply:

To recap, Todd has spent the last six years of his career at Acme (five years in sales and now one full year of marketing/key accounts). Having worked at Acme in various roles, He was confident in his understanding of the company culture, both in concept and in practice. The culture was a great fit for him, especially regarding communication.

Todd's communication was informal and frequent. He communicated well with his previous managers, both in his current role in marketing and his previous role in sales. Todd would pass along voicemails or emails about successes or issues that he encountered as they occurred. Todd's managers would respond quickly. Communication was real-time, and they discussed the business issues that were current. His managers knew that he could handle the job and that he would produce good results. As a result, they all used a "hands off" approach and never asked for any formal reports. This suited Todd perfectly. In his opinion, this culture of frequent, informal communication was one of the reasons Acme was so successful.

And, even better, Acme senior leadership had just announced that Fridays were going to be Hawaiian-shirt day! Todd was thrilled, as this move was definitely aligned with Acme's culture of informal communication. This type of informal environment would make real communication even easier and more meaningful.

During the 12 years she worked at her previous company, Apex, Julie never experienced a Hawaiian-shirt day on Friday. But, Apex valued communication just as much as Acme. Apex valued communication so much that it didn't want to leave it to chance, so they standardized and institutionalized it. So, every Friday, Julie (along with every other Apex employee) would provide her manager with a one-page, written report summarizing the events of the week. This report contained a list of business activities completed, potential opportunities identified, and threats that required attention. Julie would still reach out to her manager in the case of a true emergency, but this weekly report was the foundation for the vast majority of Apex's business communication.

Julie loved this system, as it forced her to organize her thoughts in a succinct manner and really understand her business. Her old manager embraced this system because it allowed her to maintain a real-time understanding of her peoples' situations: the good, the bad, and the ugly. So not only did this system of standardized communication force Julie to decide what was truly meaningful and what was fluff (in condensing her business to a single-page report), it allowed her manager visibility into what really mattered. There was no wasted time with confusion over the meanings of emails or the nuances of voicemails.

Julie was excited about starting at Acme as she respected and admired the value that senior management placed on communication. She was sure that she would fit right in, as she had learned the tremendous value of communication at Apex.

From the above, we know that both Todd and Julie take communication very seriously. Although they both have solid communication skills, they have very different styles. And, while you would assume that two individuals who both value communication and have been successful at communicating would be able to connect with each other, you know that is not necessarily the case. This story has two very different potential, and predictable, endings.

Fairy Tale or Horror Story?
"Let us make a special effort to stop communicating with each other so that we may have some conversation."
    - Judith Martin

What is the difference between a happy ending and a sad ending? The Adult Learning Model. If Julie and Todd are operating out of Conscious Competence (aware of what they know), then the story of differing communication cultures will end well. But, if they have bought into the myth of conventional leadership, and are operating out of Unconscious Competence, then this story has the potential to become scary.

This would be the fairy-tale ending:

Todd meets with Julie during her first week on the job. Among other things, they discuss communication and expectations. He asks how she would like for him to communicate with her. Julie explains her weekly report system. Todd expresses his concern, and talks about his informal style and the culture at Acme. Julie absorbs this new information, and proposes some sort of new idea, a blend. Todd will meet with Julie once a month to discuss the business in a formal way. The report template can change, but it needs to be written. Outside of that meeting, Todd will call Julie not just for emergencies (like she was used to), but for anything that he deems relevant for her to know in real-time. Julie also makes a mental note to call Todd once or twice a week just to say "Hey" and see how he is doing.

This innovative blended approach will allow Julie to acclimate to the Acme culture. It provides her an opportunity to learn the business while not making Todd feel suffocated and micromanaged. While Todd and Julie experience some of the expected initial speed bumps (Todd's reports aren't concise enough for Julie, Julie doesn't respond quickly enough to Todd's voicemails), within six months they have found a good rhythm.

This would be the horror-story ending:

Todd meets with Julie during her first week on the job, and she explains her weekly reporting system. Todd thinks that this is ridiculous, but is hopeful that Julie will adjust to the Acme culture. Todd reaches out to Julie during the week, but she is slow to respond. Todd is frustrated at Julie's lack of interest in his business needs—he wouldn't be calling her if he didn't need to discuss something. Unfortunately, during the Friday sessions, Julie becomes increasingly frustrated with Todd. He doesn't seem to be getting the system. Worse, he doesn't seem to care. His reports are unorganized and incomplete. After one Friday, Julie wonders how a "successful" businessman could "forget the report."

Todd wonders how long it will take her to adapt to the Acme culture. This isn't Apex! How could his "strategic business partner" be so unwilling to adapt and throw in the towel on her "proven system"?

Four months have passed since Julie started and this situation hasn't improved. Their communication has remained poor and the Friday meetings painful. In light of her recent discovery and confrontation regarding Todd's increased spending, Julie is considering putting him on official warning. At the same time, frustrated about Julie's indifference towards him and the business, Todd is considering reporting her to Human Resources. Their inability to communicate has led to several missed business opportunities that have made both of them look incompetent.

Survival of the Fittest

What was the difference between the endings? It isn't their ability to communicate, as both Todd and Julie value it and have histories of successful communication. The difference is their current location within the Adult Learning Model. Fairy-tale ending: stage three, Conscious Competence. Horry-story ending: stage four, Unconscious Competence.

Julie's environment has changed; she works for a new company. Todd's environment has changed; he has a new manager. The degree of success within their communication will be largely determined by their degree of awareness of these changes.

Their previous success in communication, and the actions that led to that success, are meaningless in this new environment. Simply repeating what they did yesterday will not generate impactful communication today.

Success depends on the ability to examine the external environment, collect relevant information, sense changes, and make internal adjustments. It is about adaptation. Darwin called it "survival of the fittest." Yet if you are at stage four and Unconsciously Competent, you cannot adjust. You cannot survive.

Unfortunately, this is the fallacy of conventional leadership. Unconscious Competence is the goal. At best, this myth is ineffective; at worst, it is dangerous.

And this myth is everywhere. We have been told that we need to become experts in our field, so that we can perform our work with muscle memory, out of habit, like riding a bike. Conventional leadership places a tremendous value on experience. Why? Because it falsely believes that the behaviors that led to success yesterday will lead to success again today.

This is why, as a hiring manger, you are praised by conventional leadership for hiring an individual with 16 *years* of experience in a particular market. It doesn't matter that the market underwent a drastic transformation 16 *months* ago, rendering the skills that previously contributed to success useless. And what of the pending, and predictable, failure that is about to occur? The conventional leader can't even see it coming.

So where do we go from here? As conscious leader, your first step is to figure out your starting point. You need a map. And you need to learn how to navigate with it.

Conscious Navigation

"The traveler is active; he goes strenuously in search of people, of adventure, or experience. The tourist is passive; he expects interesting things to happen to him."
- Daniel J. Boorstin

Conventional leadership doesn't like maps and prefers not to use them. Consistently busy and rushed, it believes that maps require too much time and effort. Conventional leadership is only concerned about one thing—arriving at the destination in as little time as possible. It doesn't matter how you get there, just get there fast! And you can get there fast if you've been provided a 3-D image of the landscape and real-time, turn-by-turn instructions by a lady with a British accent.

Ironically, conventional leadership, which was founded on a myth, has embarked on the quest to find the mythical leadership GPS. Unfortunately, driving and leadership are not synonymous. You can drive across the country and arrive at your target destination without the slightest idea of how you got there. But you can't lead like that.

Leadership doesn't come with a GPS; but it does come with a map. And you must learn how to use the map if you don't want to stay lost forever. So how do you use it?

To navigate effectively with a map, you need three basic elements:
- **Humility:** You must admit that you are lost.
- **Self-awareness:** You must identify your current location.
- **Confidence:** You must move forward.

Just as these three components are critical if you are to be an effective navigator, they are also critical if you are to be an effective leader—a conscious leader.

Navigating the Leadership Map—Humility

"To be conscious that you are ignorant is a great step to knowledge."
 - Benjamin Disraeli

I might be lost. Humility is a term that is not really in vogue today. In fact, it probably has never been in vogue. It's not a conventional term, and that's the problem. Without humility, you will never admit you are lost. But if you can't admit you are lost, regardless of the resources available, you will never arrive at your destination.

Humility allows you, as a conscious leader, to pull out the map. If you don't think you are lost, you will never open a map (or ask for directions). It is unfortunate when a lack of humility prevents conventional leaders from recognizing the need for a map. It is tragic when a lack of humility prevents a conventional leader from opening the map that he has already been given.

"Wait a minute," you might say. "No one is that arrogant. That is an exaggeration." Is it really? Let's drop back in on Todd and Julie. If this story doesn't strike you as an exaggerated caricature, then we have made our case. Most people don't have the humility to admit when they are lost.

Todd and Julie are driving to meet a new potential vendor, Fox Paper. This is a big meeting because they are going to have the opportunity to sign an exclusivity agreement for Fox's new, proprietary web-portal ordering system. They have a 1:00 pm meeting with the Vice President. Neither has been to Fox's facility before, but they print out directions before they leave. Todd's car doesn't have GPS, but he is confident that if they leave at 12:00 pm, they can arrive by 12:30 pm, giving them a 30 minute buffer.

TODD (12:04 pm): This trip should be a breeze. I've been to this area of town before. We will just hop onto the interstate. So, what are your predictions for this meeting with Fox Paper?
JULIE (12:06 pm): We will see. I hope the live model works as well as the demo we received in the mail. This could be a huge win for us. Hey, did you grab the directions off the printer?
TODD (12:06 pm): No, I thought you did.

JULIE (12:06 pm): No, I thought you did. Oh well, no big deal. Do you want to turn back around and get them? We have plenty of time.

TODD (12:07 pm): Nah, it'll be okay. I've been to this area before. I called on them as a sales rep a few years back. They are just a few exits up the road.

JULIE (12:21 pm): Are we getting close to the exit?

TODD (12:21 pm): I think it is either this one or the next...wait... here it is, exit 54.

JULIE (12:28 pm): Are we close? I wanted to make sure we had time to prep for the meeting.

TODD (12:28 pm): Very close. It's just a couple more streets up.

TODD (12:32 pm): Wait a minute. My bad, I took a left back there when I should have taken a right. Let me do a quick U-turn and we will be there in no time.

JULIE (12:33 pm): Hey, there is a convenience store. Why don't you pull in and ask for directions? Or see if they have a map?

TODD (12:33 pm): What'd you say? A map? No, don't worry. We will be there in a snap.

JULIE (12:41 pm): Todd, come on. It's obvious that you don't know where this place is. It's no big deal; let's just find a gas station and ask for directions or get a map. I'll run out and do it.

TODD (12:44 pm): Okay, that's fine. Wait, I recognize that blue building. It's all coming back to me now. A couple of left turns and we are there. Promise.

JULIE (12:49 pm): Todd, you have passed four convenience stores. Let's just stop and ask.

TODD (12:51 pm): We still have plenty of time. It's right across from this shopping center.

JULIE (12:55 pm): Todd, will you please stop and ask?! We are going to miss this meeting.

TODD (12:56 pm): If it's not right past the next stoplight, we will stop.

JULIE (12:58 pm): When do we get to the next stoplight?

TODD (12:59 pm): This is weird. I could have sworn this road was one-way. Must have done some construction. Stoplight is right around this curve...

JULIE (1:00 pm): You have got to be kidding me. Did that sign just say "Welcome to Rhode Island"?

We really hope that this doesn't stir up any old, bitter, personal memories. Ladies, take a deep breath. It's not his fault—something to do with males and the Y chromosome.

The sad part is that we all can relate to this story. While we can laugh and joke about driving incidents, there is a serious principle at work here. And it has to do with another myth of conventional leadership:

- **Myth:** Confidence is the defining character trait of a leader.
- **Truth:** Humility is the defining character trait of a leader.

We aren't saying that confidence isn't important for a leader. In fact, it is one of the three essential characteristics of a conscious leader, which we will discuss in detail shortly. But confidence isn't as critical as humility.

Ironically, confidence and humility are related. It requires a tremendous amount of confidence to be humble. You can be humble and still not be a good leader. But you can't be a good leader and not be humble.

Humility allows you to view yesterday's success with the proper perspective. Without that perspective, we tend to believe that the behaviors that led to yesterday's success become a prerequisite for today's success. This is why, devoid of humility, conventional leadership places such a tremendous value on what worked yesterday. And it is also why conventional leadership is not working today. Without humility, it is almost impossible to generate impact.

Humility is the first key component required of a conscious leader. It is a conscious leader's defining characteristic. Humility says, "I might be lost. I need to open a map." But once the map is open, then what?

Navigating the Leadership Map—Self-Awareness

"The first act of leadership is coming to grips with yourself, who you are, and what is of value to you, and shaping yourself by acts of conscious will into what you want to become."
     - Fenwick W. English

You are here. Have you ever visited a large shopping mall and wondered why they provide you with two maps? In addition to the folded brochure/map you get from the visitor center, you also have access to the illuminated kiosks/directories placed every one hundred yards. The kiosks show the exact same map as you received in the folded brochure. It seems like a waste of money to duplicate the map in your hand. So why are those kiosk/directories needed? Because they have the red dot with a "You Are Here" sticker.

You have to know where you are in order to figure out where you are going. This is called self-awareness. And it is critical to conscious leadership.

You can't *change* what you don't *understand*. And change is essential to leadership and impact.

Unfortunately, conventional leadership doesn't understand self-awareness.

Although self-awareness is a conventional buzzword, conventional leadership makes self-awareness impossible to achieve. As we stated earlier, conventional leadership ignores the belief component of the outcome model. Conventional leadership focuses on the outcomes, and sometimes, although rarely, the behaviors that led to those outcomes. But it never deals with beliefs; it doesn't even acknowledge them! Yet if you don't know why you behaved in a certain manner, how in the world are you supposed to change your behavior?

Think about that. Self-awareness involves more than just comparing my behavior with my circumstances. It involves knowing and understanding why I behaved in a certain manner. Without the "why," there is no self-awareness. And while intuitively we recognize that self-awareness sounds like a good thing, we don't know where to look for it.

Start looking at your beliefs. By definition, self-awareness is about understanding our beliefs. Then you can see what caused your behaviors. Ironically, and unfortunately, while conventional leadership is throwing around the term "self-awareness" as the latest fad, it is instructing you to progress to a state of Unconscious Competence and to focus on your outcomes and behaviors.

We will spend more time on self-awareness (especially at the belief level) throughout this book. This portion is intended simply to introduce it as one of the fundamentals required for conscious navigation.

Humility allows the conscious leader to open a map. Self-awareness allows him to pinpoint his current location. Confidence allows him to go forward.

Navigating the Leadership Map—Confidence

All aboard. Given today's culture and environment, it shouldn't be hard to convince you of the important role that confidence plays within leadership. As we stated earlier, conventional leadership hails confidence as the defining character trait of a leader. Conscious leadership values true confidence, which might look different than its current caricatures. Unfortunately, conventional leadership sometimes confuses confidence with cockiness:

- Confidence allows you to admit that you are lost. Cockiness claims to never get lost.
- Confidence allows you to admit that just because you were successful yesterday doesn't mean that you will be successful today. Cockiness claims that success is inevitable.
- Confidence allows you to embrace new, better ways of business. Cockiness will loudly assert that its way is the best way.
- Confidence allows you to admit that you were wrong so that you can learn and grow. Cockiness will never acknowledge failure.
- Confidence allows you to read the map, asking others for help along the way. Cockiness doesn't believe that it needs help.
- Confidence allows you to progress forward without all of the information, knowing that you might need to make adjustments mid-journey. Cockiness will rationalize the delay, afraid of moving forward without guaranteed results.
- Confidence allows you to press forward, aware of and in spite of your doubts. Cockiness is not aware of its doubts.

- Confidence allows you to keep moving forward, even in the face of criticism. Cockiness, unwilling to make a difficult decision, is never criticized.
- Confidence allows you to challenge the consensus and adopt viewpoints contrary to the status quo. Cockiness, never straying from the crowd, always sides with the majority.

Like most of the lists in this book, this one isn't exhaustive. But you can see the differences between confidence and cockiness. Confidence is quiet, reserved, and often lives under the surface. Cockiness is loud, brash, and in-your-face. But when the pressure heats up, cockiness crumbles into powder and soot, whereas confidence is transformed into a diamond.

Confidence is valuable to a conscious leader because it allows him to fully leverage the power of humility. It also allows him to ask the penetrating questions, without being afraid of the answers capable of truly defining his current location. It then allows him to move forward regardless of opposition.

You will never have all of the answers. As a leader, you aren't supposed to. When you are looking at your map, you will never know for certain that a particular route will take you to your desired destination. Confidence is okay with that, and tells you to move forward anyway.

Conventional leadership discourages you from opening a map. It subsequently renders it impossible for you to identify your current location. But it demands that you move towards a destination with speed and confidence (or cockiness).

MIRROR, MIRROR ON THE WALL...

———

A quick disclaimer: Humility, self-awareness, and confidence are cornerstones of conscious leadership. While we will address all three in this book, we will spend a disproportionate amount of time on self-awareness. Self-awareness is a skill that can be taught, learned, and applied. Confidence is an overarching attitude that serves as a background for the conscious leader. Humility is a decision.

Offered to all leaders, it can be accepted or rejected. You, the reader, can either decide to be humble or decide not to be humble. Humility can be chosen, but it can't really be taught (at least not in this context). So please don't interpret the focus on self-awareness as a devaluation of humility or confidence. Instead, interpret it as though we have made the assumption that you have confidently decided to be humble.

If you haven't decided to be humble, then we want to take this opportunity to be truthful with you. For you, this book will be less impactful than it will be for the leader who has chosen to be humble. You will still gain some value, but that value will be muted. Without humility, it is very difficult for a leader to consistently generate sustainable impact.

With that disclaimer out of the way, let's continue.

As we have discussed, self-awareness is a cornerstone of conscious leadership. As its name implies, for you to be effective and impactful, you must be cognitive of leadership. Not only do you need to be aware of your changing environment, but you also need to be aware of yourself, and the interaction between you and the environment. You need to know not just what you do, but you need to understand why you do it. You need to move back a level in the Adult Learning Model. You need to return to stage three, Conscious Competence. You need to be aware of your ability, and why it may or may not be effective in a given situation.

This is difficult. It requires a tremendous amount of effort and energy to remain at the conscious level. It is much easier to drive when you are not thinking about driving. We would all rather zone out and sing along to the radio than concentrate on the traffic around us while focusing on our actions. Yet, when it starts pouring rain, or when the streets are covered with snow, you instinctively turn the radio down, put both hands on the wheel, and drive at a conscious level. Why? The environment has changed, and you are required to operate at the level of Conscious Competence. Your driving is now more effective. But it is not easy.

Self-awareness is not a new concept, regardless of what conventional leadership books claim. Socrates discovered this principle over two thousand years ago when he memorialized the maxim, "Know thyself." Today's research has proven that an increase in self-awareness leads to an increase in social skills and an increase in interpersonal relationship skills. Research has also proven that those interpersonal relationship skills are a key determinate of business, and leadership, results. This shouldn't really surprise us; we know that those interpersonal skills are important. We don't need any new research or information about self-awareness, we just need application. What does self-awareness look like? How do you achieve it?

You start by using a mirror. You look in the mirror, and you study what you see, focusing on transforming who you are, not what you do. The mirror doesn't lie. Mirrors allow for the process of reflection.

Reflection is the critical factor in the application of self-awareness. Reflection is defined as, "an image, a representation, or a careful consideration." Reflection involves the examination and interpretation of our past experiences. Reflection requires first observing the "what" (the outcomes) and the corresponding "how" (the behaviors). At that point, we are ready to move to the "why" (the beliefs).

Reflection involves looking backwards to fully understand what happened, how it happened, and why it happened. What did we achieve, how did we act, and what did we think? If you don't understand the details of yesterday, it is difficult to put the dynamics of today into proper perspective. There is no better, or alternative, way to develop self-awareness than through the practice of reflection. Thus, reflection is instrumental for the conscious leader. So how do you reflect?

Start broadly, and ask yourself a question: What do you believe? Let's narrow that question down a little start by looking at your calendar. How do you spend your time? Not in theory, but in reality? We have asserted that your beliefs and your behaviors are linked, and that your beliefs drive your behaviors. *What we do* is a great indicator of *what we believe.*

For instance, all conventional leaders say that they believe in training and developing people. But do you really believe that? How can you tell? Your calendar is one indicator. Look at your calendar over the last four weeks. How much time have you spent coaching, training, or developing people over the past month? Barring some crazy life event or exception, if you really believed that training people was important, you would have done it. So how much time did you really spend developing people over the past four weeks? This is another reason why conventional leadership doesn't really embrace self-awareness. Done well, it is painful. Always. Don't panic, this is a good thing. We will discuss this aspect of self-awareness and conscious leadership in the next chapter.

Skeptical? We respect that. Consider today's most advanced leadership schools (we are not going to throw the baby out with the bath water). The most advanced MBA programs involve some sort of mountain hike or expedition. They require you to travel to a foreign land to perform a foreign activity. Why? So that you can experience two of the pillars of conscious leadership examined thus far: the importance of beliefs and self-awareness.

Reflection does not happen by accident, especially in today's society. If you wait for the right moment for things to slow down to allow you to reflect, it will never happen. To be effective, reflection must be intentional. It must be constant, disciplined, rigorous, and facilitated. A base camp on Mount Everest forces this situation. There are no cell phones, no laptops, and no Internet. The stillness forces you to silence your mind and experience a heightened level of self-awareness.

As the vast majority of us are not expert climbers, we cannot operate out of habit. We have to move back from Unconscious Competence. The foreignness of the situation forces us to remain conscious of *what* we are doing, and more importantly, *why* we are doing it. The expedition forces us to be conscious of our behaviors and our beliefs.

And it is in those types of environments that true growth is possible. Those excursions are designed to force people to function at the conscious level (behaviors and beliefs) and then provide an environment to reflect on those behaviors and beliefs. This is the crux of conscious leadership. And this is also why these expeditions can be successful in helping people grow as leaders.

But what about those of us who have never been on a climbing expedition? There is good news. You don't have to climb a mountain or go on an African safari to develop as a conscious leader. The principles apply regardless of the situation. Mountain climbing is not a prerequisite for reflection. You can reflect on anything. And, you can be conscious of your beliefs and behaviors regarding any topic. Conscious leadership is about applying these principles to your Tuesday afternoon budget meetings.

But, when dealing with your everyday experiences, there is one more element that needs to be accounted for—one that you didn't have to deal with while you were on the mountain—unlearning.

Unlearning

"When I let go of what I am, I become what I might be."
    - Lao Tzu

Another current buzzword of conventional leadership is "synergy." Synergy is based upon the principle that $1+1=3$; in other words, the whole is greater than the sum of the individual parts. And we wholeheartedly embrace this principle...most of the time.

Our past experiences and success have ingrained within each of us certain behaviors and fostered certain beliefs. No one is a blank slate. From as early as five years of age, we have formed certain beliefs. Your beliefs continue to be molded and shaped throughout your developmental years. This is why psychologists spend so much time digging into the past. Those beliefs that were formed in the past impact our behavior in the present. There are probably very few arenas in life where you have no preconceived ideas or rooted beliefs. You definitely don't encounter anything on a day-to-day basis where you are not impacted by previous experiences and held beliefs. Those activities where you are a blank slate are incredibly rare.

Why is this important? It is in this area of beliefs where conventional leadership's unequivocal support of the synergy principle fails. Beliefs don't operate in a synergistic fashion. Said differently, you cannot hold a particular belief, add to it another belief, and expect a fruitful outcome. If the belief that you added in any way contradicts the belief you already possess, you will experience internal conflict

What's the take-home point here? Whenever we are introduced to a new belief we want to assimilate into our character, we must first unlearn previously held beliefs. Sometimes we are aware of this process; sometimes we aren't. Unlearning isn't always a sequential process. In some cases, unlearning presents itself as openness to new ideas and willingness to admit you were wrong.

This introduction to unlearning has been presented from an abstract point-of-view. What would a concrete example of this look like? Consider the four-minute mile. For decades, this feat was considered impossible. Scientists concluded that the human body was not capable of running one mile in less than four minutes. Since the inauguration of the IAAF (International Amateur Athletic Foundation) in 1913, no one had broken the four-minute mark.

But in 1954, Roger Bannister changed the belief of the world when he finished one mile in 3:59.4. The four-minute glass ceiling, which had remained intact for decades, was shattered; and within a just few days, the four-minute mark was eclipsed again by John Landy. In fact, within 20 years of Bannister's feat, the glass ceiling would be broken by high school runners. Today, a four-minute mile isn't considered the *ceiling*, but the *standard*, for middle-distance runners.

What happened? Runners everywhere, with the help of Roger Bannister, unlearned the "fact" that a four-minute mile was impossible. Beliefs have incredible power. For decades, believing that the four-minute mile was impossible, the world was incapable of achieving this feat. As soon as this myth was debunked, a new belief was introduced to runners everywhere. Believing that this time could be broken, runners across the world broke it again and again and again. Success hinged on unlearning an old belief and embracing a new one.

Just as we must uninstall old computer software before we install new software, we must discard old ideas before we can embrace new ones. To achieve synergy as a conscious leader, you must unlearn your current set of beliefs before you adopt a new one. If you have changed your stance with regard to politics at some point in your life, you have experienced unlearning.

This makes sense, right? The concept of unlearning is incredibly intuitive, yet it is often ignored. Like most of the principles of conscious leadership, unlearning, albeit intuitive, is difficult. Why is it so hard?

First, you cannot unlearn what you don't understand. Said differently, you cannot embrace a new idea if you cannot unlearn an old idea. And you cannot unlearn an old idea if you are not even aware of the old ideas that you are currently embracing. A high level of self-awareness is required for unlearning. Unfortunately, as we have already discussed, self-awareness is rare, especially in today's era of conventional leadership.

Second, beliefs have an emotional component. You don't believe something (consciously or subconsciously) by accident. There is a legitimate reason, at least from our perspective, behind each belief that we embrace. You become emotionally attached to your beliefs. And when you are unlearning an old belief, you are essentially saying, "I was wrong." The emotional factor to unlearning is real and powerful. It requires both humility (to admit that you were wrong) and confidence (not only to admit you were wrong, but to embrace a new belief). This is another reason why the conscious leader is characterized by humility, self-awareness, and confidence.

For those of you who prefer the concrete to the abstract, let's look at a tangible example of unlearning that will illustrate the power of emotions. Let's talk about clothes.

First, think of the last time you hosted a garage sale. Specifically, think about the internal struggle you experienced as the big day drew near. At a garage sale, you get rid of items you don't want or need anymore. You undoubtedly found some old socks and sweaters with which you were glad to part. But, being honest with yourself, there were many items that you were unwilling to part with for no rational reason. But there was an emotional reason. You wanted to hold onto the quilt that your friend gave you when you were eight, now grease stained from being buried under the toolbox for the last 10 years. And you found yourself unwilling to part with the security uniform that you wore to your first job after college (even though it is now three sizes too small).
Now, think about your last trip to a department store. When you saw a new outfit that you wanted to purchase, you didn't experience that same intense emotional conflict. You came; you saw; you purchased.

The principle that is at work when we are buying new clothes or discarding old clothes is the same principle that governs our emotional attachment to our intangible beliefs. It is much more difficult to let old ideas go than to embrace new ones. And while difficult, the ability to unlearn is pivotal to your success as a conscious leader.

So What Now?

"The world is full of people whose notion of a satisfactory future is, in fact, a return to the idealized past."

- Robertson Davies

We have provided you with this framework so that not only will you better understand leadership, but so that we can better communicate leadership. Leadership is complex. It is simultaneously intellectual and intuitive, rational and emotional, logical and unreasonable. While this framework is intellectual, rational, and logical, it doesn't devalue the intuitive, emotional, and unreasonable components of leadership—it *explains* them! Conscious leadership recognizes that the most impactful leaders are those who can harness the power of intuition and can tap into the strength of emotion (often through storytelling).

The conscious leadership framework will enable you to comprehend intuition, understand emotion, and analyze that which lacks logic. If these "softer" elements of leadership can be understood, then they can be trained and developed. This development is not easy, nor is it a quick-fix (unlike the conventional leadership mantra of today); but it is powerful.

At its core, conscious leadership is about belief change. True, there are other components of conscious leadership, but the reflection, self-awareness, and unlearning are supporting structures. Belief change is the cornerstone. If you cannot change your beliefs, then you will never be a great leader. If you don't have a system for intentionally introducing yourself to new ideas and new thoughts (the most powerful of those ideas coming as a result of your reflection on your own experiences), then you will stagnate. You might have your 15 minutes of fame when your beliefs (and the subsequent behaviors) align with the circumstances in the environment. But without the ability to change your beliefs, you will find it difficult to make a lasting impact.

That could be an intimidating thought because belief change sounds scary, unreachable, intangible, and vague. So what now?

Skipping the Summary

At the end of every chapter, from this point forward, we will provide you with the chance to peer into the mirror. This will give you an opportunity to apply what you have just read, as well as reflect on what you really believe.

We are conscious of the fact that in your typical conventional leadership books, the "summary" section is normally nothing more than a regurgitation of previous points (which, to the credit of conventional leadership, is consistent with the definition of a summary). However, regardless of its definition, you, like us, probably skip most summaries.

Please don't skip this. At the end of each chapter is not a summary, but a section entitled "Mirror, Mirror on the Wall…" We won't ask you, "Who is the fairest of them all?" but we will provide you with the "Conscious Leader's Toolbox" at the end of each chapter. The Toolbox is filled with some practical ways to help you identify what you really believe as well as provide some guidelines to help you implement what you have learned. Implementation is required for impact.

These tools are practical and intentional. They aren't designed to tell you what to *do* as a conscious leader; they are designed to help you *become* a conscious leader. At the conclusion of the book, if you can describe conscious leadership, but you actually aren't in the process of becoming one, we have missed our mark. The Toolbox is designed to help you write your story and write it with impact, not just read about the impact of others.

The Toolbox contains new information that complements the material in each chapter. After the Toolbox, you will find a section entitled "Reflection Points" which summarizes some of the key themes in the chapter. Although we wish that you wouldn't skip over this section either, we understand that it is a behavior you must unlearn, and we are conscious it might happen anyway.

Your Story

As you are writing your story, it is often helpful to study the stories of others. Painful as it might be, you need to study the myth of conventional leadership. The better you understand its beginning origins (where it came from), the better you will understand its outcomes (where it's going). And conventional leadership's story doesn't end with meaningful change and significant impact; it ends with normalcy and status quo.

But your story doesn't have to be normal, nor does it have to be fictional to be impactful. You can write a meaningful story—a legendary story—that others will want to read, but you can't do it out of muscle memory and habit. You will have to let go of the old and embrace the new.

You need humility, allowing others to edit and proofread your work. You need self-awareness to recognize which chapters to emphasize and which chapters to delete. And you need confidence to keep writing—even during those times when you feel that no one would ever want to read your story.

Because they will read it—if it's impactful. Stories of impact are *always* read. Be conscious of the story you are writing.

Mirror, Mirror on the Wall…Chapter 2

The Conscious Leader's Toolbox

1. **Questions:** In regards to the Adult Learning Model, do you more naturally function at the Conscious Competence level or the Unconscious Competence level? Why? Thinking about your work experiences over the past six months, provide two examples of each.

2. **Questions:** Have you decided to be humble? Why or why not? Was it a difficult decision? Why? How does that decision impact your leadership?

3. **Questions:** Are you self-aware of your self-awareness? Do you think that you have a high level of self-awareness? Why or why not? Would others agree? What have you done recently to improve it?

4. **Questions:** How do you reflect on your experiences? What is your method of reflection? Are you intentional? Is your reflection constant, disciplined, rigorous, and facilitated? When was the last time you reflected on an experience? What was that specific experience? What learnings or insights (be specific) did you gain?

5. **Questions:** Are you confident? Chances are, your confidence level varies per subject. Where are you most confident? Why? Where are you least confident? Why? Are you confident in your leadership ability? Are you confident enough to be humble?

6. **Questions:** Is unlearning hard for you? What beliefs are you currently holding on to that have a large emotional component? What would it take to let them go?

7. **Questions:** How do you follow? Followship is a great predictor of leadership. The way you follow says a lot about the way you lead. Who do you currently follow? How do you follow when you agree with the leader? How do you follow when you disagree?

8. **My Leadership Journey:** Following are graphs (and examples); "time" is the X axis and "emotion" is the Y axis. Map out your life, starting as early as you like. What were the major moments of your life? What were your most meaningful experiences, both positive and negative? What impact have they had on you, especially your beliefs about leadership? List your two high points and two low points. Specific to those events, what have you learned about leadership? Go into as much detail as your comfort level allows. Your graph should contain both professional and personal experiences. The personal moments have probably impacted your beliefs more than your professional moments.

9. **Leadership Philosophy:** What is your leadership philosophy? What do you currently believe about leadership? Think about it. Say it aloud. Then write it down. As the saying goes, "You don't know what you mean until you see what you say." There is no right or wrong, there is just awareness. Are you surprised by what you wrote? Would those you lead agree with your philosophy? Would they say that your actions and behaviors really line up with those beliefs?

10. **Strength Identifier:** Complete the exercise to identify some of your leadership strengths.

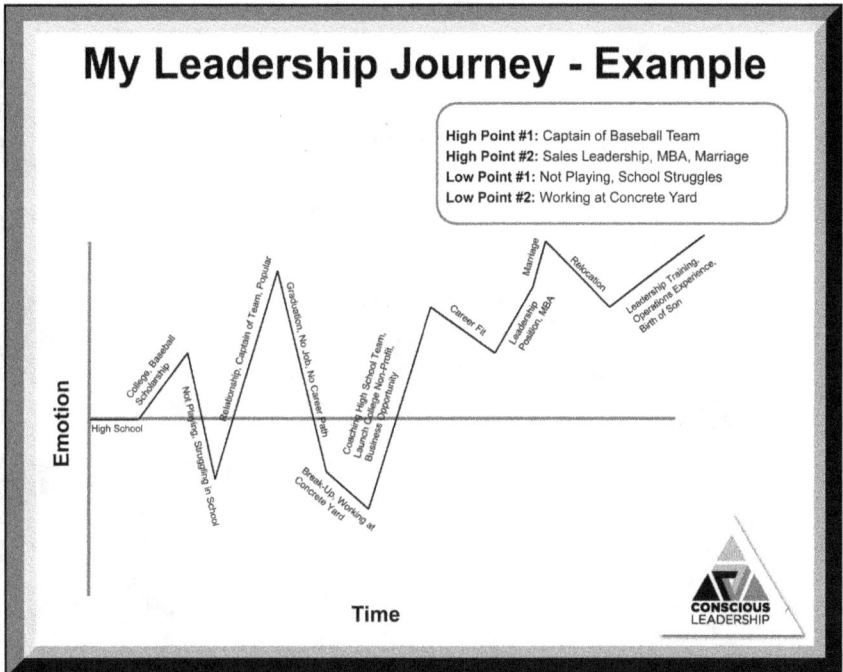

My Leadership Journey - Example

High Point #1: Captain of Baseball Team
High Point #2: Sales Leadership, MBA, Marriage
Low Point #1: Not Playing, School Struggles
Low Point #2: Working at Concrete Yard

Emotion

High School

College Baseball Scholarship

Not Playing

School Struggles in Business

Relationship, Captain of Team, Popular

Graduation, No Job, No Career Path

Break-Up, Working at Concrete Yard

Coaching High School Team, Launch College Non-Profit, Business Opportunity

Career Fit

Leadership Position, MBA

Marriage

Relocation

Leadership Training, Operations Experience, Birth of Son

Time

CONSCIOUS LEADERSHIP

My Leadership Journey - Example

High Point #1

Description: Captain of college baseball team, became leader within team, performed at a high level

What I learned: I liked leadership (and being responsible for younger players); really enjoyed being a part of a team (it was more than just playing baseball)

High Point #2

Description: Finished MBA, Leadership position, married

What I learned: MBA exposed me to multiple aspects of business (which I enjoyed); learned how to create and lead a team; my wife

Low Point #1

Description: Not playing on college team, struggling in school

What I learned: I was failing and was not in the spotlight; I had to learn patience, humility; developed discipline to be ready should I get a chance

Low Point #2

Description: Working at concrete yard (after graduation from college), no job, no career path

What I learned: Humility; experienced pain that judgment causes; understood the value of money

Notes:

CONSCIOUS LEADERSHIP

49

My Leadership Journey

High Point #1:
High Point #2:
Low Point #1:
Low Point #2:

Emotion

Time

CONSCIOUS
LEADERSHIP

My Leadership Journey

High Point #1

Description:

What I learned:

Low Point #1

Description:

What I learned:

High Point #2

Description:

What I learned:

Low Point #2

Description:

What I learned:

Notes:

CONSCIOUS
LEADERSHIP

Strength Identifier

Rating

- You are going to identify your strengths and weaknesses
- List your 5 biggest strengths and 3 biggest weaknesses
  - Rate yourself on a scale of (**-5 to 5**)

Strengths

Description	Rating
1.	-5 ——————— 5
2.	-5 ——————— 5
3.	-5 ——————— 5
4.	-5 ——————— 5
5.	-5 ——————— 5

Weaknesses

1.	-5 ——————— 5
2.	-5 ——————— 5
3.	-5 ——————— 5

Notes

CONSCIOUS
LEADERSHIP

Leadership Philosophy
Writing It Down

- This exercise is designed to help you clarify current leadership principles
- It will help you identify some beliefs which currently drive your leadership

Leadership Philosophy

- Why are you a leader?

- What do like most about leadership? Least? Why?

- What is your vision for the team you are leading? Why?

- What do you expect from your team? Why? Has this been communicated?

- What can your team expect from you? Why? Has this been communicated?

- What critical tasks will you set out to accomplish in this particular situation? Why?

- What values do you hold in high regard for a leader? Why?

- Who is the best/worst leader you have ever worked for? Why?

Notes

CONSCIOUS
LEADERSHIP

Strength Identifier

Clarification

- This exercise will help you gain clarity about your self-perception
  - Utilize the strengths and weaknesses you previously identified

Strength

- Complete this pie chart representing your total % of strengths and your total % of weaknesses

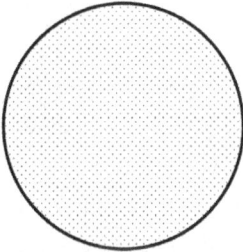

Out of 100%:

What % of your pie chart is strengths?

What % of your pie chart is weaknesses?

- How did you feel when you identified each strength?

- How did you feel when you identified each weakness?

- Which strength do you think is most unique to you?

- What is your current perception of yourself?

Notes

CONSCIOUS
LEADERSHIP

Reflection Points

- Belief → Behavior → Outcome
- "Why" → "How" → "What"
- Who you *are* → What you *do* → What you *produce*
- Beliefs drive behaviors that influence outcomes
  - What you do stems from who you are
  - Changing circumstances render behaviors obsolete
  - Conventional leadership only focuses on outcomes and behaviors
    - What you should do
  - Meaningful, lasting change comes from belief change
    - Who you are
  - Belief change consistently generates sustainable impact
- Adult Learning Model
  - Four stages
    - 1. Unconscious Incompetence: You don't know what you don't know
    - 2. Conscious Incompetence: You know what you don't know
    - 3. Conscious Competence: You know what you know
    - 4. Unconscious Competence: You don't know what you know
  - Conventional leadership pursues stage four (Unconscious Competence)
  - Conscious leadership pursues stage three (Conscious Competence)
- Three characteristics required of a conscious leader:
  - Humility
    - Admit that you are lost (open the map)
    - The defining characteristic of a conscious leader, a decision
  - Self-awareness
    - Identify your current location (read the map)
    - A skill that can be taught, a focal point of this book
  - Confidence
    - Move forward towards your destination (use the map)
    - An overarching attitude
- Self-awareness
  - Required for belief change
  - Reflection is the best way to increase your self-awareness
  - Must be intentional, disciplined, and focused

- Unlearning
    - o Uninstall old software before you install new software
    - o Unlearning is required for synergy at the belief level
    - o Difficult
        - Requires a high degree of self-awareness
        - Currently-held beliefs have an emotional component

CONSCIOUS
LEADERSHIP

CHAPTER 3

OLD DOGS
AND NEW TRICKS

"The trouble with most of us is that we would rather be ruined by praise than saved by criticism."
- Norman Vincent Peale

"Criticism may not be agreeable, but it is necessary. It fulfils the same function as pain in the human body. It calls attention to an unhealthy state of things."
- Winston Churchill

So far, you have been introduced to some of the foundational principles of conscious leadership. While some of them might be new to you, none of them are overly complex. However, they should help you see that there is a vast difference between conventional leadership and conscious leadership.

We are now going to present you with another model and another myth. They are both fundamental to conscious leadership and impact. Because they are closely related to each other, you need to understand the model to debunk the myth. First, the model:

Conflict → Change → Impact

Conscious leadership is about impact. Impact requires change, specifically change at the belief level. And change is impossible without conflict, as conflict is the universal change agent.

What is conflict? We will show you what it looks like later in the chapter, but its official definition is worth noting: "Discord of action, feeling, or effect; antagonism or opposition, as of interests or principles; a striking together; a fight, battle, or struggle."

We will continue to explore the relationship between conflict, change, and impact throughout the chapter. It was important, however, to provide you with a basic understanding of the model before we expose you to the myth. This myth is powerful, because if accepted as truth, it will severely limit your ability to generate impact as a conscious leader. In addition, this myth partially explains why there are so few conscious leaders as compared to conventional leaders:

- **Myth:** People can't change, especially at the belief level.
- **Truth:** People can change, but people avoid change.

Old dogs can be taught new tricks! To claim that people can't change is an easy cop-out for every party involved. "Leaders" tacitly use this myth to excuse themselves from the responsibility of fostering meaningful change in their followers. Likewise, followers use this myth to absolve themselves from the responsibility of changing, developing, and progressing.

Avoiding Impact

Conscious leadership believes that people can change, even on a belief level. And this change is what is required to generate sustainable impact. Without change, leadership becomes impotent. The failure of conventional leadership is evidence of this principle.

Change is essential for leadership. Change is a common theme in the stories written by history's great leaders. Not surface-level change, but deep, belief-level change.

Consider Martin Luther King Jr. He impacted the world by constantly striving for belief change; behavior change wasn't enough. The official legislation of the United States

Government, specifically Constitutional Amendments 13, 14, and 15, put an official end to racial discrimination and slavery. Well, it put an official end to the behavior of slavery and racial discrimination. However, that official legislation didn't generate change at the belief level. And so, America saw the rise of Jim Crow, "Separate but Equal," laws.

This wasn't good enough for King (and it wasn't good enough for many other American citizens either). King wasn't satisfied with simply changing behaviors; he wanted to change beliefs. His "I Have a Dream" speech wasn't about changing actions, it was about changing thoughts. Why? Meaningful change that creates sustainable impact requires belief change. Further debunking the myth, beliefs did change. And today, that story is told around the world.

But that change didn't happen apart from conflict.

Unfortunately, most conventional leaders fail, not because they can't change, but because they *avoid* change. But they don't do so directly. They avoid change by avoiding conflict. And by avoiding conflict, conventional leaders also avoid impact.

Conflict is so central to impact that we will eventually arrive at a place where we invite it into our lives. But, to do that, we must understand why we so desperately try to avoid it. We will do this by exploring the ways we are both "hard-" and "soft-wired" to avoid conflict. First, we will explore the former.

Nature
"Whatever has overstepped its due bounds is always in a state of instability."
- Seneca

We are born with a natural drive to be at equilibrium. By equilibrium, we mean stability, or at peace with the environment around us. In other words, we all just want to get along! Think back to the last holiday you spent with your family. If everyone was getting along, chances are you had a good time. But if there was disagreement and conflict, chances are it wasn't such a good time.

This principle (people want to get along) applies outside of the holidays. At work, no one really enjoys difficult conversations. You might be able to have those conversations, but you probably don't really enjoy them. Most people would rather give a great performance review than a terrible one. You enjoy hiring people much more than firing people. As people, we are all naturally wired to desire peace and equilibrium in our relationships. None of us are wired to desire conflict.

This push towards equilibrium is evidenced outside of people and relationships. There are other examples of this principle (the desire to maintain status quo) in the non-personal realm of physics:

- **Newton's First Law (The Law of Inertia):** Bodies in motion will stay in motion, and bodies at rest will stay at rest until acted upon by an outside force.
  - o Change must be forced
  - o Physical objects won't change from current state unless forced to do so
- **Second Law of Thermodynamics (The Law of Entropy):** In a system, energy is equally distributed until equilibrium is reached.
  - o Example: Ice cubes + room temperature water = melted ice cubes + colder water.
  - o But over time: Ice cubes + room temperature water + the weekend = room temperature water
  - o Over time, physical systems naturally move towards equilibrium (status quo)

If you aren't a science person, or an abstract person, don't worry. You don't need to have a complete mastery of these laws of physics to understand the main point, which is this: there is a natural tendency to be at peace with the world around us. Nature designed both personal and non-personal systems to gravitate away from conflict and towards stability. Conflict avoidance is a universal desire. We are naturally designed to resolve and remove conflict.

Not sure how this relates to the lack of conscious leaders, or the requirements for belief change? Hold on, we will get there. Before we do, however, let's look at the other piece of this equation, nurture.

Nurture

"Nature" is used to describe how we start, the raw materials from which we were built. "Nurture" is used to describe what happens to us from that point forward, what is done with those raw materials. While some of the "nature" principles above apply to the physical world in general, the "nurture" principles are more unique to living creatures, people in particular.

From an early age, we all learned a simple, but pivotal, lesson, "You go along to get along."

Think back to your days in elementary school. If there was a bully in your class, you went along with his demands to avoid a black eye. If there was a teacher with whom you disagreed, you still followed her orders and commands to avoid detention and public chastisement. You learned to be quiet while seated, you learned to walk in a straight line, and you learned that you could only have five seconds at the water fountain before your turn was over. In short, you learned "pack mentality." Going along made it possible for you to get along. Conflict was to be avoided.

In fact, it was almost impossible to get along without going along. Those that didn't go along were labeled rebels or misfits. Your teachers could hold you back. Your principal would identify you as a "problem child." You might be without friends.

This pressure to go along to get along doesn't go away as we get older. In fact, it gets stronger with time. We just call it something different.

As adults, and as business professionals, we now consider ourselves "flexible." We get a unanimous group consensus before making a decision. We "compromise." Regardless of the verbiage used, the principle is the same. We adopt a pack mentality and go along to get along. Fortunately, for the sake of the dignity of business professionals everywhere, conventional leadership has disguised this principle with several new names.

Modern psychology is responsible for the creation of one of these new names. It refers to the "go along to get along" principle as "peer pressure." Even though we are cognizant of this principle, we see kids, and adults, do the most ridiculous things for the sole reason that everyone else is doing it. Peer pressure intensifies with age. An elementary kid will make fun of the new guy at school. A teenager will experiment with drugs. An adult will cheat on his taxes and lie during business negotiations to close the deal. Why? Because everyone else is.

Regardless of age, no one likes conflict. We don't want to buck the system. We have a desire to fit in, to conform, which has been nurtured since grade school.

There is a tremendous societal pressure to conform. We see it everywhere. We aren't saying that this pressure is always negative. At work, your company undoubtedly has a system of corporate values. New hires are exposed to these values in an attempt to get them to conform to the culture of your organization. These values are communicated, and conformity is requested to create unity. Those who don't buy into the organization's values (and culture) will eventually be terminated, or they will leave voluntarily. In this case, we would submit that this "go along to get along" mentality is a good thing. You want your company's employees to be aligned around its core values.

Our goal in this section is to raise the power of this "go along to get along" mentality to a conscious level. It is ubiquitous; it impacts people at all ages, and it is very strong. People are nurtured to avoid conflict and to fit in. There are certain circumstances where it can be positive. Most of the time, however, avoiding conflict is negative.

And it is fatal to impactful leadership.

Wanted: Conflict

"One who accepts the general ideas of his time gets along smoothest, but he does the least for progress."
   - Lewis F. Korns

Why are these concepts, nature and nurture, so powerful? They address, and explain, a basic human principle—people don't like conflict. We are naturally wired to remove conflict, and we are nurtured to avoid conflict. This is unfortunate, as per the "Conflict ➜ Change ➜ Impact" model, impact ultimately requires conflict.

The concepts of nature and nurture, however, are very helpful in understanding, and eventually debunking, the myth that people can't change. The truth is that people can change; they just avoid it by avoiding conflict.

Let's pause for a moment. A lack of change means a lack of leadership. A manager (conventional leader) is one who promotes stability, safety, and sameness. A leader drives change. And a prerequisite for change is conflict. Beliefs are not changed without conflict. Even behaviors are not altered without challenge.

Due to the influence of nature and nurture, we don't like conflict. In fact, it is natural to fear conflict. Conventional leadership, lacking the humility, self-awareness, and confidence, won't admit this fear of conflict. And paralyzed by fear, it denies the capacity for change, sabotaging any potential impact that it might have generated.

A conscious leader is not someone who has developed a masochistic desire for the pain caused by conflict. A conscious leader is simply someone who values the positive results of change *more* than the pain of conflict—someone who has embraced the truth that impactful change is impossible without conflict.

However, embracing conflict can get easier. First, simply being aware of the pain that conflict can create helps mitigate and dampen it. Conscious leadership provides you a rational framework to understand the emotional component of conflict. By understanding it, you can begin to anticipate and control it. Conflict becomes less scary, and the pain less intense. Second, embracing conflict is a muscle and a skill. Like most skills, the more you practice, the better you become, and the easier it gets.

For a concrete example, think about the last fitness program that you started. Maybe you enlisted a personal trainer, purchased new workout clothes, joined a gym, and then started a new type of workout program (weights, running, biking, swimming, yoga, etc.). Your body develops strength through conflict and challenge. When you lift a weight, you are actually creating microscopic tears within your muscle fiber. You are breaking down your muscle tissue. After the workout, the body begins to rebuild itself, healing those tears within the muscle tissue. It grows stronger. For your body to grow stronger (change), you must expose it to intentional, frequent, breakdowns (conflict).

Remember the morning after your first workout session? You were sore—so sore that it hurt to get out of bed. Yet, after a couple of months, the soreness dissipated. You could perform the same workout without experiencing that initial level of pain. As you embrace conflict, and intentionally increase your exposure to it, it becomes less and less painful. And you become stronger.

A conscious leader doesn't love the soreness that comes from starting a new fitness program. That would be crazy! He just values the positive impact of the fitness program more than the soreness.

Universal Relationships

"You don't get harmony when everyone sings the same note."
      - Doug Floyd

That was a lot to digest. Eventually, we will revisit Julie and Todd to see how they handle conflict. Before we do, however, we want to make you conscious of the fact that the relationship between conflict and change is not unique to people. This relationship affects just about everything, including personal and non-personal systems. Its influence is just as extensive as the natural desire to pursue equilibrium we explored earlier.

As we said earlier, conflict is the universal change agent.

Category	Status Quo	Conflict	Change/Impact
Nature	Finches in the Galapagos Islands have the same style beaks	Food shortage - some islands have food (bugs) hidden in trees and some have food (nuts) hidden in shells	Finches develop specialized beaks - long beaks for reaching bugs and short beaks for cracking nuts
Music	A pleasant melody	Dissonance - introduction of another melody which conflicts with the original tune	Harmony - a blend of tense and relaxed chords resolving into a new consonant chord and pleasing tune
Philosophy (Hegel's and Kant's Theory of Progress)	Thesis - the current or original state of being	Antithesis - introduction of a state of being which conflicts with the original thesis	Synthesis - combination of thesis and antithesis resulting in an improved state of being

We are conscious that these are only rudimentary representations of some major tenets of complex disciplines, and that we failed to do them justice in our explanations.

But these crude descriptions serve our purpose by illustrating another key relationship, the beneficiary/benefactor. Ultimately, the system benefits from the change created through conflict. Conflict produces change, and this change ultimately improves or enhances the system.

Not only are these relationships universal, they are also ironic. Consider this:

- **Conflict:** By nature, systems universally desire to pursue equilibrium and avoid conflict
- **Change:** Conflict is the universal requirement for change
- **Impact:** Systems benefit from the change produced by conflict

Status quo, peace, and equilibrium are universally desired. But to create change, conflict is universally required. Change results in impact.

Back to Beliefs

"The highest possible stage in moral culture is when we recognize that we ought to control our thoughts."

    - Charles Darwin

This relationship is of critical importance. It provides the context for conventional leadership and conscious leadership. The desire for status quo and equilibrium is natural, normal, and...conventional. Following this desire, conventional leadership conforms to its natural design, striving to maintain the status quo while avoiding conflict. But it does so at a cost, ignoring the requirements for change. Conscious leadership, being... conscious...of this requirement, resists the urge to conform and embraces conflict.

So where does this leave us in regards to conventional leadership, conscious leadership, and the "Conflict ➔ Change ➔ Impact" model? It all depends on what you believe.

Conventional leadership believes (unconsciously) that conflict isn't required for impact. Thus, following its natural desire to maintain the status quo and pursue equilibrium, it avoids conflict. It also avoids impact.

Conscious leadership believes that conflict is a prerequisite for impact. Thus, it decides to intentionally embrace conflict in order to create meaningful change. The outcome is the generation of impact, which benefits the entire system.

Exposed

Hopefully by now, this principle has begun to crystallize. Conscious leadership is all about change; and change is impossible without conflict. No one enjoys conflict for the sake of conflict, yet for the conscious leader, the reward (impact) justifies any temporary discomfort. And, by embracing conflict, understanding it, and exposing yourself to it regularly, the discomfort will become more and more minimal.

Challenge and conflict expose our true beliefs. The best way to see if we really believe what we say we believe is through challenge. When challenged, our resulting behavior will be the litmus test of our beliefs. We will act out of what we *really* believe (albeit perhaps subconsciously), not what we *claim* we believe. This is yet another reason why conflict is so powerful.

So as a conscious leader, we must manage our learning. We must actively invite conflict. We must intentionally seek challenge. A critical component of leadership is defining how you view and take on new challenges. Being self-aware of our natural (and nurtured) tendency to avoid conflict, we must be intentional. Ideally, this is orchestrated so that we can control our level of exposure to conflict. This ensures that we don't become stagnant in our beliefs and mindsets while simultaneously avoiding exposure to dangerously high levels of conflict too quickly. We will explore this idea of orchestrated conflict further in the next chapter.

Even with managed learning, however, exposure to conflict can be difficult. Conscious leadership is not for the weak. Conflict often presents itself in the form of criticism. The truly great leaders have the ability to bear, internalize, and grow from external criticism, without allowing it to get them down. We cannot overstate the fact that this is not easy. Embracing conflict requires a huge amount of internal strength, confidence, and courage. Julie and Todd at Acme Office Supply illustrate just how much strength embracing conflict requires, but also just how power it can unleash:

Even with the advent of Hawaiian-shirt Day, Todd continues to be frustrated. The communication issues he is having with Julie are not getting any better. Every single one of his previous managers have commended him for excellent communication, but he can't seem to get through to Julie. She continues to focus on those weekly reports. Todd recognizes that he is not on a good path, and that things can't continue to progress in this fashion. He is conscious that he has only a couple of choices.

He can either initiate conflict with Julie about this issue, or he can wait for her to bring up the topic and initiate the conflict. It is always dangerous to confront your direct manager. It would be much easier for him to go along to get along. But, that is what he has done for the previous six months, and it has gotten him nowhere. And she has not said anything directly to him. So, Todd decides to initiate the conflict. He doesn't sleep at all Thursday night and has nightmares about the meeting. Friday morning, palms sweating and heart racing, he opens up the meeting with the following:

TODD: Julie, I have something I want to talk to you about. I hope you are okay with me bringing it up. It's been on my mind for some time now, and I really want to address it with you. I don't think that we are communicating well. I feel very disconnected from you, and it is frustrating to me. And I sense that it is frustrating to you as well. I feel that you are upset with me. I am not sure what the issue is, as I have not had communication issues with my previous managers. But I know that something isn't working here, and I really would like for us to fix it. What are your thoughts?

Todd has not said anything that is disrespectful or accusatory. He has merely been truthful. Imagine yourself having this conversation with your boss. Not fun. You probably wouldn't have slept on Thursday night, either. Knowing that your palms would be sweating, you would probably have that opening sentence role-played and rehearsed verbatim. It is scary to initiate conflict, especially with your manager. Especially when you sense that she is frustrated with you already. Ideally, if there is an issue, it should be the manager who is initiating the difficult conversation, not the report. You see the strength and courage that this requires from Todd.

Now let's consider Julie. First, she is undoubtedly aware of the issue. Even though she hasn't brought it up with Todd, you can be sure that she is frustrated. Like all of us, she has probably had multiple imaginary conversations in her mind where she chews

Todd out (we can't be the only ones who launch into those mental tirades). Like Todd, she has also been commended by her previous managers and employees for excellent communication. And now Todd, by raising this issue with her directly, is implicitly criticizing her. And she is the boss. She is his boss. She couldn't get to where she is now without being able to communicate, and communicate well.

Todd has touched two important areas with Julie. First, he brought up the communication issue. Apart from the actual issue, this might touch a nerve with Julie. Deep down inside, she knows that, as the boss, it should be her responsibility to initiate this conversation. Second, and this area is perhaps more flammable than the communication issue, Todd is implicitly criticizing her communication style. If he thought her style was perfect, he would have adjusted his style to match hers. There would be no need for this conversation. By not adjusting his behavior, he believes that his communication style is superior to hers. So, what are Julie's options?

If she concedes too much, then it might give off the appearance of weakness. Yet if she doesn't get some resolution to this issue soon, things will deteriorate to the point where she will have to initiate the termination process with Todd, who has a great reputation within the company. Undoubtedly, this would lead to undesired questions from upper management. Common sense tells Julie that if this issue could be resolved, she would be able to sleep much better at night. However, all of these points are weighed against the tension of being right (because she is the boss).

Finally, this situation exposes Julie's core beliefs. Having been challenged, her next actions will indicate what she really believes. Does she believe that the boss is always right, that the employee should always cater to the boss's preferences, and that a display of managerial vulnerability should be avoided at all costs? Or does she believe in doing whatever is necessary to move forward and progress? Does she appreciate the courage of Todd, or does his criticism make her want to lash out at him?

A Stubbed Toe

Julie's response to this conflict requires just as much strength and courage as Todd required when he initiated the conflict. For Julie, the response also requires humility. It is only out of deep inner confidence that Julie could respond in the following manner:

JULIE: First, Todd, thanks for bringing this up. Truthfully, I should have brought this issue up weeks ago. Yeah, like you, I am frustrated by our lack of ability to communicate effectively. Like you, I have received praise in the past for excellent communication, which makes this current situation even more puzzling and confusing. I know that there is a lot of frustration from both of us about this issue. But I don't want to start a blame game. I am sure that there are things that we both could have done better. Even more importantly, I am sure that there are things that we can both do different going forward. So why don't we rewind all the way back to the beginning and start from there? We could both share our thoughts on communication. How have you communicated in the past? What is your ideal method of communicating with me? I can also share with you my experiences and my ideal way of communicating with you. I'm sure we will land in a good place this morning..."

Challenge reveals not just who we are, but importantly, who we are not. Conflict has the unique ability to expose our true beliefs and mindset. If you have a core belief that is challenged, you will be forced to either defend it (thus further strengthening that belief in your life) or change it. Conflict and challenge will inevitably clarify our beliefs—both what we believe and what we *don't* believe.

Pause for a moment and think about the big toe on your right foot. Is it there? Are you sure your big toe is there? How do you know? You can go through most of the day, perhaps most of the year, without being aware of your right toe. Yet you use it constantly, every time you take a step. With regards to your big toe, you are at a level of Unconscious Competence. You use it expertly, out of habit, yet you aren't even aware of it.

This situation is fine for a big toe, but it's a problem if that analogy relates to your beliefs. However, this is often the case. It is possible to go through days, years, seasons of life without being aware of beliefs. So what can you do to change this situation?

Pick your right foot off the ground. Now point your big toe downward and gently kick the floor with it—gently! Is it there? Can you feel your big toe? How do you know it's there? Are you aware of it?

What just happened? Through the process of stubbing your big toe (gently, we hope), you become aware of it. The conflict of your toe hitting the ground increased your awareness of it. There is a principle buried within this example: Conflict increases self-awareness.

Conflict is so central to conscious leadership that we will revisit it again in a later chapter, exploring this relationship from a different angle. But the core principles will remain the same. Conflict increases self awareness, and conflict is required for the meaningful change that leads to impact. By ignoring beliefs and avoiding conflict, conventional leadership has reduced its level of self-awareness, and rendered itself ineffective at creating significant, meaningful change. As a conscious leader, the only way you will be able to truly generate a lasting impact is by embracing conflict.

Your Story

All good stories have conflict.

It's natural to want to avoid conflict. We are instructed by both nature and nurture to avoid conflict. The pursuit of the status quo is natural, normal, and conventional. We all desire to be at peace with our environment.

No one wants to sail on a boat that is being rocked by wind and battered by waves. But everyone wants to read a story about that boat.

Although smooth sailing might be appealing, you don't want to read about it. And deep down inside, you don't want to write about it, either.

Your desire to create meaningful change outweighs your desire for peace and stability. And you know that you cannot create that change, or generate significant impact, without conflict.

Don't run away from conflict; run towards it. It is powerful. If you leverage that power to write your story, people will want to read it.

Mirror, Mirror on the Wall...Chapter 3

The Conscious Leader's Toolbox

1. **Questions:** What was the best piece of feedback/criticism that you have received within the last six months? Was it proactive (you sought it out) or reactive (it sought you out)? Who did it come from? Why was it valuable? How can you get more feedback like that?

2. **Questions:** How open are you to feedback and criticism? Now...answer that question honestly. Your behavior is indicative of what you really believe. What is the last piece of criticism/challenge that you received? Who was it from? How did you react?

3. **Questions**: What scares you the most about criticism? Whose criticism do you fear the most? Why? Whose do you value the most? Why? What do your reactions say about you?

4. **Exercise:** Fold your arms across your chest. What hand (right or left) is on the top? Now switch (top hand on bottom and bottom hand on top). Does that feel weird? Conflict, and the subsequent change that it introduces, will always feel uncomfortable at first.

5. **Start/Stop/Continue:** Conduct the Start/Stop/Continue exercise with your direct reports. Have each of them answer the questions on the page. Once they have completed the survey, have them all send their answers to a member of your team. Have this person compile the team's answers and send them to you. This ensures that the feedback is anonymous. Do this every six months.

6. **Follow-up Questions:** What does your emotional reaction to the Start/Stop/Continue exercise tell you about your beliefs? Do your reports feel free to challenge you as their boss? How did you react to the feedback? Did you excuse it or embrace it?

Start, Stop, Continue

360° Survey

- This survey can be given to:
  - Direct reports, colleagues, other stakeholders, mentors, mentees
- To be effective, this must be anonymous

Completed For:

- What is 1 thing that you would like me to **START** doing?

- What is 1 thing that you would like me to **STOP** doing?

- What are 3 things that you would like me to **CONTINUE** doing?

- What are my 5 biggest strengths (be specific)?

- What is my 1 biggest area for development (be specific)?

- Other

Notes

CONSCIOUS
LEADERSHIP

Reflection Points

- Conflict ⇒ Change ⇒ Impact
  - o Sustainable impact requires meaningful change
  - o Meaningful change is impossible without conflict
  - o People can change, but they avoid it by avoiding conflict
- We tend to avoid conflict because of nature and nurture
  - o Nature
    - All systems (personal and non-personal) were designed to pursue equilibrium, peace, status quo
  - o Nurture
    - "Go along to get along"
    - Peer pressure doesn't diminish over time
- Universal paradox
  - o Universal desire to pursue status quo and avoid conflict
    - Conventional leadership
  - o Conflict is the universal requirement for change and impact
    - Conscious leadership
- Don't avoid conflict, intentionally invite it
  - o Orchestrated conflict
  - o Value of progress outweighs pain of conflict
- Conflict can be painful, but it lessens over time
  - o Understand the cause of your emotions
  - o Develop this skill, practice it often
- Conflict provides clarity and self-awareness
  - o What we believe
  - o What we don't believe
- Conflict forces us to adopt new ideas or solidify old ones
  - o Impactful leaders will embrace conflict

CONSCIOUS
LEADERSHIP

CHAPTER 4

ENVIRONMENTALLY FRIENDLY

"Do not go where the path may lead, go instead where there is no path and leave a trail."
  - Ralph Waldo Emerson

"Belief in the truth commences with the doubting of all those 'truths' we once believed."
  - Friedrich Nietzsche

A conventional leader, following his natural desires, pursues equilibrium, avoids conflict, maintains the status quo, and strives for normalcy. In contrast, the conscious leader intentionally decides to embrace conflict to create change and beneficially impact the system.

So if conflict is required for change, then how do you generate conflict? Should you start acting like a 13-year-old: picking fights, calling people names, and generally becoming a bully? Not exactly…but kind of. You don't start picking fights, but you do engage in another behavior indicative of 13-year-olds…the DTR talk.

Define the Relationship (DTR)

Are you familiar with this term? If not, your children might be. The DTR talk is typically had between two teenagers in a quasi-romantic relationship. Their relationship has progressed to a point where they are more than friends (they have been flirting as only teenagers can). This romantic tension has blurred the conventional boundaries of their relationship. The goal of the DTR talk is to define those relational boundaries; are they just "good friends" or are they both comfortable being labeled as "going out?"

As a conscious leader, you also need to have the DTR talk; but you need to define a different relationship, your relationship with the system. Said differently, your ability to orchestrate conflict—and ultimately generate impact—is dependent on your relationship with the system.

Practically speaking, what does that look like? Allow us to engage you, the reader, in a DTR talk. Our relationship is probably not characterized by romantic tension, but we would like to take it to the next level. We are about to intentionally generate conflict and challenge your beliefs (Chapters 5-11). This chapter is our modified version of the DTR talk.

Why do we want to engage you in a DTR talk? For the same reason we are encouraging you to have the talk—it will increase our ability to successfully orchestrate conflict with the system (you are our "system"). We want to start the process of defining our relationship by defining a couple of terms.

In the previous chapter, we introduced the "system." As we were discussing scientific principles and some laws of physics, "system" was an appropriate term. Moving forward, we want to substitute the word "environment" for "system." What do we mean by "environment?"

By "environment," we don't mean the trees, birds, clouds, and flowers. The environment refers to everything outside of you. It is everything external. Paradoxically, conventional leadership having an internal focus but lacks self-awareness, and conscious leadership, having an external focus, possesses self-awareness. Self-awareness is gained through a combination of internal reflection and external relationships.

We will explore the relationship between internal/external focus and self-awareness throughout the remainder of the chapter. If you want to create transformational change as a leader, you need to define your relationship with your environment.

Looking Outward

"We are enslaved by anything we do not consciously see.We are freed by conscious perception."
- Vernon Howard

The purpose of an external focus is not merely to observe the environment as a stand-alone entity. Rather, the goal is to be aware of the environment in terms of your interactive relationship with it and the context it creates for your leadership. The conscious leader needs to be aware not only of his decisions and the environment, but also of the interaction between the two. Although the environment is the final piece of the leadership framework we have been creating, it is really the starting point of conscious leadership and the focal point for the conscious leader.

Why? Leadership doesn't happen in a vacuum. It happens in the context of the environment. There are two simultaneous forces at work between the conscious leader and the environment. First, the conscious leader is pushing outward and exerting influence on the environment. At the same time, he is pulling inward and drawing in new ideas, learnings, and beliefs. A conscious leader's relationship with the environment is defined though a series of continual push/pull, import/export interactions.

Without this push/pull relationship with the environment, conscious leadership cannot exist, and the conscious leader is powerless to create meaningful change. The importation of ideas from the environment provides him with a source of new beliefs. It also ensures that he maintains a proper perspective and remains relevant. It is difficult to create an impact without relevance.

It is this importation of ideas that makes his exportation of influence so impactful. Exportation of influence, by itself, is nothing special. Conventional leadership can push their will and influence outward. Without the continuous renewal that comes from pulling in, however, the outward pushing becomes less and less impactful. Said differently, your degree of impact is directly related to your ability to import.

Importation of new ideas provides the conscious leader with challenge to his beliefs, which increases self-awareness and clarity of who he is and who he isn't. On occasion, the conscious leader might assimilate some of these new ideas into his core belief system.

In addition, pulling in of new ideas allows the conscious leader to understand the context and environmental currents that affect his leadership. By comprehending his circumstances, the conscious leader can adapt his behaviors, ensuring that they are relevant and aligned with the environment, allowing him to produce continued positive outcomes.

This push/pull relationship with the environment is made possible through self-awareness, and it also increases self-awareness. Unfortunately, the pace of change and the cadence at which society moves today makes it very difficult to maintain this relationship. This explains why it is so easy to have your focus drift inward. This cadence is also why the conscious leader must be intentional about directing his attention outward.

Understanding the environment is a tall order. It can be somewhat daunting. After all, if the environment includes everything except for you, it is pretty big. Within the framework of conscious leadership, we have designed a construct that allows us to break the environment down into three smaller sections. These sections, or domains, provide a manageable framework from which you can understand the environment. These are the three domains of conscious leadership:

People—Process—Performance

People, interacting through process, deliver performance.

It is important to note that there is a causal relationship between these categories, although to a lesser degree than you have seen in previous models, "Belief ➔ Behavior ➔ Outcome" and "Conflict ➔ Change ➔ Impact". There is no "➔" linking the different components of the "People, Process, Performance" model. Although they are inter-related—an input/output relationship is present between the categories—they exist independently of each other. As a leader, your individual beliefs within each domain are independent of your beliefs outside that domain.

It is also important to note that these categories are not arbitrary. Although different people might assign them different names, the substance and content of the categories would remain intact. The titles might be interchangeable, but the content is not. In addition, the order in which they are presented (people, process, performance) is also intentional.

People

"A life is not important except in the impact it has on other lives."
        - Jackie Robinson

The people domain is first, and it is first for a reason. People are the cornerstone of every organization. Nothing happens without people. As has been said (but not always done) by others, the primary endeavor for any organization should be getting the right people on the team, and then getting those people in the right roles. Everything else should be secondary.

When all is said and done, every business—regardless of whether the company produces laundry detergent, provides financial consulting, or develops the latest solar cell technology—is a people business. *Your* business is a *people* business.

Conscious leadership is about leading people. There is a big difference between leading people and managing people. Managing people is about controlling them with a focus on regulating their behavior. Leading people is about motivating and directing them, aligning their beliefs and unlocking their potential. Leading people is about helping them write a story that they want to write and that others will want to read.

Conventional leadership believes that people are complicated. This is a myth. People aren't complicated, but they are complex. The conscious leader believes in and embraces this complexity. People's complexity is a result of their duality; a person is both rational and emotional. To be an impactful leader, you must engage your people both rationally and emotionally. Conventional leaders run away from the emotional element. Conscious leaders run towards it. We will explore the "why" and "how" of emotional engagement and avoidance during the subsequent chapters.

The best systems, technologies, and innovations cannot reduce the importance of people. People build those systems, implement those technologies, and communicate those innovations throughout the organization. People matter most. And what you believe about people will impact how you behave towards them.

Julie is meeting with Todd today to discuss the creation of his appraisal/review methodology for the following year.

JULIE: Todd, today we have a couple of decisions to make. First, we need to determine the components that will make up your performance review for the coming year. Second, we need to determine the relative weightings of those components. Do you have any initial thoughts?
TODD: Well, I don't think that we need to invent a whole new list of categories. Some of the categories from last year should work well, based on where we are trying to go as a company this year. How about the following:

Business Results:	25%
New Product Development:	20%
Market Expansion:	20%
Budget:	10%
People Development:	25%
Total:	100%

JULIE: Okay, I agree with your components, but I disagree with your weightings. I think they are off. Each objective should be weighted according to its relative importance. The most important objectives should be weighted heavier. Remember, Todd, you role is marketing and key accounts. The crux of your job is new products, new channels, and new customers. You need to have your appraisal weightings proportioned and scaled to reflect that. Let's go with these weightings:

Business Results:	35%
New Product Development:	25%
Market Expansion:	25%
Budget:	10%
People Development:	10%
Total:	100%

What does this simple dialogue say about what Todd and Julie really believe about the importance of people? Julie believes that people are a means to an end. She thinks that the marketing position is all about new products, new customers, and new channels. As a result, she wants to weight Todd's appraisal to reflect those priorities. What she doesn't understand is that it is Todd's team of people that will develop those new products, discover those new customers, and penetrate those new channels. Todd's department, and your department, is only as good as the people who work in it.

Conventional leadership either doesn't understand this principle or chooses to ignore it. At best, it assumes that people are only one component out of many required for delivering performance, no more valuable than technology or infrastructure. At worst, it assumes that people are a commodity. Of course, a conventional leader will never verbalize this. They don't have to; their behavior speaks to what they really believe.

There is no such thing as a legendary leader who is not a "people person."

This doesn't mean that a conscious leader has to be extroverted, or charismatic, or the life of the party. But you do have to value people and care about them, believing that they are the most important asset in your organization. You do have to understand them and be able to communicate with them, both rationally and emotionally. You do have to be able to understand a person at an individual level, and you do have to understand the dynamics of multiple persons working together in teams. If you don't really believe that your people are the backbone of your organization, your foundation will be weak. And eventually, under the pressures of today's environment, it will crack.

Your favorite stories—the ones that are so inspirational and moving that you read them again and again—are stories about people.

Process

After people, the next domain we need to explore is process. Process is about interaction. Process is concerned with both personal interaction (people to people) and non-personal interaction (people to things). Although it could be argued that there is a third form of process, another non-personal interaction (things to things), we think that our original category of non-personal interactions has included those types of processes. Those processes (things to things) are still set up and initiated by people.

An example of a personal interaction could be the process teams go through when trying to reach a group decision. An example of a non-personal interaction could be the process you go through when organizing your day.

People who work in operations or manufacturing encounter process on a daily basis. The primary function of your role, or your department, might be the discovery and implementation of better processes. Process improvement is the primary revenue generator for some companies. These organizations understand process, and they understand its importance. So how would they define process?

Process is the link between inputs and outputs. For the conscious leader, process is the link between people and performance. It is a loose link, unworthy of an "➡," but ultimately, the combination of people and process results in performance.

Process never stands alone. Without inputs and outputs, people and performance, process doesn't exist. There is no such thing as a process that is devoid of people and performance. In practice, this means that the boundaries are sometimes blurred between people and process as well as performance and process.

However, just because it doesn't stand alone doesn't mean that process isn't essential for a conscious leader. Process improvement will increase the generation of impact.

Todd understands the importance of process. He is engaging Julie in a conversation about their personal interactions, specifically, an element of the feedback process:

Todd and Julie are having their usual Friday 1:1 meeting.

TODD: I've got a unique request to make of you today.

JULIE: Okay, I'm all ears. But if you are looking for tickets to the company's box at the playoff game this weekend, you might be disappointed...

TODD: No (although that would be great). This is a different type of request, and this might sound a little weird. You know that my department is launching several new initiatives over the coming months. As those initiatives develop, and we approach their launch, I want to ask if you would disagree with me more often. Well, I don't really mean "disagree with me more often," but rather "disagree with my decisions more often." Or I guess I'm asking you to challenge me more frequently.

JULIE: You are right; that's a unique request and much more unusual than asking for box tickets. Can I ask why? Why do you want me to challenge you more frequently?

TODD: As you know, my department has several new people. These new hires are still getting comfortable with Acme and our culture. Until they get comfortable with the culture and with me, they tend to just agree with everything I say. We end up reaching a unanimous consensus, quickly, on just about everything. No one ever challenges my decisions, and that's not good. Ideas will go stale and performance will suffer without some healthy debate. I need someone who can provide that contrarian viewpoint. But until these new hires acclimate to the culture and begin to trust me more, they won't challenge as often as I need them to.

JULIE: Hmmm. That's well thought out. Still an unusual request, but it makes a lot of sense. Okay, can you be specific? What exactly do you want this to look like?

TODD: I'm not 100% sure what this will look like down the road, but here's my initial idea. During our 1:1s, I'll give you an update with regard to our current progress. I need you to intentionally challenge me. I need you to intentionally push me and force me to defend my ideas.

JULIE: Okay, that works for me. We can definitely give it a try. Even though it makes sense, I still have to admit, this is one of the more unusual 1:1s I think I have ever had.
TODD: Great! Again, I really appreciate this. I know this is a little out of the ordinary, but all of the group consensus within my department right now could really hurt us down the road.

This dialogue is an example of process—a personal interaction between Julie and Todd about how they will work together. This dialogue illustrates that process can involve both people and performance. It is the conduit. If you can improve that conduit, you can improve performance. Process is about people and their interactions with each other (personal) and with the surrounding infrastructure (non-personal).

A good process is not one that is absent of people (a contradiction of terms). Nor is a good process one that is absent of accountability for performance (again, a contradiction of terms). A good process is one that strengthens the link between the two and facilitates those interactions. People, interacting through process, deliver performance.

Performance

Performance is the output.

Ultimately, high performance is the result of impactful leadership. Performance can be defined in many different ways, and it can be evaluated over different periods of time. Regardless of how it is defined or when it is measured, performance is related to leadership.

The leadership/performance relationship, however, is in need of a DTR talk. Like any relationship, the more you understand it, the better it becomes. And this relationship is not easy to understand. There are enough myths and rumors about the leadership/performance relationship to fill a tabloid magazine! It's critical that we accurately understand this relationship. Why?

Performance matters. For all leaders, not just conscious leaders but also conventional leaders, it matters a lot! And it should. If your organization isn't performing well, then you have an issue. An organization cannot survive long without good performance.

Leadership focuses on performance not just because of its importance, but because of its visibility. Performance, or lack thereof, is obvious. Of all of the domains, performance is the most visible and tangible. Thus, out of all three domains, because of its importance and visibility, both conscious and conventional leadership observe performance first.

So if both consider performance of critical importance, and both observe it first, then what is the difference between conventional leadership and conscious leadership in regards to performance? Perspective.

Conventional leadership deals with performance first, and then subsequently considers process and people. And to be fair, that intuitively makes sense. Performance is the most visible domain, and it is critically important. A company can have poor processes, and still keep paying its bills if the performance is good. A company can hire mediocre people, and still keep generating profit. Right?

For a while—but not forever. Conscious leadership has a different perspective on performance. Although conscious leadership observes performance first, it actually deals with it last, after people and process. Performance is addressed last not because of its relative importance, but because of its relative position.

It's about cause and effect. Performance is the effect. People and process are the causes. Good performance is a result of good people interacting effectively through good process. Performance is the output; people and process are the inputs. If you want to impact the output, then you need to change the input.

Our belief about the relative position of performance does not diminish our belief about its importance. In fact, it augments it. You can still have individual, stand-alone beliefs about performance. Our beliefs about performance will trickle down and influence both the processes that we establish and the people with which we have those interactions.

The following is an interaction between Julie and Todd that reveals what Julie believes about the nature of performance. Note that although the belief about performance stands alone, it influences how she behaves with regard to process and people:

JULIE: Todd, Q3 ends in two weeks, and we are tracking behind our budget. Can you put together some sort of program, discounted rates or extended terms or something, that will "push" some product out the door? We need numbers now.

TODD: We could do that, but I'm not sure we should. The results wouldn't be very good. It's not just that the program would be far from ideal, it might actually be counter-productive. Right now, we don't have enough inventory in our new product lines to conduct any sort of seeding campaign. We have lots of inventory in our existing product lines, but those are products that customers are already purchasing on a consistent and regular basis. So if we discounted the price on that inventory, we could "push" it out the door and get some orders now. But the orders would be nothing more than customers buying next month's inventory early—and at a discounted price. We would literally be doing nothing more than throwing away margin dollars.

JULIE: That makes sense, but we need to hit our numbers for the quarter.

TODD: Can you tell senior management that if we miss Q3 (by just a little bit), we will hit our numbers, both revenue and profitability, for not only Q4, but for the entire year? We can always discount the existing products in Q4 if we have to. By then, we will have enough new product inventory that we could create a special promotion to seed the market (which would be incremental business) while still maintaining high margins on existing products. They just need to wait 90 days...

Although she would vigorously deny it, Julie believes that it makes sense to give up an advantageous, long-term position for a short-term gain. How do we know that this is what she believes about performance? Through the observation of her behaviors.

She is sacrificing long-term performance (hitting Q4 and the full year numbers) for short-term gain (hitting Q3 budget). She is also sacrificing senior management's long-term perception of her for their short-term perception of her (they will be much happier with her if she hits the full year but misses Q3 than if she hits Q3 but misses the full year).

It is worth noting that her belief about performance (short-term versus long-term) is impacting her behavior towards people (Todd and senior management) and process (discounting/terms/inventory management).

Performance is critical. A conscious leader must deliver performance. However, performance is a result of people and process. Although time lags might make this causality difficult to observe at times, performance always stems from people and process.

If performance begins to suffer, then as a leader, you are responsible to remedy the situation. The remedy you choose will be dependent on how well you understand the relationship between leadership and performance. As we will eventually discover, poor performance is cured by delivering medicine to people or process.

Compare/Contrast

"The key to every man is his thought…he can only be reformed by showing him a new idea which commands his own."

> - Ralph Waldo Emerson

You now have the entire framework for conscious leadership. To help solidify this framework, we are going to juxtapose conscious leadership and conventional leadership. Sometimes, the best way for a leader to understand who you are is to understand who you are not. The following contrasts should help you further understand the distinctions:

Conventional Leadership	Conscious Leadership
A myth, written through plagiary, that is unremarkable and quickly forgotten	A unique story, full of impact, that others want to read
Observes and focuses on the outcome (and sometimes behavior) portion of the model; is not aware of beliefs Belief → **Behavior** → **Outcome**	Observes outcomes and behaviors, and then focuses on the belief portion of the model **Belief** → Behavior → Outcome
Leadership is about control, stability, normalcy, and predictability	Leadership is about change, specifically belief change
People cannot and will not change	People can and will change (they just typically avoid it)
Behaves, as though the environment is static (unaware of his belief)	Believes that the environment is changing and behaves accordingly
Leadership is influence	Leadership is an activity
Instinctively functions at stage four of the Adult Learning Model (Unconscious Competence)	Intentionally functions at stage three of the Adult Learning Model (Conscious Competence)
Low levels of self-awareness resulting from a degree of cockiness	Through humility and confidence, proactively develops a high level of self-awareness
Is not aware of a need to unlearn old ideas (attempts synergy through addition)	Unlearns old ideas in order to learn new ones (addition by subtraction)
Follows the natural desire to pursue equilibrium, continues to "go along to get along," provides no benefit to the system	Embraces requirements for change, intentionally generates conflict, ultimately produces benefits for the entire system
Inward focus; he is central	Outward focus; the environment is central
Sole focus on exportation of ideas (pushing influence outward)	Simultaneous importation/exportation of ideas (pushing influence out while pulling ideas in)
Maintains status quo and normal	Generates impact

For those of you who like tables and charts, hopefully the above was helpful. For those of you who prefer more abstract thinking, we will now conduct the same exercise, comparing/contrasting the visual models of conventional and conscious leadership.

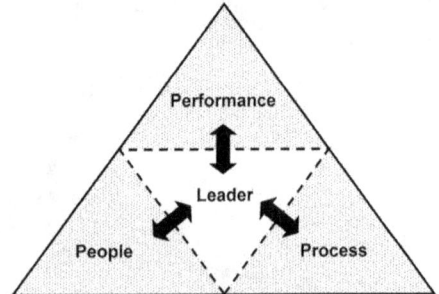

Conventional Leadership

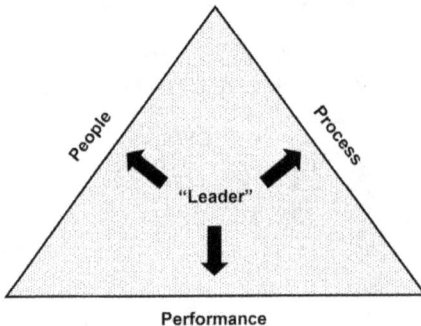

People   Process

"Leader"

Performance

Conscious Leadership

Performance

Leader

People   Process

Let's examine these models briefly.

Conventional leadership starts with the "leader." The "leader" is placed first, creating the center, and then the triangle, which represents the environment, is drawn around him. He is the focal point of the model. Lacking self-awareness, there exists a continual "barrier" separating him from the outside environment and limiting his impact on people, process, and performance. Unaware of beliefs (his own or others'), the conventional leader exerts his influence on his environment. The unidirectional arrows represent his outward pushing, regardless of context and oblivious to its dynamic nature. He believes (subconsciously) that either he can't change or that he doesn't need to change. Functioning at a level of unconscious competence, the same ideas the created limited success in the past will now facilitate his failure.

Conscious leadership completely flips this model upside-down. Performance is the base of conventional leadership, and although this might appear proper, it's actually a myth. The base is not where performance belongs. Performance is the result of good leadership, not the cause of it. Performance is the pinnacle of conscious leadership, with people and process forming the base.

Conscious leadership starts with the environment. Because he is externally focused, the outer triangle representing the external environment is drawn first. From there, the environment is compartmentalized into the three domains: people, process, and performance, represented by the three grey triangles. The intersection of these three triangles actually creates the space for the leader. So although he is centrally located, he isn't centrally focused. The dotted line represents the conscious leader's filter—a result of self-awareness. He maintains a healthy relationship with the environment, simultaneously pushing his ideas outwards while pulling other ideas inward. Represented by the bidirectional arrows, he is exporting influence and importing new ideas. The constant importation of ideas, having passed through his filter, actually creates his belief system.

Story Restoration

"Stories are the creative conversion of life itself into a more powerful, clearer, more meaningful experience. They are the currency of human contact."
- Robert McKee

You are now ready to begin your journey towards conscious leadership; the framework is complete. You have the right gear and a trustworthy map, both essential requirements. There is only one requirement left that must be fulfilled for you to begin creating change and generating impact. What's left?

Conflict—the universal requirement for change. Don't worry; we've got that one covered. For the next seven chapters, we are going to intentionally create conflict by challenging some widely held beliefs of conventional leadership. Although generally accepted as truth, they are myths.

These myths must be debunked for the story of leadership to be restored. Embrace this conflict to increase your self-awareness and expose your true beliefs. Do you really believe what you say you believe? Challenge will force you to articulate, at least to yourself, what you actually believe. In some cases, you might not know what you believe. This is okay, because conflict will not only expose beliefs of which you are conscious, it will also surface those beliefs that might be at the subconscious level.

As you experience challenge, you will also gain clarity. With increased discernment and self-awareness, you will be able to distinguish truth from myth. Ultimately, you will be able to change your beliefs and generate impact.

But you will have to debunk the myths of conventional leadership. You might have accepted some of these myths as truth for a long time. Although parting with those old, familiar, comfortable beliefs might be painful, you know it is the right thing to do.

Your story depends on it.

The process of orchestrated conflict is neither natural nor normal, but it is required if you want to create transformational change. Conventional leadership is both natural and normal, but it is incapable of generating impact. And this is why you embrace the conflict—you are tired of typical, average, usual, ordinary, and common. You are tired of normal.

Conscious leadership isn't typical; it's transformational. Although impact isn't routine, it's real. It's not a myth, and it could define your leadership. The conscious leader will:

- Generate sustainable impact consistently
- Create transformational, substantial change—in yourself and others
- Perform at levels of excellence
- Work more efficiently and effectively, producing positive results in less time
- Connect with and motivate people through meaningful relationships
- Discover new ideas and breakthrough innovation
- Challenge conventional boundaries and normal solutions
- Develop other leaders

This is a picture of impact. This is the story of conscious leadership.

Orchestrated Conflict

"A very popular error: having the courage of one's convictions. Rather, it is a matter of having the courage for an attack on one's convictions."
    - Friedrich Nietzsche

Only once you know what you believe, and why you believe it, are you in a place where you can really learn new ideas. Our ultimate desire is belief change. Our goal is that through your external environment (this book), you will import some new ideas and change some of your beliefs.

And new beliefs will drive new behaviors, which will influence new outcomes. Said differently, belief change leads to impact.

To create this conflict, we are going to do a "deep dive" into each of the three domains—people, process, and performance. Within each domain are two or three core axioms, which we believe not just to be true, but to be foundational to conscious leadership. Each core axiom contains one or two sub-principles, which further expand the original belief.

The exploration of these axioms will be both abstract and concrete. We are conscious that different people learn differently. Therefore, we will intentionally provide you with both theoretical and tangible perspectives throughout each chapter. Some of you will relate more to the concrete; some of you will relate more to the abstract.

Our goal isn't simply to challenge your beliefs for the sake of challenge. Our goal is challenge for the sake of change. By intentionally orchestrating conflict, as opposed to randomly experiencing it, you can control how hard you stub your toe. This somewhat limits the pain of conflict while leveraging its power. To help you best leverage that power, we exhort you to explore the Conscious Leader's Toolbox at the end of each chapter—especially this chapter.

The Toolbox at the end of this chapter contains the resources that you will need throughout the rest of the book. Any knowledge gained from this book will be powerless without application. The Conscious Leader's Toolbox, contains equipment that will help you convert that knowledge into something meaningful that contains the potential for impact.

Setting Expectations

We are conscious that you will *not* agree with all of the axioms and sub-principles that we are about to share with you. You might agree with some of them, or you might agree with most of them. Hopefully, you will *not* agree with all of them. Complete agreement was never our *intention,* so please don't make it your *expectation.*

There are three outcomes that you can expect from the remainder of this book, and each reader will probably experience all of them to some degree:
- **Awareness:** You will gain an awareness of your current belief system
  - o What you believe and why you believe it
- **Acceptance:** You will accept some of the axioms/sub-principles as truth
  - o Unlearn your current ideas
  - o Import these new ideas into your belief system
- **Rejection:** You will reject some of the axioms/sub-principles
  - o Clarify what you do believe by discovering what you don't believe
  - o Strengthen your current belief system

The Roadmap

Chapter 5: People, 1 of 3
- <u>Axiom</u>: I don't believe in doing the fair thing; I believe in doing the right thing.
  - o Sub-principle: Truthful, not Transparent
  - o Sub-principle: Motives, not Mechanics

Chapter 6: People, 2 of 3
- <u>Axiom</u>: I don't believe in being flexible; I believe in being malleable.
  - o Sub-principle: Depth, not Breadth
  - o Sub-principle: Make a Difference, not a Point

Chapter 7: People, 3 of 3
- <u>Axiom</u>: I don't believe in knowledge; I believe in wisdom.
  - o Sub-principle: Chess, not Checkers
  - o Sub-principle: The 5i's

Chapter 8: Process, 1 of 2
- <u>Axiom</u>: I don't believe in prioritization; I believe in triage.
  - o Sub-principle: Important, not Urgent

Chapter 9: Process, 2 of 2
- <u>Axiom</u>: I don't believe in agreement; I believe in alignment.
  - o Sub-principle: Contrarian, not Complementary

Chapter 10: Performance, 1 of 2
- <u>Axiom</u>: I don't believe in objectives; I believe in outcomes.
  - o Sub-principle: Diagnosis, not Development
  - o Sub-principle: Productivity, not Activity

Chapter 11: Performance, 2 of 2
- <u>Axiom</u>: I don't believe in best practices; I believe in better practices.
  - o Sub-principle: Embrace Failure, but Challenge Faults

Your Story

Todd and Julie, our friends from Acme Office Supply, will continue the journey with us. We will read their story and look at their leadership through the various lenses presented above. You will be able to see how their behaviors are a reflection of their beliefs, and you will be able to relate to their experiences. Why are we so confident in that statement?

Because this story belongs to you, the reader. This story also belongs to us, the writers. If you were satisfied with the status quo and content being average, ordinary, and normal, you wouldn't be reading this book. If we were satisfied with the status quo and content being typical, common, and normal, we wouldn't have written this book. Like us, you recognize that conventional leadership hasn't delivered on its promises. Like us, you have been a victim of its myths. You have been frustrated by conventional leadership, and now you are fully conscious of the source behind those frustrations.

You are frustrated with the status quo because you don't want more of the same; you want transformational change. You are frustrated because you know you're not ordinary; you're different and unique, and capable of generating tremendous impact. You are frustrated because you don't want to be a normal leader who maintains the current standard; you want to be an impactful leader who creates transformational change.

If you weren't a member of that select group of individuals, who want to make a meaningful difference and recognize that there has to be something more, you wouldn't still be reading this. Instead, you would be content with the normal "leadership" seminar offered annually.

Like us, however, you are not content with the status quo. You aren't okay basing your leadership on myths. You don't want your story to be normal; you want it to be legendary.

Let's start writing that story…

Mirror, Mirror on the Wall...Chapter 4

The Conscious Leader's Toolbox

"All men can see the tactics whereby I conquer, but none can see the strategy out of which that great victory is evolved."

    - Sun Tzu

The Strategic Map:

1. Overview
2. Business-Focused Strategic Map Definitions
3. Acme Office Supply Strategic Map[1]
4. Leadership-Focused Strategic Map Definitions
5. The Conscious Leader's Strategic Map[2]
6. Blank Strategic Map Template[3] (for you to fill out)

1. **Overview:** Tell your story through a strategic map. Leadership is both profound and practical. The strategic mapping process is a powerful tool that will help you take the profound (team identity) and convert it to the practical (tangible business decisions). We will look at a typical strategic map used in business[1] (this one borrowed from Acme Office Supply), explore how to leverage it for conscious leadership[2], and then provide you with a blank template[3]. You can always download more strategic map templates from our website, www.debunkingtheleadershipmyth.com.

2. **Business-Focused Strategic Map Definitions:** In the marketplace, a strategic map is used to guide decisions, check progress, and provide feedback. A strategic map can be used by an entire company, a team within a department, or a single individual. Regardless of its owner, it consists of several foundational components:

    A. **"Today"** statement reflects your perception of "Where you are now." For a company, it refers to the current state of business. For a leader, it reflects your current state of leadership.

B.   **"Tomorrow"** statement reflects your perception of "Where you want to be," or the ideal condition you wish to attain. It refers to your desired future state, either as a company or as a leader.

C.   **"Vision"** contains details of the company's future. With a focus on tomorrow, it creates an image of the future. It is a leader's responsibility to craft a powerful vision statement. It should be memorable, portable, and inspiring. It informs your mission statement. The vision/mission statements provide the link between today and tomorrow.

D.   **"Mission"** is your purpose, reason for being, or simply "who we are and what we do." The mission statement is concerned with what your organization is about. It is informed by your vision. Your mission statement describes how you will turn your vision into a reality. If a vision cannot be implemented through a mission, then it won't be impactful.

E.   **"Critical Success Factors (CSF)"** are the high-level, strategic imperatives that must occur for you to be successful. They will enable you to move from where you are now (today) to where you want to go (tomorrow). These are the three-to-four key items that are vital to your success. You should focus your energy here, because if you don't execute these, then you will not achieve your mission, and your vision will not become a reality.

F.   **"Programs"** are the business plans and tactics that help you achieve the critical success factors. These are the specific actions that you will execute to achieve success.

G.   **"Visual Layout"** is where you map your programs across your CSFs. This allows you to see if your planned actions are aligned to your CSFs. Some programs will cross over multiple CSF, while some programs will only touch one CSF.

3. [1]**Acme Office Supply's Strategic Map**

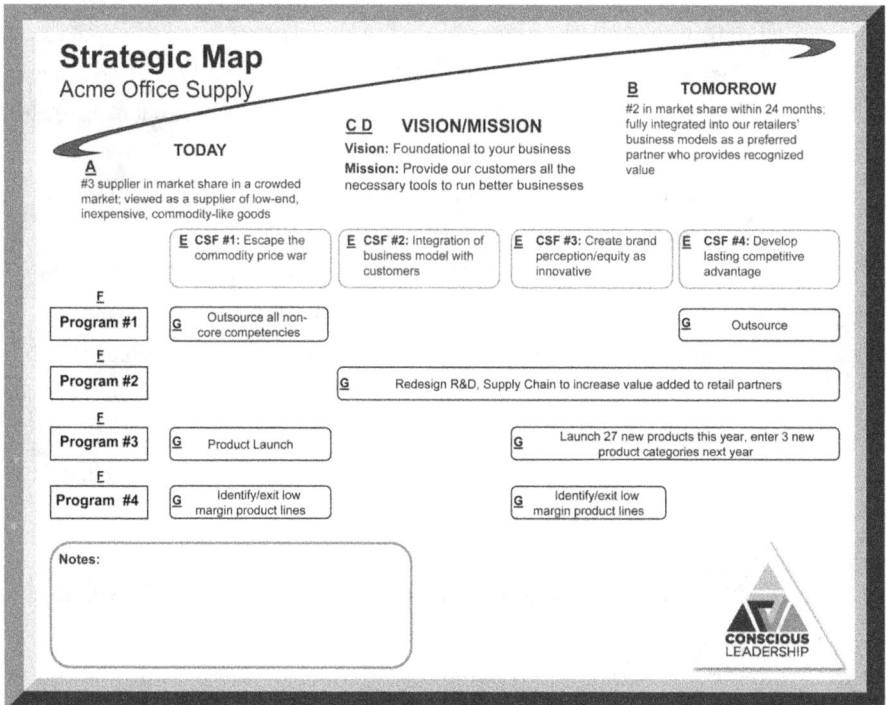

Strategic Map
Acme Office Supply

A TODAY
#3 supplier in market share in a crowded market; viewed as a supplier of low-end, inexpensive, commodity-like goods

C D VISION/MISSION
Vision: Foundational to your business
Mission: Provide our customers all the necessary tools to run better businesses

B TOMORROW
#2 in market share within 24 months; fully integrated into our retailers' business models as a preferred partner who provides recognized value

E CSF #1: Escape the commodity price war
E CSF #2: Integration of business model with customers
E CSF #3: Create brand perception/equity as innovative
E CSF #4: Develop lasting competitive advantage

F Program #1 — G Outsource all non-core competencies — G Outsource

F Program #2 — G Redesign R&D, Supply Chain to increase value added to retail partners

F Program #3 — G Product Launch — G Launch 27 new products this year, enter 3 new product categories next year

F Program #4 — G Identify/exit low margin product lines — G Identify/exit low margin product lines

Notes:

CONSCIOUS LEADERSHIP

4. **Leadership-Focused Strategic Map Definitions:** The Conscious Leader's Strategic Map is listed below, followed by a blank strategic map template. It is a slightly modified version of the strategic map used in business. Although it appears different, its purpose remains unchanged—to serve as your guide and your map. The "Today/Tomorrow" and "Vision/Mission" sections are the same. The "CSFs" have been replaced by "Beliefs" and the "Programs" have been replaced by "Behaviors." The goal is to fill this in as you progress through the book. Don't try to fill it in all at once; you will fill in different areas at different times. Here are some definitions to help you make the transition from Acme Office Supply's Strategic Map to The Conscious Leadership's Strategic Map.

   A. **"Today"** statement reflects your current state of leadership. What is your current leadership philosophy? How would others describe you as a leader? Is your current state of leadership delivering on its promises? Are you satisfied with its results?

      i. Fill this in now. If you need help, revisit your "My Leadership Journey" and your "Leadership Philosophy" found at the end of Chapter 2.

B.   **"Tomorrow"** statement reflects where you want to go and who you want to be as a leader. What kind of impact do you want to make? Where do you want to make it? What do you want your leadership philosophy to look like? How do you want others to describe you as a leader? What is your desired outcome?

      i. Fill this in now. You can revise it as necessary, but you should have an idea of what this looks like now.

C.   **"Vision"** contains details of your future as a leader. Focusing on tomorrow, it creates an image of the future. It is a leader's responsibility to craft a powerful vision statement. It should be memorable, portable, and inspiring. It informs your mission statement. The vision/mission statements provide the link between today and tomorrow.

      i. You don't have to fill this in now, but you should fill it in shortly. It is difficult to fill in the mission/belief/behavior sections without this portion completed. You can always come back and change it.

D.   **"Mission"** is your purpose, reason for being, or simply who you are and what you do. The mission statement is concerned with what you are about. It is informed by your vision. Your mission statement describes how you will turn your vision into a reality. If a "Vision" cannot be implemented through a "Mission," it won't be impactful.

      i. You don't have to fill this in now. In fact, you might want to fill in some of the beliefs/behaviors before you fill in your mission. However, this will help you implement what you discover, so make sure you complete it at some point during the book.

E.   **"Beliefs"** replace critical success factors. These are new beliefs that you acquire throughout this journey. These are what you deem as critical to the realization of your leadership vision.

      i. Fill these in throughout the following chapters. Choose beliefs that you want to enter into your strategic map carefully. If you recognize that you are completely aligned with an axiom then don't enter it. Or, if you are 100% misaligned with an axiom, don't enter it. Enter and track the ones that challenge you, that are new to you, and with which you are partially aligned. These will be the beliefs that if accepted as truth, have the potential to generate the most impact in your life.

F. **"Behaviors"** represent those actions that you would exhibit if you truly believed what you said you believed. As you identify new beliefs which you would like to change, identify the corresponding behaviors that would accompany your new belief/idea.

   i. Fill this in during Chapter 12. Sometimes, a behavior can cross over multiple beliefs. You should be able to hold yourself accountable to these behaviors, as should others.

G. **"Visual Layout"** is where you map your behaviors across your beliefs. This allows you to see if your planned actions are aligned to the beliefs that you identified. Some behaviors will cross over multiple beliefs, while some behaviors will only touch one belief.

5. [2]**The Conscious Leader's Strategic Map**

6. ³Blank Strategic Map Template

Reflection Points

Conventional Leadership	Conscious Leadership
A myth, written through plagiary, that is unremarkable and quickly forgotten	A unique story, full of impact, that others want to read
Observes and focuses on the outcome (and sometimes behavior) portion of the model; is not aware of beliefs Belief → **Behavior** → **Outcome**	Observes outcomes and behaviors, and then focuses on the belief portion of the model **Belief** → Behavior → Outcome
Leadership is about control, stability, normalcy, and predictability	Leadership is about change, specifically belief change
People cannot and will not change	People can and will change (they just typically avoid it)
Behaves, as though the environment is static (unaware of his belief)	Believes that the environment is changing and behaves accordingly
Leadership is influence	Leadership is an activity
Instinctively functions at stage four of the Adult Learning Model (Unconscious Competence)	Intentionally functions at stage three of the Adult Learning Model (Conscious Competence)
Low levels of self-awareness resulting from a degree of cockiness	Through humility and confidence, proactively develops a high level of self-awareness
Is not aware of a need to unlearn old ideas (attempts synergy through addition)	Unlearns old ideas in order to learn new ones (addition by subtraction)
Follows the natural desire to pursue equilibrium, continues to "go along to get along," provides no benefit to the system	Embraces requirements for change, intentionally generates conflict, ultimately produces benefits for the entire system
Inward focus; he is central	Outward focus; the environment is central
Sole focus on exportation of ideas (pushing influence outward)	Simultaneous importation/exportation of ideas (pushing influence out while pulling ideas in)
Maintains status quo and normal	Generates impact

- Define the Relationship (DTR)
    - o Define your relationship with the system
    - o Create beneficial impact for the environment
    - o Understand the context for your leadership
    - o Environment includes everything outside of yourself
- Conscious leadership has an external, outward focus
    - o Allows for a push/pull relationship with environment
        - Import new ideas
            - Eventually become your beliefs
            - Potential to generate impact is related to your potential to import new ideas
        - Export influence
            - Generate impact in your environment

- Environment consists of three domains
  - People
    - All business is people business
    - Foundation of conscious leadership
  - Process
    - How people interact with other people (personal) and their environment (non-personal)
    - Link between people and performance
  - Performance
    - Critically important
    - Pinnacle of leadership
    - Results from people interacting through process
- Orchestrated Conflict
  - Next seven chapters will challenge your beliefs
  - Debunk myths of conventional leadership
- The Conscious Leader's Strategic Map
  - Your map to becoming a conscious leader
  - Increases your potential for impact

CONSCIOUS
LEADERSHIP

CHAPTER 5
LOWEST COMMON DENOMINATOR

"The educated man, particularly the educated leader, copes with the fact that life is not fair. The way to deal with failure is not to invent scapegoats or to lash out at followers."
> - James Stockdale

"The truth of the matter is that you always know the right thing to do. The hard part is doing it."
> - Norman Schwarzkopf

Introduction—People Domain

The first domain within the conscious leadership environment (people, process, performance) that we will explore is people. All organizations are people organizations. Performance, good or bad, is ultimately a result of people and process. Performance is the output; people and process are the inputs. And people are more important than process.

As a leader, there is nothing more critical than the way that you view, value, and relate to people. This includes the people who report into you, the people who are your colleagues, and the people to whom you report. Chances are, your biggest stressor at work (or at home) is not due to a process, procedure, or a policy, but due to another person. People are the primary source of performance, both positive and negative. Thus, leadership is all about people.

Leadership and relationships go hand-in-hand. They are inseparable. A leader has to be able to influence people. As we started earlier, leadership is an activity, and influence is the result of that activity. Specifically, your ability to influence others is a result of your activity (or your behaviors). And your behavior is a result of your beliefs.

Ultimately, you cannot influence people and make an impact as a leader if you cannot connect with people. This doesn't mean that you have to be charismatic, but it does mean that you have to understand and value people. Remember, people are complex. To be an impactful leader, you have to be able to communicate with both the rational and emotional halves of a person. You cannot be an effective leader, who influences people and creates transformational change, when you can only connect with half of a person.

For most leaders, it is easier to connect with the rational half of a person than the emotional half. This is probably a result of another myth of conventional leadership that claims that emotions should be divorced from business.

Regardless of the cause, as a conscious leader, you have to embrace the emotional component of people for two main reasons. First, leadership often involves, at some capacity, a team. A team is comprised of individuals, each possessing a unique set of skills and competencies. So, what is the difference between a group of individuals working together and a team? The difference is the degree of emotional connectedness among the individuals. This emotional energy magnifies the existing skills and competencies, creating the synergistic effect that is often observed among high-performing teams. If you don't understand people, and if you can't relate with them both emotionally and rationally, it will be difficult for you to create or lead a high-performing team.

Second, leadership is about belief change, which, as we have discussed, requires unlearning. Because it is an emotional process, unlearning is difficult, much like giving away a favorite pair of old jeans. To facilitate this emotional process, you must be able to connect with other people on an emotional level.

What is required to be able to connect with another person on that level? Trust.

Leading people requires trust. The followers need to trust their leader. The leader needs to trust his followers. The relational aspect of leadership is fueled by trust. Trust allows people to work together with less friction. Trust is the "oil" that allows for effective, productive relationships. Trust fills in the gap when there are questions and unknowns. Trust makes it possible to give the benefit of the doubt.

And yet today, more than ever, trust is broken. Relationships are defined by controversy, not connectedness. The issue is a faulty belief system. The erosion of trust, and the loss of impact, is a result of the acceptance of myth as truth. The intensity of today's pressures has exposed this myth, serving as a catalyst in the erosion process.

We observe strained relationships, ineffective communication, and an ever-increasing need to involve human resources as relationship referees. Human resources are being pulled in on both ends of the spectrum, facilitating the most basic forms of communication while also buffering the most outrageous scandals. All of this is evidence that trust is lacking within our relationships.

The erosion of trust isn't the only damage that these myths have caused. Trust is just one example. But, if we want to restore trust, meaningfully connect with people, and create transformational change, then we must debunk some myths and change our beliefs. This brings us to an important question: What does a conscious leader believe, and not believe, about people?

<u>Axiom:</u>
I don't believe in doing the fair thing;
I believe in doing the right thing.

Let's start off with a concrete example. This will help illustrate not just this axiom, but the sub-principles that follow. Why don't we drop in on Julie and Todd at Acme Office Supply? After they finish discussing the measures and weightings of next year's review process, they have the pleasure of conducting this year's review. This includes not just the appraisals but also the corresponding merit increases. Julie's reaction to this time of the year, appraisal time, is similar to yours and and ours:

Julie is stressed this morning. She has now been with Acme for almost a year, and it is time for her to deliver her first annual appraisals to her team. She is not looking forward to the next couple weeks. She has some big decisions to make. The company has given her a fixed pool of money. From this pre-defined pool, she is to distribute raises to her team.

Julie's pool is based on a 3% average merit increase, meaning that her pool is worth 3% of her direct reports' combined salaries. She has been given the freedom to distribute this money to her direct reports in any manner that she chooses; but the total amount of money in the pool is fixed.

This freedom is her problem (and is also why she is stressed). All of her reports, because they also manage people, know that she has this freedom. They know that she can distribute the money from the pool in any manner she chooses. So if one employee gets an increase less than 3%, it is because another received an increase of greater than 3%. Her reports understand this.

This freedom wouldn't be a problem if the performance of all of her employees this year was the same. If that was the case, then Julie could equally distribute the money from the pool, giving everyone a 3% merit increase. But, as you would expect, all of her employees did not perform equally well this year. (Did we mention that Julie was stressed?)

Although Julie and Todd had a rough start in regards to communication, once it was resolved, Todd emerged as the star of Julie's team. The department's success and ultimately, her success (and her anticipation of a positive review from her manager) was largely a result of Todd's work.

Whereas Todd performed at the highest level this year, Julie has two individuals on her team who significantly underperformed. Unfortunately, this wasn't the first year they have struggled. Both reports had been with the company for many years, and had difficulty adapting to the changes in the marketplace. Their inability to adapt resulted in very poor performances. To make matters worse, not only were they struggling to adapt, but they were also keeping their colleagues from adapting. If not checked, this negative influence could threaten the performance of Julie's collective team.

Both of these underperforming individuals were extremely vocal. They were great at pointing out flaws with the "new" system. And they complained without ever really offering any constructive solutions. As a result of their tenure, they had the "ear" of most of their colleagues. Their constant, vocal, reminders of "the good old days when we used to..." lowered the overall morale of the entire team.

And so Julie had a difficult decision to make. Todd definitely performed at a level that was well above average and these two individuals performed at levels that were well below average. Yet if they received a merit increase less than the average 3%, they would not only know that Julie chose to give "their" merit increase to someone else, but they would also make sure that the entire team knew it, as well. They would use this as another opportunity to disparage Acme Office Supply— and Julie—to their colleagues.

Julie recognized that she had two options. She could give these underperforming, divisive employees a 3% raise along with everyone else in her department. Everyone would get an even

3%. Or, she could give a portion of "their" increase to a high performer like Todd. She played out each scenario in her head, again and again and again. Aware of the vocal tendency of the two underperforming veterans, as well as the level of attention that they received from the rest of her team, Julie knew that giving them less than 3% would create an explosion. They would complain, gossip, and slander. This would threaten the team culture that Julie had worked so hard to create.

If she gave them the average 3%, however, she would only have the average 3% left to give to her highest performer, Todd. Julie knew that Todd was a true team player. She was aware that while he would be disappointed with a 3% raise, he would not say or do anything to bring down the team. Julie knew that, regardless of his raise, he would remain positive and do his best to help the team perform at the highest possible level.

And so, as Julie sat down at her desk to enter the merit increases into the system, she felt a little better. She had arrived at a conclusion. She would distribute 3% evenly to everyone in her department. "After all," she rationalized, "the overall health and morale of the team outweighs individual concerns. And besides, Todd just got promoted last year, so he might not be expecting a raise anyway. And on top of everything else, I have only been with Acme Office Supply for one year. Who am I to make these sweeping judgments about people in such a short time period? I'll be fair and give everyone a 3% raise. At the end of the day, we are all on the same team. People will respect this decision."

No, they won't. We don't. You don't. Todd definitely doesn't respect this decision. And deep down inside, Julie's other reports, even the two who are struggling, won't either. While no one respects this decision, everyone recognizes it. This scenario plays out every year in thousands of organizations. At some point in your career, you have experienced this first-hand. Maybe you experienced it last year. Like Todd, you might have been the employee who knew you deserved more than the average raise. Or, like

Julie, you might have been the boss who rationalized the benefits of giving everyone, regardless of performance, the same raise. Or, you might have gone through a season of failure. Conscious that your performance was below average, you knew you didn't deserve the average raise that year. You probably didn't challenge the decision, but you still didn't respect it (we don't blame you for not offering to return the money).

You can relate to this situation; and that is why you don't respect it. But if this type of decision isn't respected by you, me, Julie, Todd, the underperformers, or the top performers, we should ask ourselves some questions:

- Why is this situation so common?
- As the high performer, why do we have such a hard time challenging when we experience this?
- And why, if we are truthful with ourselves, have we all been guilty of playing the role of the spineless, but seemingly equitable, boss?

Fairly Attractive

"The idea that men are created free and equal is both true and misleading: men are created different; they lose their social freedom and their individual autonomy in seeking to become like each other."
- David Riesman

The concept of fairness is incredibly attractive. Fairness means equality. After all, wasn't America founded on the concept that all men are created equal? Yes. Then why is this situation different? The Declaration of Independence is speaking about equality with regard to the people's rights and opportunities. It is not speaking about equality of outcomes. It is saying that all people are created equal and deserve equal opportunities to achieve their own level of success. It is not saying that all people deserve equal levels of success, regardless of their behaviors or beliefs.

"Equal rights" is different than "equal rewards."

And yet we miss this. Fairness is ubiquitous, and it is deeply ingrained in our society and culture. The fairness doctrine is distributed, well...fairly, across the country, ignoring age, race, gender, and socio-economic status. Every four years, we hear about fairness in the political arena. Candidates tell us to vote for them because they are fair, and their opponent is unfair.

We learn about fairness as a child. If you are a parent, you have heard these words often, "But Daddy, why can't I do [fill in the blank]? That's not fair!! Billy's parents let him do [fill in the blank]." And what's your response? "Well son, life's not fair."

And Dad—you're right. Life isn't fair; and this isn't always a bad thing.

Fairness has drawbacks that we don't often explore. Why? Because it is taboo to question a virtue as universally celebrated as fairness. Questioning fairness would be heresy! But we want you to consider some of the consequences of adhering to the fairness doctrine, especially in the context of people.

Fairness often results in diminished accountability, as it is easy to hide behind. Fairness provides a way out from making difficult decisions. In fact, it sometimes removes the decision-making responsibility altogether. Julie appealed to the fairness doctrine to absolve herself from making several tough decisions. These included the decision to distribute the merit increases unequally (giving Todd a higher percentage than the veteran under performers) and the decision to confront the underperformers about the truth of their position. By invoking the fairness doctrine, Julie was able to avoid these difficult situations altogether. Fairness diminished Julie's accountability by making all of the decisions for her.

When you abdicate decision-making to fairness, you surrender the potential for impact. Fairness won't generate impact; but it will maintain the status quo.

Fairness has a leveling effect—it levels *down*—often to the lowest common denominator.

If you think about this conceptually, it makes sense. When pursuing fairness, it is much easier to reduce those at the top than to raise those at the bottom. Pushing down requires less effort than pulling up. It is far easier to *ignore* performance (treating high and low performers as average) than it is to *recognize* performance (rewarding high performance and confronting low performance).

Instead of recognizing Todd's good performance, Julie ignored it for fairness's sake. Despite Julie's attempts to rationalize the situation, fairness didn't provide justification for the equal rewards. It was just much easier to give Todd a lower raise than it was to demand better performance from the two veteran employees.

Boring your Best

"Mediocrity knows nothing higher than itself. But talent instantly recognizes genius."
   - Sir Arthur Conan Doyle

Consider another example. Pretend that your boss is conducting a department-wide training on a technical skill—"How to use computer-based spreadsheets." The spreadsheet training can be customized either to an advanced level or a basic level. There is only budget to perform the training once, so a choice must be made about its difficulty level. Within your department are two general types of people: those who use spreadsheets on a regular basis and those who almost never use them at all. The frequent users are probably somewhat advanced, possessing at least a moderate degree of spreadsheet proficiency. The other group of people, who never use spreadsheets, probably possesses only the most rudimentary skills and little to no proficiency.

Based on this background information, should the training be customized to an advanced level (which would go over the heads of the non-user group) or to a basic level (which would be useless for the advanced group)? Although neither situation is ideal, you are forced to make a choice. To make the best decision—the decision which would create the most impact for the department—we need to ask another question: Which group of people, the users or the non-users, would benefit the most from spreadsheet training?

The users! Common sense tells us that those who use spreadsheets most frequently would benefit the most from spreadsheet training. As a result, given that you can only perform this training once, if you want to create as much impact as possible for the department, the training should be customized for the advanced group.

Yet, we would bet that, in most organizations today, the spreadsheet training would be tailored around the needs of those at the basic level instead of those at the advanced level. Why? Because conventional leadership believes that it wouldn't be fair to the group at the basic level if the training was designed for the group at the advanced level. Everyone needs to be able to understand and participate. So after a day of spreadsheet training, what is the outcome (besides the jitters caused by drinking too much coffee to stay awake)?

The non-user group (with basic skills) now understands the fundamentals of spreadsheets. The user group (with advanced skills, having already mastered the fundamentals) has collectively beaten Solitaire thirty-four times. They were bored to tears, so that group can also boast of thirteen updated Facebook profiles. Ultimately, the group of advanced users, who actually use spreadsheets frequently, got nothing out of the training.

It wasn't impactful; but it was fair.

In the pursuit of fairness, however, the training was leveled down to the lowest common denominator. And the company gained nothing from the training. It was a waste of money.

To be fair (pun intended) to the training, it never really had a chance. It was destined to be meaningless. When "leaders" invoke the fairness doctrine to make their decisions and absolve them of accountability, the chances of impact creation are very slim.

Fairness is fundamentally concerned with sameness. Sameness can be achieved either at a high level or at a low level. A high level of sameness (all parties producing and performing with excellence) could be used to describe a high-performing team. The combination of sameness, excellence, and consistency could be used to describe impact. However, impact is rare. The achievement of sameness occurs most often at a low level.

Doing the fair thing levels down to the lowest common denominator.

Difference and Excellence

So what should a conscious leader do? Instead of asking yourself, "What is the fair thing to do?" ask yourself, "What is the right thing to do?" This question will provide clarity many difficult decisions. It won't make the decision for you, and it won't necessarily make the decision easy, but it will make the decision simple.

Doing the right thing doesn't level down. In fact, sometimes doing the right thing can level up.

Doing the right thing doesn't remove the need for social justice. The right thing to do is to ensure that everyone is given equal opportunities and that all people are treated with equal value. The right thing to do is to pursue equality in civil rights. The right thing to do is to recognize that everyone is endowed with certain inalienable rights. If you believe that doing the right thing is more important than doing the fair thing, your behavior will consist of doing right things. The outcome? Society is leveled up.

When you do the fair thing, it is easy to ignore performance. Ignoring good performance allows you to avoid dealing with poor performance. You just rename and redefine performance. Poor performance is redefined as average or slightly below average). Excellent performance is redefined as average or slightly above average. The fundamental issue of poor performance is ignored, and excellent performance is leveled down—to the lowest common denominator.

But when you do the right thing, not only is it hard to ignore good performance, it is almost impossible to avoid dealing with poor performance. You can't simply rename it and call it something different. You can't pretend that it doesn't exist. You are forced to deal with it in your efforts to ultimately improve it. There are several ways to do this, and none are easy. Doing the right thing is rarely easy.

Just as doing the right thing forces you to deal with poor performance, it also forces you to deal with good performance. It demands that you recognize excellence. And the only way to recognize excellence is to make the statement, publically, that other levels of performance are not excellent. You have to recognize, and communicate, that all outcomes are not equal; there are different levels of performance, and they will be rewarded differently. Julie would have to publicly recognize that Todd's performance was different, and better, than the two vocal under performers.

Doing the right thing celebrates differences. Difference paves the way for excellence. When you believe in doing the right thing, you don't just tolerate—you celebrate—difference. You call attention to uniqueness and distinction.

Difference is a prerequisite for excellence. You cannot recognize excellence if you don't allow for difference. Fairness, by minimizing or ignoring differences, eliminates excellence.

Excellence demands difference. Sameness will not, and *cannot*, generate excellence—ever.

However, if you recognize differences, then you also must make decisions. You cannot absolve yourself from accountability by relying on the fairness doctrine to make decisions for you. This is rarely easy. But if you want to do the right thing, then you must embrace accountability and make decisions.

Popularity Contest

Doing the right thing recognizes that certain outcomes are better than others. Thus, it rewards not only superior outcomes, but also superior performers. Conversely, doing the right thing will confront both poor outcomes and poor performers. We will discuss these confrontations in depth in a later chapter.

These confrontations, however, are one of the major reasons that conventional leadership neglects doing the right thing—it requires difficult decisions and difficult conversations. It is impossible to lead others unless we first lead ourselves. Your child may not do what you say, but he will do what you do. If we can't make those difficult decisions and have those difficult conversations, how can we expect that from others?

To be able to recognize (and encourage) Todd's excellent performance, Julie must first admit that it is different. Although this is the right thing to do, it isn't always the popular thing to do.

Doing the right thing will expose you to criticism. In fact, if you haven't been criticized in a while, maybe you haven't been doing enough of the right thing. Doing the right thing requires hard conversations and hard decisions. Often, these types of decisions lead to criticism. Think back to our example. If Julie had given Todd a disproportionately high raise and thus the two under performers a disproportionately low raise, she would have needed to have difficult conversations with the low performers. She would have to explain the cause of the low raise and challenge their performance. After that difficult conversation, they would criticize her, both privately and publicly.

And that might not be the end of it. If they vocalized their discontentment within the department, and if those vocalizations led to a reduction in team morale and performance, Julie might have to make the difficult decision to terminate their employment. The unequal distribution of raises is, by no standard, an easy decision. However, by every standard, it is the right decision.

We want those who report into us to do the right thing. We want them to display "managerial courage." We want them to call "balls and strikes" and to call "a spade a spade." Perhaps most telling, we get frustrated when those around us do not do the right thing. We become exasperated when our "leaders" lack the courage to make the difficult decision that is the right decision.

Deep down inside, we really want what is right, not what is fair. If you really want your story to be significant and make an impact, it should be filled with chapters about doing things that are right, not things that are fair.

Doing the right thing, over time, leads to another benefit: trust. If you are known as a leader who does the right thing, even when it is hard, people will trust you. And as we have said, trust is essential for conscious leadership. This brings us to our first sub-principle under this axiom:

Sub-Principle #1:
Truthful, not Transparent

Imagine that you are having a conversation with someone, and he opens the dialogue with the words, "So let me be transparent with you…" What is your first reaction? How do you feel? You don't trust what they are about to say! We have the same reaction. When we hear that phrase, we don't trust what we are about to hear.

The word "transparent" almost never comes up in standard, everyday conversation. When is the last time you were having drinks with your friends, watching the TV, talking about the game, when the word "transparent" was used? Probably never. Why? It feels like a disclaimer. When you are watching TV with your friends, you usually don't need disclaimers. When you hear the word "transparent," it feels like the speaker is whispering a disclaimer, "This conversation is hard, and it might be a little awkward. I'm afraid to say something to you directly, so I won't. What I say might not be what I really mean, but you should trust me because I'm a leader doing the fair thing."

We will continue to explore this conceptually in a moment. Right now, we get to be a fly on the wall and listen to Julie give Todd his annual appraisal. His reaction to his fair, three percent merit increase, should be interesting:

JULIE: Todd, I've been looking forward to this review. It is always fun to give out good reviews. And yours is good! It's true that we had our issues with communication when we first started working together. I want to thank you for being direct with me and initiating what some might call a difficult conversation. It made a huge difference! As soon as we got through that issue, it has been nothing but smooth sailing! You have done an excellent job this year and have initiated many breakthrough projects for the department.

TODD: Thanks, Julie. You were right in that we were not communicating well when we started, but I'm glad we are aligned now. I have enjoyed working on your team, and am glad that some of these projects are beginning to show positive return. I appreciate you mentioning those projects here during our review. Sometimes it is difficult for a person to make a big impact right out of the gate when joining the home office.

JULIE: I'm glad you brought that up. Because Todd, as good as your performance has been over the past 12 months, this is still just your first official year inside. You still have lots to learn about how to navigate the corporate environment... all first-year employees do. Don't worry; it will come with time and experience.

TODD: Okay, well, I guess I don't quite understand. I thought you said that I was performing great. And as you have said, a large part of my ability to drive these breakthrough projects has been my ability to form solid relationships with other internal stakeholders. And now it sounds like you're saying that I need to work on my ability to network within the office.

JULIE: Don't get me wrong. You have done an excellent job. I just want you to recognize that this is still your first year inside, and it takes a long time to become an expert at navigating this environment. But as you said, you have driven some breakthrough projects, and so (handing Todd the paperwork) I am extremely pleased to be able to give you a 3% merit increase for your work this year. Nice job!

TODD: Thanks...but I have a question. Isn't 3% the company average? I thought you just said my performance was excellent. You even said breakthrough. That's much different than average. Yet 3% is only average. I don't understand...

JULIE: Todd, I want to be transparent with you for a moment. Please don't let this conversation leave these four walls. I really do think you have done a great job. And I tried very hard to get you a raise higher than 3% but was told "No" by the company. I didn't have a choice; it wasn't my decision. The 3% merit increase is the standard company policy for first-year employees, and this is officially your first year in the home office. It wouldn't be fair to give you something different than everyone else.

TODD (interrupting): Wait. This is good news. I talked with human resources about this during my interview process. I am almost certain that the 3% rule you are talking about is for first-year employees who are new to the company, not existing company employees who took a new position. I have been with the company for six years. Can you look into that for me? This should be an easy fix.

JULIE (looking a little flustered): Todd, I recognize what you have brought to this department and the organization as a whole, and so does senior leadership. You just got promoted last year, and if you keep up the great work, I am sure another one is right around the corner. I will do some research into the policy, but I am almost positive that I interpreted it correctly—3% for the first year in a new position. I do promise you, however, that if the policy is different, I will do whatever I can to get you additional compensation. In the meantime, Todd, keep doing what you are doing. This team responds to your ideas and needs your leadership. Don't take your foot off the pedal now..."

Sound familiar? If so, then you can feel confident that you have been exposed to a myth, because this conversation is typical when "leaders" do the fair thing instead of the right thing. Julie can't really recognize excellence if she doesn't acknowledge difference. Although she says that his performance is excellent (and different), her actions reveal what she really believes. She won't officially recognize the difference. This lowers Todd's trust.

But there is something else going on here. What do you think that Todd's chances are of getting a higher merit increase? Right, pigs don't fly yet. We also see Todd's reaction to a transparent conversation. There is something about being "transparent" that just rubs us all the wrong way. What is it? What bothers us so much about that word? Why does Todd's trust in Julie decrease after she commits to transparency?

Transparency Gaps

Transparency has several subtleties which make it very detrimental to trust and dangerous for leadership.

First, if I announce that I am being transparent for this particular conversation, you can infer that there are conversations where I haven't been transparent. You can infer that there are times where I have filtered the message that you received. I filtered my message not to be a safeguard for the company, but to control your reaction. If I have to announce when I am transparent, the natural conclusion is that there are times when I am not transparent. If I were completely transparent on all occasions, there would be no need for the grand announcement, as transparency would be my default status in communication. But it's not, so your trust is diminished.

Second, you can conclude that while I might do the right thing on this occasion and draw back the curtain so that you can have a clear view into my intentions (being transparent), I have the right to keep the curtain closed if I so choose. The implication is that while I am doing you a favor by offering you transparency during this interaction, it is my right and privilege to do so. Thus, I have the right to be less than transparent during our next interaction if I choose. As the sender of the message, I own the power in the interaction. An announcement of transparency means that you, the receiver of my message, do not have the right to honest communication; it is a privilege that has been given to you by me.

The third subtlety inherent with "transparency" is that there are naturally several different degrees of transparency. You, as the listener, don't know which "version" you are receiving. The power to decide the level of transparency of this interaction is with me, the sender. For instance, consider a frosted shower door. It lets light through, but not without some level of distortion. You might be able make out vague shapes, but it is designed for only partial visibility. In the same way, within communication, there are different degrees of clarity and visibility. By offering the overarching disclaimer of being "transparent," the extent of that clarity is left to the discretion of the one who is delivering the message.

All three of these inferences create a somewhat jaded view of transparency. While on the surface it seems like a positive concept, its use in corporate communication has actually eroded, not created, trust. The corrosive effect of this word is not due to the actual behavior of being transparent, but to the core beliefs that accompany it. And whether you are aware of those beliefs, either on a conscious or subconscious level, they are the reason you cringe when someone opens a conversation with, "Let me be transparent."

Transparency, contrary to both its current definition and probably its original design, now implies anything but honest, genuine communication. Transparency is linked to manipulation and deceit. The myth of conventional leadership is that transparency creates trust. If we have debunked the transparency myth, then what's the truth? What creates trust?

You Can't Handle the Truth

"Truth is both arms and armour."
- Edward Counsel

Truthfulness, not transparency, creates trust.

The biggest distinction between these two ideas is the intrinsic right of the message sender. Whereas transparency acknowledges, albeit tacitly, the right of the sender to manipulate and distort the message if so desired, truthfulness denies this right to both the sender and receiver of information. The sender does not have the freedom to distort the message. Truthfulness is an entitlement, not a privilege. Thus, the receiver does not have to worry about the "degree of truthfulness" that she is receiving.

Truth is truth. Truth leads to trust. A truthful conversation is an impactful conversation.

Just as transparency inferred several nuances, so does truthfulness. Truthfulness implies getting down to the core of the issue. It boils away all other motivations and distortions, and allows both parties to deal with the real situation. It dissolves the shadow of manipulation and distrust that often cloud our interactions. Truthfulness also implies that "what you see is what you get." The receiver of the message can rest assured that there are no hidden agendas. Thus, as the receiver is not trying to decipher hidden meaning and secret goals, she can focus on actively listening and understanding the message that is actually being delivered.

Truthfulness doesn't mean that some information isn't privileged and confidential. There is some information that truthfully, shouldn't be communicated. Truthfulness gives you courage so that you don't have to shrink from those encounters; you can feel good about saying, "I can't discuss that right now."

Truthfulness also doesn't mean naïveté or gullibility. It doesn't mean that you are easily manipulated, nor does it mean that you are incapable of negotiation. It doesn't mean that you open yourself up so that others might take advantage of you. You can be truthful and still be a good poker player; you don't have to wear your heart on your sleeve to be truthful.

But it does mean that you do have to say what you mean, and mean what you say. And this requires self-awareness, confidence, and courage. Conscious leadership is not for the faint of heart.

120

You should know that a reputation of truthfulness isn't something that is developed over a 30-day plan. The benefits of truthfulness will come to fruition when the receiver is confident that the sender is being truthful (which implies that the sender has built a historical record of truthfulness). Truthfulness begets trust, but not immediately. Trust takes time to develop, but good leaders, understanding the importance of trust, are willing to invest over the long-term.

So why does conventional leadership favor transparency over truthfulness? Truthfulness is difficult. It is hard. The truth can hurt. It requires a tremendous amount of courage, both from the sender and the receiver of the message. Yet, it is the way that you want to be treated. You expect (or at least hope) that others are truthful with you. And while the truth may hurt, anything less kills. Anything short of truthfulness will destroy trust and diminish impact.

In our original example, let's assume that Julie had already made the fair decision to give everyone a three percent raise. Although Julie didn't do the right thing in distributing raises, what if she at least did the right thing in her dialogue with Todd? What if she told Todd, truthfully, that she didn't want to create dissension on the team in her first year, and so she made the decision to give everyone the same raise? She could acknowledge his disappointment, but she would be able to talk to him about how much she valued the team morale. She doesn't have to discuss the vocal low performers with Todd; that is none of his business. But she didn't have to be transparent, she could have been truthful. Truthfulness would have fostered trust.

Often, doing the right thing requires truthfulness. It requires the difficult, but honest, conversation. Conventional leaders shy away from truthfulness for the same reason they shy away from doing the right thing—it is difficult. Although being truthful demands a high price, the conscious leader considers it a sound investment.

The return on the investment of truthfulness is trust. Transparency, while easier in the moment, over time, erodes trust. Truthfulness, while temporarily more challenging, over time, builds trust. And trust makes impact possible.

The concept of truthfulness provides the framework for our final sub-principle in this chapter:

Sub-principle #2:
Motives, not Mechanics

If you manage people in the corporate environment, you will inevitably be invited to trainings and seminars this year. We would bet the farm (okay…being truthful, we don't really have a farm) that one of those trainings is on communication. The idea behind these trainings is that if we can communicate better as an organization, we will be more efficient and more productive. Better communication between people will lead to better outcomes from the organization. We don't disagree; this truth is self-evident.

These trainings, and the books that accompany them, often focus on mechanics of communication. You will learn the best techniques for: properly coaching your employees, challenging your manager, leveraging your network, setting goals, holding people accountable to those goals, confronting poor performance, and effectively recognizing success.

These trainings can teach you how to ask better questions. You can master the mechanics for making a job offer to a potential employee. You can study the techniques for the best way to terminate that employee without a lawsuit ensuing.

We don't need to visit Acme Office Supply to see the examples of this type of training. Let's play a game—and don't cheat! Be truthful with yourself. Answer these questions:

Critical Communication Components

1. Fill in the blanks:
    o Communication is _____% verbal (the words you use), _____% para-verbal (the tonality, speed, pace of your words, etc.), and _____% non-verbal (body language).

Communication Spectrum of Richness

2. Rank the following media in order of least to greatest effectiveness within the "Communication Spectrum of Richness":
    o Webcast, Text, Voicemail, Email, Ping, Phone, In-Person

See below for answers.

Answers:

Critical Communication Components

1. Communication is **7%** verbal, **38%** para-verbal, and **55%** non-verbal.

Communication Spectrum of Richness

2. The "Communication Spectrum of Richness" ranks these media in the following order from least-to-greatest effectiveness: **Ping, Text, Email, Voicemail, Phone, Webcast, In-Person**

So this exercise was kind of ridiculous. And the term "Communication Spectrum of Richness" is very ridiculous. But...what is even more ridiculous?

We bet that you got that quiz almost 100% correct. If you didn't know the exact percentages for communication, you were probably pretty close. What does this tell us? Two things:

- We invest lots of time and money on training communication mechanics.
- This myth of conventional leadership is widely accepted as truth.

The corporate world has recognized that there is a large communication disconnect within their people (especially managers and their reports). It also has recognized the lack of trust among teammates. The result is that billions of dollars are spent each year by organizations trying to solve this problem. Regardless of the company, the solution is always the same—train communication mechanics and techniques. Unfortunately, the results are also often the same—nothing.

This communication gap, and the inability of conventional leadership to close it, can be explained by the "Belief ➔ Behavior ➔ Outcome" model:

- **Belief:** Mechanics matter most in communication
- **Behavior:** Train communication techniques
- **Outcome:** Communication gap

This myth of conventional leadership claims that if you change and upgrade the communication mechanics of your people, then they will communicate better, and the performance of your organization will improve. Yet we know that isn't true. We experience it everyday. But this myth is widely accepted as truth. And so year after year, the focus remains on communication mechanics, and, year after year, the disconnect remains.

Why? The question is the answer…

Why? vs. How?

"The more elaborate our means of communication, the less we communicate."
        - Joseph Priestly

"People don't care how much you know until they know how much you care." This old adage is true (as are most old sayings). Conventional leadership focuses on the mechanics, or the "how," of communication. Conscious leadership, without dismissing the "how" (more on that in a minute), believes that your motives, the "why," are the most important element in effective communication.

Your people (your reports, your boss, and your teammates) are more heavily influenced by "why" you are communicating your message than "how" you are communicating your message. If people trust your motives (which is a result of being truthful about doing the right thing over time), then they have a much greater chance of being receptive to your message. If your motives are pure, then the listener can actively focus on what is being said, trusting that you mean what you say. The listener does not have to worry about finding the real meaning skillfully buried within your transparent dialogue.

If your employee trusts your motives, then you can tell them just about anything, and they will receive it positively. Feedback is transformed into a truly valuable tool and not merely a passive-aggressive attack. There is the possibility for coaching; and there is the potential for impact.

You will never completely agree with every portion of someone's critique of your performance. However, if you trust the motives of the person providing the critique, you will look for (and find) the portion of the feedback that is true and applicable. If you don't trust their motives, you will look for—and find—the portion of the feedback that is untrue and irrelevant. Trust increases the potential for feedback to be well received. When I trust the motives of another person, not only does it provide freedom for me to challenge them, but also for them to challenge me. Pure motives make all the difference.

Consider our previous example. Julie has just told Todd that he is going to get a three percent raise. Do you think that his reaction will be impacted more by how well she delivered the message (mechanics), or by how much he trusts her (motives)? Read the dialogue again and think about that question:

TODD (interrupting): Wait. This is good news. I talked with human resources about this during my interview process. I am almost certain that the 3% rule you are talking about is for first year employees to the company, not existing company employees to a new position. I have been with the company for six years. Can you look into that for me? This should be an easy fix.

JULIE (looking a little flustered): Todd, I recognize what you have brought to this department and the organization as a whole, and so does senior leadership. You just got promoted last year, and if you keep up the great work, I am sure another one is right around the corner. I will do some research into the policy, but I am almost positive that I interpreted it correctly—3% for the first year in a new position. I do promise you, however, that if the policy is different, I will do whatever I can to get you additional compensation. In the meantime, Todd, keep doing what you are doing. This team responds to your ideas and needs your leadership. Don't take your foot off the pedal now..."

The mechanics of Julie's communication are almost irrelevant. Todd's reaction will be based on his level of trust in her motives. If he believes that she is looking out for his best interest, and that she will research the policy and try to make it right for him, even if she can't get him an extra penny, he will continue to work hard for her. If he doesn't trust her motives, however, he will begin to disengage, even if human resources were to send him an unexpected bonus.

Being truthful, however, we do want to pause for a moment here. As a conscious leader, you should recognize the value of mechanics in communication. We are not trying to discount the value of communication technique; we are simply trying to augment the value of motives. There is skill involved in communication. This skill can, and should, be trained and developed. Don't miss this point. Even if you have pure motives, and your people trust you implicitly, you can improve your ability to relate and connect with people by refining your mechanics. Just remember, the "why" always trumps the "how." The best mechanics in the world, without proper motives, will fail.

Demonstrate What?

"Subtlety may deceive you; integrity never will."
        - Oliver Cromwell

Although this concept is extremely intuitive and grounded in common sense, it is ignored by conventional leadership every day. Conventional leadership continues to focus on the "how" instead of the "why." Ironically, even when conventional leadership does recognize the power of motives, it doesn't address the foundational issue (what are your true motives, the "why"). Instead, it focuses on how to more effectively communicate your existing motives (going right back to the "how"). The enlightened conventional leaders talk about the "How" of the "Why." In other words, conventional leadership isn't that concerned with the quality of your current motives (challenging you to change). It is concerned with changing other's perception of those motives, regardless of their actual quality.

Conventional leadership is concerned with *demonstrating* the quality of its motives to others. Conscious leadership is concerned with *developing* the quality of its motives within ourselves.

Why is conventional leadership blind to the "why," especially in regards to communication? It goes back to the original myth of conventional leadership: what you do versus who you are. A simple translation will help illustrate:

The Conscious Leader's "Communication Spectrum of Richness"

Belief ➔ Behavior ➔ Outcome
"Why" ➔ "How" ➔ "What"
Motives ➔ Mechanics ➔ Impactful Communication

Conventional leadership can't address the motives driving communication for the same reason it can't address anything else at the belief level—it isn't even conscious that they exist! And so conventional leadership focuses all of its efforts to improve communication on the only portion of the model it can—the "how."

Predictably, conventional leadership's communication is standard, safe, familiar, pretty, fluffy, and politically correct. Also predictably, it is powerless to create significant, meaningful change. A change in the "how," a surface-level behavior change, might feel good. But it can't make a real difference. It doesn't go deep enough.

For your communication to elicit transformational change, you must go beyond the "how" and get to the "why." You must address beliefs (your motives), not just behaviors (your mechanics).

Unfortunately, because conventional leadership is unable to penetrate behaviors and deal with beliefs, it can never address the fundamental issue and ask the exposing question: "What are your true motives?"

Regardless of your technical communication skills, eventually your true motives will be exposed. The heat and pressure of today's environment, increased scope/size, faster cadence, economic downturn, push all leaders to their limit. And at some point, their armor cracks. Once armor cracks, true motives are revealed. Pressure will reveal, or in some cases expose, our true motives.

Motivating Motives

As we near the end of this axiom, we want to ask you the real question, "What are your motives when dealing with people?" If you don't know, ask someone who works for you. We guarantee that they know. You can't hide motives. Over time, they will be revealed.

Motives are communicated through consistency. Rarely will a single event change others' perception regarding your motives. They will be communicated through good times and bad times, success and failure, easy decisions and difficult decisions. Consistent behaviors, driven by defined beliefs, will inform others about your motives.

Trust begets trust. If your team doesn't trust your motives, start by trusting theirs. Make them feel valuable and important. Earn their trust. What are some ways to show them that you trust them? What you do to earn trust flows from who you are:

- Who you are
  - Be vulnerable.
- What you do
  - Admit when you are wrong. Then make it right.
  - Allow them to see you for who you really are (including your weaknesses).
    - Share your "My Leadership Journey" with your team (Chapter 2).
  - Give intentional, personal, and real-time feedback:
    - Specific praise.
    - Specific constructive criticism.
    - Specific goals.

Your Story

Conscious leadership is focused on beliefs—who you are. In the realm of communication, conscious leadership is concerned with motives. Don't ignore mechanics, but don't focus on them either. The level of impact that your communication generates will be proportional to the quality of your motives. Once they are pure, then you can worry about mechanics.

Even if your story is good, if people doubt your motives, they won't let you tell it. But if people trust you, then they'll listen. Then your story has the opportunity to not just resonate with the audience, but to *captivate* them.

What if your motives aren't pure? Don't worry—there is good news. Just because your motives are currently tainted doesn't mean that they have to stay that way. You can change them.

Start by focusing on doing the right thing, instead of the fair thing. Make the difficult decision, and then communicate it truthfully. Face the subsequent criticism with confidence, believing that you did the right thing. When you are wrong, be humble enough to admit it; and then do whatever you can to make it right. Be motivated by their best interest, not yours.

People will begin to see that you aren't normal or conventional; they will believe that you are different. And then, you'll be able to make a difference.

Mirror, Mirror on the Wall…Chapter 5

The Conscious Leader's Toolbox

1. **Questions:** Think about the last time someone did the fair thing, as opposed to the right thing, with regard to you. How did that make you feel? Why? Now, think about the last time you avoided a difficult decision by invoking the fairness doctrine. What were the circumstances? What was the right thing to do? Why was it hard to do? Would you do anything different now?

2. **Questions:** Reflect on annual appraisals. Specifically, think about the last three reviews you received. Were they right, or were they fair? What about you—do you give all of your reports the same (or very similar) reviews? Does their performance warrant that degree of equality in regards to rewards? Who is the highest performer on your team? Have you rewarded her disproportionately? Who is the worst performer on your team? When will you have that difficult conversation with him?

3. **Exercise:** Over the course of the next week, listen for the phrase, "I want to be transparent…" Who said it? How did it make you feel? How truthful do you think the conversation was? What was the intention of the speaker? Did you say it? What was your intention?

4. **Questions:** How specific are you in your communication with your people? Is your praise/feedback general (i.e., "great job on that project") or specific (i.e., "I loved the way you answered that tough question during your presentation")? How often do you give praise compared to critical feedback?

5. **Exercise:** Have you shared your exercise from Chapter 2 (My Leadership Journey) with your team? With anyone? Can you do that this month? Have each of the individuals on your team made their own Leadership Journey? Have they shared them with you?

6. **Questions:** How good are you at showing weakness and vulnerability? When is the last time you admitted that you were wrong? Publicly or privately? Who did you admit it to? Is there an opportunity to do that this week?

7. **Personal Brand:** Branding is very important. Companies spend billions of dollars each year trying to build brand equity, both of their company's brand and of their individual products. At its core, a brand is about how you are perceived in the minds of others. Strong brand equity is the best defense against commodity-status. Just as products and companies have brands, so do people. What is your personal brand?

Your Brand

Personal and Professional

- Your brand is how you will be thought of in the mind of others
- You can have a personal brand or a professional brand
- For thought starters, look back at your "Strength Identifier" and your "Start/Stop/Continue" exercises
- Personal – transcends jobs. It is who you are at the core. It should be derived from your strengths, passions, and values.
- Professional – will change from job to job. It is how you want to be known at your place of employment. It will also reflect your strengths and passions, but will vary depending on the context and circumstances.
- Your final brand should be short, simple, and concise (3 words)
  - Start by writing down potential descriptors and narrow:

Personal Brand

- Word #1:
- Word #2:
- Word #3:

Professional Brand

- Word #1:
- Word #2:
- Word #3:

Notes

CONSCIOUS LEADERSHIP

Your Brand

Brand Equity

- Brand equity is a measure of the "power" of your brand
  - It can be created, changed, and destroyed
- It is a reflection of whether others perceive your brand the way you desire
- Here are several questions to measure your brand equity:

Brand Equity

- How often did your personal or professional brand (3 words) come up in your 360° review?

- How often did your brand appear in your strategic mapping exercise?
  - Today/Tomorrow statements?
  - Vision/Mission statements?
  - Critical Success Factors/Beliefs?

- Why or why not?

- Ask those outside of work to describe you in 3 words. What are they?

- Are there similarities/differences between your branding at work and your branding away from work?

- Why do you think that those differences/similarities exist? What insights can you draw?

Notes

CONSCIOUS
LEADERSHIP

Your Brand

Making Changes

- What happens if your brand equity is low and doesn't resonate with others?
  - They don't associate you with your brand
- How do you re-brand yourself?
  - Often, our brand is created by our behaviors, which impacts the way others perceive us
  - Our behaviors are shaped by our beliefs
  - The strength of a brand is often determined by consistency of behaviors
- What behaviors would demonstrate alignment with your desired brand?
  - What beliefs need to change for those behaviors to materialize?
- This exercise should align with your strategic map:

Changing Brand Perception

- Desired Brand #1:
- Needed Behavior #1:
- Changed Belief #1:

- Desired Brand #2:
- Needed Behavior #2:
- Changed Belief #2:

- Desired Brand #3:
- Needed Behavior #3:
- Changed Belief #3:

Notes

CONSCIOUS
LEADERSHIP

Reflection Points

- I don't believe in doing the fair thing; I believe in doing the right thing.
  - The fairness doctrine allows people to avoid making difficult decisions
  - It is easier to push people down (high performers) than to pull people up (low performers)
  - Fairness has a leveling-down effect to the lowest common denominator
    - Doing the right thing levels up
  - Doing the right thing requires courage and difficult decisions
- Truthful, not Transparent
  - Tricks of Transparency
    - Communicator has right to not be transparent
    - Communicator has history of not always being transparent
    - Communicator has power to control degree of transparency
  - Truthfulness increases the effectiveness of communication
    - Listener is not concerned with deciphering true meaning
  - Truthfulness is not naiveté or gullibility
  - Truthfulness requires courage
    - Often difficult conversations
  - Accurate communication is a right, not a privilege
- Motives, not Mechanics
  - Focus on the "why" not the "how"
  - "I don't care how much you know until I know how much you care"
  - Focus on developing the quality of your motives, not demonstrating your motives to others
  - If your people trust you, then your communication will be well-received
    - Mechanics can increase the effectiveness of communication, but not to the degree of motives
  - If your motives are not pure
    - Change is possible
    - Work on improving the quality of your motives, making them pure (changing your core beliefs),
    - Don't work on improving the quality of how you communicate impure motives

CHAPTER 6
THE FOUR THINGS

"A man who trims himself to suit everybody will soon whittle himself away."
- Charles Schwab

"An appeaser is one who feeds a crocodile—hoping it will eat him last."
- Winston Churchill

<u>Axiom:</u>
I don't believe in being flexible;
I believe in being malleable.

Much like the word "transparent," the word "flexible" is a big buzzword in today's corporate world. We are all expected to be flexible: flexible with our schedules, our agendas, and our opinions; flexible in the way that we lead other people, and flexible in the way we allow ourselves to be led; flexible to adjust and adapt to a changing environment.

On the surface, this seems like a worthwhile pursuit. Recognizing the speed of change at the workplace, flexibility seems capable of enabling us to adapt to this rapid cadence. On Monday, we think that option "A" is the right target to pursue, but on Tuesday, we receive some new market information. Based on these new data, option "A" now no longer seems like the right course to pursue; instead, option "B" now looks desirable. It is flexibility that allows us to course-correct in the middle, right?

Perhaps. Truthfully, there is some merit in being flexible regarding tactical decisions. Flexibility is the proper term to describe the manner in which tactics are executed. But is flexible really the proper term to describe a leader's capacity for adaptation? Perhaps not. There is a big difference between the execution of tactics and the character of a leader. So let's examine the idea of flexibility. Let's look at it first from the abstract, conceptual perspective, and then we can explore it using concrete examples.

Think about a couple of items in your daily life that are flexible. A plastic sword that your kid plays with—you can bend it in any direction and it bounces right back. That's flexible. Gumbi is flexible. You can twist, tie, and contort him all day long; but as soon as you stop applying pressure, he returns to his original shape. The $12 plastic souvenir cup that you purchased at the last concert you attended is flexible (it seemed like a bargain at the time).

Let's focus on the plastic sword. If you bend a plastic sword a little bit, it will return to its original shape as soon as you stop applying pressure. If you bend it too far, however, it will snap. The sword snaps because it is weak; it is not strong enough to withstand the pressure. That weakness is exactly why plastic swords are sold as kid's toys. The plastic sword is not strong enough to cause physical damage.

This illustration of a plastic sword's flexibility is somewhat frivolous. But it illustrates two characteristics of flexibility that are much more somber: weakness and the tendency to return to the original state.

Anything, Everything, and Nothing…or Something

"Internalization. This occurs when you've exploited impact, when you've molded the standard material to your needs and made it yours, when you've made your new skills strong through hard use. All of a sudden these new concepts stopped churning within you, and a new reality is born: You and the concepts are one. They have literally become you. You have become them."

- Tom Hopkins

Generally speaking, if an item is flexible, it's not that strong. If a "leader" is flexible, it means that he will bend to the current circumstance and yield to the current pressure. A "leader" that is truly flexible resembles a chameleon more than anything else. Flexibility enables the conventional leader to sit on the fence, standing for anything and everything. Simultaneously, flexibility absolves him from the responsibility of making a decision, enabling him to stand for nothing—including principles, ideals, and the people that he "leads." And adage goes, "If you don't stand for something, you will fall for anything." In the corporate environment, however, "falling" isn't respectable. And so the conventional leader doesn't "fall," he "flexes."

You have witnessed flexibility at work (and probably outside of work), and it drives you crazy. It might even make you mad. It should frighten you. Why? Flexibility in leadership is dangerous. When a "leader" is really flexible, the people that he is leading will invariably get hurt.

A conscious leader makes decisions, and he stands for something, especially for the people that work for him. A flexible "leader" will say whatever needs to be said and do whatever needs to be done to alleviate the current pressure and appease his superiors. Unfortunately, this is often at the expense of those who work for him. In America, we have a word for these types of two-faced, smooth-talking, double-sided, flexible individuals, "politicians." There is a reason why a good portion of our country is disillusioned by politics and dissatisfied with politicians. The stereotypical politician is a conventional leader who excels in flexibility. The same individual will tell two completely different stories on different days based on what is expedient—the epitome of flexibility.

So if at the core, if you don't really respect flexible "leaders," why is that term so prevalent? Why is it so widely accepted? It's the same reason that hundreds of millions of dollars are spent each year training the mechanics of communication—the original myth of conventional leadership. The myth confuses what you do and who you are. This confusion is always harmful, but confusion regarding the nature of flexibility is particularly destructive.

Dare (to Do) or Esse (to Be)

When flexibility is used to describe behaviors—what you do—the results are positive and potentially impactful. Behaviors should be flexible to adjust to changing circumstances. This is the only means of consistently producing positive outcomes in a dynamic environment. Behavioral flexibility allows for successful adaptation.

However, when flexibility is used to describe beliefs—who you are—the results are dangerous and potentially damaging.

Conventional leadership is drawn to flexibility for two reasons. The first appeal of flexibility is its capacity. Flexibility has tremendous power and potential, and when used appropriately, it can produce transformational results. The second appeal of flexibility is its comfort. Flexibility touches the deepest and most familiar level of conventional leadership—behavior.

The conscious leader, having a well-defined set of beliefs, can harness the power of flexibility by constraining it to what he does. The conventional leader, however, lacks awareness of a well-defined belief system. In this situation, absent of boundaries and constraints, flexibility begins to expand its scope of influence. Eventually and unconsciously, flexibility permeates the beliefs of the conventional leader. Flexibility now describes not just what he does, but who he is.

Flexibility, in its ideal state, describes behaviors—what you do—in the presence of a well-defined belief system. The result is powerful. When flexibility describes an unconscious set of beliefs—who you are—the result is a politician. Why?

As a belief, flexibility doesn't function well within a well-defined system. It actually undermines and uproots other beliefs. If you are flexible, you don't have to be conscious of what you believe, nor do you need to know why you believe it. Today's behavior is no longer determined who you are—you are flexible. Today's behavior is determined by whatever is currently convenient. And in the minds of those "leaders" who are flexible, that's not a shortcoming to challenge, that's a success to celebrate!

The flexible conventional leader believes, thankfully only subconsciously, that his decisions should be made based on what is best for him at the moment. Today's convenience and pressure often define that decision. While this seems selfish, remember, the conventional leader is inward-focused. In his mind, he is the focal point of his environment. So from his perspective, as the "leader" in the center, it is only fair that his behavior, today, should be determined by what is best for him, today.

From our perspective, it is easy to understand why the conventional leader who is flexible is incapable of generating impact. He has believed a myth. So what now? Let's debunk this myth of flexibility. That starts by asking a question of ourselves. As conscious leaders, if we believe that flexibility is a myth, what should we pursue instead to describe who we are?

Hammers and Anvils

"We can let circumstances rule us, or we can take charge and rule our lives from within."
   - Earl Nightingale

Malleability. "Malleability" isn't a word frequently used today. Historically, it has been used to define certain characteristics of metal—specifically, its capacity to be shaped, changed, and formed. A blacksmith would take a piece of metal, and using a very hot furnace, he would heat it. Once the metal was hot (typically glowing shades of red and orange), using a hammer and an anvil, he would pound the metal, shaping and molding it into his desired form.

During a time of peace, a blacksmith would use iron ore to forge iron plows for the agricultural society. During a time of war, however, the plow could be transformed into a sword. The blacksmith would heat the iron plow to very high temperatures, and using his hammer and anvil, he would reshape and reform the plow into a sword. Once the war was over, that same sword could be transformed into an iron gate.

A plastic sword is flexible. It's a kid's toy, weak and bendable, incapable of providing physical defense. An iron sword is malleable. It is a warrior's weapon, forged through conflict, strong and sturdy, with the potential to generate physical impact.

Behaviors are flexible; beliefs are malleable. Behaviors should be circumstantially changed; beliefs should be intentionally molded.

Think about the implications for leadership. Within the context of a dynamic environment, malleability allows for a behavioral adaptation without a fundamental alteration. What you do should change based on external circumstances; who you are should change based on internal convictions. Malleability allows you to mold your beliefs as new ideas are introduced without compromising your integrity. It allows for and encourages change, but not change that is flippant or whimsical.

The same piece of iron can be forged into both the plow and the sword. Intense conflict, extensive heat and pressure, are required to reshape iron. It doesn't take more than circumstance to bend plastic.

A conscious leader strives for malleability. It allows for the consistency of pure motives required to generate trust. Malleability enables the strength required for a conscious leader to stand for something. It provides the fortitude to do the right thing, even in the face of criticism. It allows for challenge.

When you move into the realm of beliefs, you enter into an area of strength and power. The idea of strength is foreign to the flexible "leader." The strength of the malleable leader is derived from his belief system. He knows who he is, and who he isn't. He knows the areas where he can adapt and the areas where he will not budge. This strength allows him to tolerate ambiguity while not being ambiguous.

Conventional leaders prefer stability and fear change. Why? No one, even flexible "leaders," enjoy being blown around in the wind. But when beliefs are absent, flexibility is the only option. Malleability requires awareness of beliefs. The malleable conscious leader isn't threatened by uncertainty. His leadership is built on a bedrock of principles. Malleability allows a leader to support his people and defend his principles while still adapting to change.

A conscious leader is forged by beliefs that are malleable. This allows him to generate impact by fashioning behaviors that are flexible.

The Wind Blows

What do these conceptual ideas of flexibility and malleability look like in the real world? Let's revisit Julie and Todd:

Todd's primary focus this year at work is a new project named project Sandstorm, which he and Julie initiated six months ago. Project Sandstorm involves Acme's entrance into the distribution chains of their customers, allowing Acme to achieve full integration into their businesses. This would provide Acme a meaningful competitive advantage in the market. Senior leadership approved this project, and the respective budget increase, four months ago. The size and scope of this project required Todd to hire two more individuals, who both relocated their families across the country to work at Acme just three months ago.

Yesterday, senior management came to Julie and Todd and announced budget cuts. Specifically, they wanted to postpone Project Sandstorm for a full year. They requested that Julie and Todd return the budget originally allocated to the project. This would result in the laying off of both individuals who just relocated to work at Acme. Julie has called a meeting with Todd.

JULIE: So, we are in a difficult situation with Project Sandstorm. Senior management didn't give me the exact reason for the budget cuts, but I overheard them talking about dividends and maintaining value for shareholders. Regardless, I have no doubt that once management provides us with the proper funding, Sandstorm will be a huge success. They told me to expect a full year's delay, and at that point, we could resume the project with the originally allocated budget. But right now, we need to immediately stop work on the project and return the entire amount of the project's previously allocated budget.

TODD: This is frustrating, because they approved the money for Sandstorm four months ago, knowing that we would have to hire new employees to launch the program. Now, not only is this project delayed for a year, but we have two extra employees on payroll who just relocated. Their decisions to relocate were based on my communication to them about this project, its impact, their role on the team, and potential opportunities at Acme in the future. And now I am supposed to lay them off after I hired and relocated them only 90 days ago? That's not right, and we need to tell that to senior management. Surely there is another solution.

JULIE: I know it's tough. But Todd, this is good for your development as a leader. Leadership requires tough decisions. The stock price is down, and senior management is making difficult decisions, including cutting costs, to maintain value for the shareholders. They are accepting responsibility and making tough decisions, and so should we.

TODD (sarcastically): Of course they are. Even though they own thousands of shares of Acme stock, I am sure they aren't referring to themselves when they talk about shareholder value. Look, I can delay the project, even though it is a tough decision that really hurts. But there has to be another alternative to these employees. I can't lay them both off within 90 days of a cross-country relocation that was based on what I initially told them. It's not the right thing to do.

As we discussed previously, doing the right thing is never easy. It will often require difficult conversations and touch choices. Doing the right thing is not conventional, or everyone would do it. Todd is discovering how hard it is to do the right thing. Fortunately, Todd's belief in doing the right thing is malleable. As you will see, this allows him to harness the power of flexibility with regard to behaviors.

JULIE: Todd, I understand that you are upset. This is a tough situation. But you have to be flexible here. We all have to sacrifice and do our part to help the greater good of the company. I'm sure that Human Resources will give them a very fair package, and that they will be able to find work again in no time.

TODD: Have you seen the recent unemployment rate? Julie, I don't know what the answer is. I don't know how to make this work. I know we have to return the budget, but I can't lay them off like this. I'm sorry; I just can't. So if we remove that option from the table completely, what else can we do?

JULIE: Your inability to adjust and be flexible is going to hurt your career. You need to know that this is a career-limiting move. Senior management wants the entire allocated budget returned. The cost of those two employees, prorated to their start date, is $50,000. If you are afraid to make the tough decision and don't want to be a team player, then you don't have to lay them off. But you must find $50,000 elsewhere. And if you want to pull that money from other projects, reducing their impact, that's your choice. You need to know that you are still accountable to hit your numbers for the year. Those numbers will remain firm. Performance expectations are not flexible. I'm not going to have my department under perform and miss my numbers because of your inflexibility.

TODD (after thinking for a while): So I have an idea. Right now, I have $60,000 allocated towards my continuing education and development. If I forfeit that program, we can use that money to pay the salary of these two individuals for the rest of this year. Next January, we can discuss Sandstorm again with senior management and see what happens. There are no promises or guarantees at that point (and if I have to let those employees go at that point, I will). But I think we can make a very good business case as to why Sandstorm deserves funding, and deserves funding in January. If they are willing, we can also re-visit my education at that point.

JULIE: That's crazy! You have been working towards this program for a long time, and this will delay your degree by at least a year! And there are no guarantees that Sandstorm, or your education, will get funding next January. Are you sure you are comfortable with this? You seem to be vacillating back and forth an awful lot. One minute you talk about your commitment to the company and your career, and the next minute you are willing to throw it all away. Let me be transparent with you for a moment— senior leadership will view your inability and unwillingness to lay these people off as a sign of weakness. They will also view your ambivalent commitment to your development as a potential red flag for your file. Just something to think about for your career goals and aspirations. Think about it tonight, and let's talk again tomorrow.

TODD (the next day): I have thought about this decision for the last 24 hours. It pains me to delay my education and degree for another year. I fully understand how this will be perceived by senior management, and the long-term implications it could have on my career. I also am aware that I am accountable for hitting my numbers and delivering performance within this department. I am aware of all of those factors. However, I have also thought about the factors involved in laying these two individuals off right now. I am very conscious of the impact that it would have not just on them, but on their families. I can't lay them off. So go ahead and clear out my education fund. I fundamentally believe that this is the right thing to do. If you can start the process of transferring those funds, I will figure out how to redeploy these individuals and make them as productive as possible for the remainder of the year.

All About Me

"Nobody speaks the truth when there's something they must have."

    - Elizabeth Brown

This is an extreme example. Sadly, you have probably experienced something similar to this. By examining behaviors of leaders during times of adversity, we can see what they really believe. Remember, pressure reveals motives. Based on the behaviors that Julie and Todd demonstrated, what can we conclude about their beliefs?

First, it is very likely that Julie is not even aware of her beliefs. If she were, she would be embarrassed. She should be ashamed. Why? Her behaviors reveal that Julie believes that her career and reputation are more important than other people. She doesn't really believe that other people are that valuable. Her decisions are based on what can benefit her the most—today. She stands for anything, everything, and nothing. Because of that, people get hurt. Julie is a flexible leader, as external pressure and convenience, not internal beliefs, drive her decisions.

Albeit unconsciously, Julie believes in flexibility.

Based on Todd's behaviors, what can we conclude about his beliefs? First, he is aware of them. He knows what he believes and what he doesn't believe. He believes that he is not at the center of the environment. He is externally focused. He believes in the value of people. He also believes in the value of his career and education. But he believes that the value of other people is greater than the value of his education, reputation, and career. He believes in doing the right thing, regardless of circumstances. He believes that his personal reputation is more important than his professional reputation. Todd is a malleable leader who is flexible in his actions. He will adjust and adapt to the circumstances (sacrificing Sandstorm and his education), but he will not bend his beliefs (sacrificing for those on his team).

Todd believes in malleability.

This example is designed to illustrate the "why" of flexibility/malleability, not the "what." We are not suggesting that you should never lay anyone off. Nor are we suggesting that you should sacrifice your education to provide someone else with employment for a few months. Every situation is unique. Based on those unique situations, leaders have to make tough, painful decisions. The conscious leader will either lay people off or terminate employees when it is the right thing to do. Over the course of a career, we promise that at least a couple of times, the right thing to do will be to terminate the employment of another person. And although you won't enjoy it, you should do it. If you can't lay someone off, or terminate employment when it is the right thing to do, then you resemble a conventional leader more than a conscious leader.

What's the application point for you? You need to know what you believe and why you believe it. This will allow you to harness and leverage the power of flexibility with regard to your behavior. You will be able to adapt to a changing environment from a solid foundation. It is the malleable leader, not the flexible one, who makes an impact.

And There's More...

"I have always thought that the actions of men were the best interpreters of their thoughts."
- John Locke

Here is another benefit of malleability. Todd, through this adversity, added a new dimension to his leadership—moral authority. Moral authority is about walking the walk after you have talked the talk. Your behaviors adapt to the circumstances while remaining aligned not just with what you believe, but with what you say you believe.

Moral authority, although hard to define, is easy to recognize. It comes about when a leader embodies the ideals that he believes. Think back to the example. What do you think the reaction of Todd's team will be the next time he asks them to make a sacrifice? They won't complain and moan; they will smile and do it gladly. How hard do you think those two individuals who relocated will work for Todd? They will be the first ones in and the last ones to leave—every day.

What type of impact do you think Todd's decision will have? What about his colleagues? Todd has set the new standard for Julie's other direct reports regarding how they treat the people on their teams. What about his reports? Do you think they trust his motives? They will be receptive to his leadership; they'll bend over backwards for him. What about the rest of the department? People will be begging to work for Todd. Who wouldn't want to work for a leader who cares that much about his people? What about senior management? It is difficult to rise to that level in an organization without some degree of leadership. At some level, they will understand what Todd did and respect him.

When you lead by example, you create moral authority. The power of Todd's moral authority allowed him to generate a tremendous impact on an entire department. In regards to people, moral authority almost always is a precursor to impact.

Malleability is possible through self-awareness. You need to be conscious of what you believe, and what you will and will not compromise. This foundation, this bedrock of beliefs, is one of the key differentiating factors separating conventional leaders from conscious leaders. This leads us into this axiom's first sub-principle:

Sub-principle #1:
Depth not Breadth

What is the primary difference between amateur sports and professional sports? A paycheck. As soon as you get a paycheck (assuming there are no violations of NCAA guidelines), you are no longer an amateur, but a professional. This paycheck principle applies to non-athletes as well. The fact that we all get paid to perform a job makes us, at least officially, a professional.

And as professionals, we are expected to act professionally. And we agree with that expectation—for the most part. But only for the most part. Acting professionally, at certain times, can reduce your potential for impact; and so there are times that a conscious leader should and should not act professionally...

At work, professional behavior should be the rule, not the exception. Boundaries should be established and respected; employees should adhere to these lines. Conscious leadership believes that, when at work, you should NOT: dance on tables, start a food fight, blare loud music from your office, or throw a toga party in the cafeteria. On the job, a certain level of professionalism is required. Now the happy hour, that's a different story...

Okay, we are done joking. Seriously, boundaries and a level of professionalism at work are good. But what level? In what circumstances? Can there be too much professionalism? What effect does professionalism have on your interactions with others? What effect does it have on trust? What impact does professionalism have on people? Here's the big idea:

What happens when personal communication is replaced by professional courtesy?

Think about your relationships at work. Everyone is encouraged to have a network. And we are given the technological tools (cell phones, computers, Internet) to stay connected to that network. What does that mean? It means that we are encouraged, both explicitly and implicitly, to create relationships that are a mile wide but only an inch deep.

This level of connection is beneficial when used to define your network relationships. What happens when this type of mile-wide/inch-deep principle defines your relationship with your team? Is this level of connection ideal when defining your relationships with the people you lead?

Before we go any further, we need to clarify our beliefs about networking and the type of relationships that it requires. Networking, both professional and personal, is a very good thing. We highly encourage conscious leaders to expand their network and broaden their sphere of relationships as far and wide as possible. By definition, your network, and thus your relationships within that network, should be an inch deep and a mile wide. The network should be broad, not deep. This sub-principle is not attempting to debunk the value of networking. It is not challenging the type of relationships required to network effectively. This sub-principle is exploring, and challenging, the type of relationships required to lead your people effectively.

So is there a difference in your relationships between those in your network and those you lead? Of critical importance, should there be a difference between those relationships? What happens when the mile-wide/inch-deep principle, which is required for your networking relationships, also describes your relationships with the people that you lead? You have a problem. You lose the potential to generate impact.

You can't lead people from a distance. Your relationship cannot only be an inch deep. Leadership requires trust. Trust requires relationship and vulnerability. Trust requires depth.

We aren't advocating that you become best friends with everyone at work. You should have boundaries—and you need to have boundaries—within your professional relationships. There is no shortage of examples demonstrating the consequences caused by inappropriate professional relationships. You want to avoid those types of relationships at all costs. But, unless you engage people at a deeper level, you will never be a truly impactful leader. Why? You won't understand them, they won't trust you, and you won't be able to communicate effectively with them.

Crossover

As a conscious leader, your professional relationships need to be characterized by personal communication.

As previously noted, people are complex. Not only do they experience life both rationally and emotionally, but also professionally and personally. We try to compartmentalize our lives, keeping the professional sphere (work) from touching the personal sphere (non-work). But most of us aren't very good at that; with most people, there is always spillover from one sphere to the other.

Think about the last time you had a rough night at home. Maybe you got into an argument with your significant other. Perhaps you were informed that your child failed his mid-term exam and was on the verge of failing the 10th grade. Chances are, the next day at work, your professional sphere was affected by what was going on within your personal sphere. Your compartments merged.

If you cannot relate to that example, reverse the order. Imagine that you had a miserable day at work. You ran from fire-drill to fire-drill, dealt with several changed deadlines, and received from your boss a "fair" merit increase that accompanied your annual appraisal (which stated that your performance was excellent). After a day like that at work, what will happen when you get home? You probably won't be in a very good mood. Your personal sphere is going to collide with your professional sphere.

Nothing new there, right? This concept is intuitive. Life experiences are inter-related. What happens in your personal life will affect your professional life. Your spheres will collide. As intuitive as that may be, conventional leadership instructs us to divorce our personal life from our professional life. Taking it a step further, conventional leadership demands that we remove personal communication from our professional relationships.

Conscious leadership, with the support of common sense, debunks this myth of completely personal and professional separation. Belief in this myth will eventually produce outcomes that are predictable. You will be disheartened because we each only live one life, and it is impossible to completely separate the personal and professional components. In addition, you will be disappointed because as your ability to compartmentalize people increases, your ability to impact people decreases.

Leaves and Roots

"The modern world is filled with men who hold dogmas so strongly that they do not even know they are dogmas."

> - G.K. Chesterton

Why does conventional leadership want to keep all relationships at a distance? Fear. Fear of a conversation that could become a Human Resources issue. Fear of being misinterpreted. Fear of being exposed. Fear of being in a complex situation and not knowing what to do or say. There is nothing inherently wrong with fear. But instead of displaying humility and confidence, and choosing to embrace that fear and work through it, conventional leadership ignores it. Denying the fear renders conventional leadership incapable of dealing with it, so it demands complete separation of the personal and the professional.

Conventional leadership won't engage professional relationships with personal communication. This is one of the reasons why conventional leadership is failing. Relationships don't work that way, people don't trust that way, and leaders don't create impact that way.

Beliefs are personal. Impact comes from changing beliefs. If you can't engage in personal communication, then you can't create impact.

Conscious leaders engage their professional relationships with personal communication— this includes communication about beliefs. This engagement allows you to create a meaningful difference. A person's behavior is nothing more than a manifestation of his beliefs. Beliefs go deep, and permeate both the professional and personal spheres.

To make a difference in the lives of people, a conscious leader looks beneath the surface issue. He looks at the root issue. Conventional leaders don't even know that there is a root issue. To illustrate this point, consider this analogy: think of people as trees. As you walk through the park, you can see the leaves on the tree, your children can swing on the branches, and you can smell the blossoms. These are all the "surface components" of a tree. We observe the leaves, branches, and flowers with ease, as they are tangible and visible.

What happens when the leaves begin to wilt or the branches show signs of disease? The park calls their arborist to treat the diseased tree. Upon arrival, he first takes note of the leaves, branches, and blossoms. He gathers all of the relevant information, observing the visible and tangible signs of disease. Drawing insights from that information, he diagnoses the tree's core problem and cause of disease. Most often, to effectively treat the disease, he won't spend his time with the tree's leaves, branches, or blossoms. Instead, he will focus his energy on the tree's roots.

With people, as with trees, the cause of the disease is not readily apparent. The symptoms of sickness are not always the cause of the sickness. The leaves are wilting because the roots are sick, but if they can be healed, the leaves will flourish. What does this tree analogy have to do with conscious leadership?

The root issue is the real issue. If you want to make a difference, you must address the root issue.

In this respect, do you see that people are no different than trees? As a conscious leader, you need to be aware that diseases often manifest themselves in the form of wilted leaves and cracked branches (behaviors). The conventional leader spends his time here. But the diseases' cause—and cure—is often found in the roots. Engaging people at their roots (beliefs) can be messy and is always complex. But it is usually the only way to create meaningful change within another person.

The conscious leader has the courage to dig, get his hands dirty, and deal with the roots. Some conventional leaders will trim the branches, but most are content with merely smelling the roses.

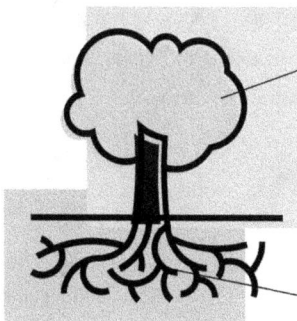

Behaviors & Outcomes: tangible, observable, surface level, we notice first, displays signs of health or sickness, where we naturally focus

Beliefs: the true source of life for the tree; invisible, underground, impacts the health of the tree, where we should focus

If you aren't an outdoors person, here is another analogy. Think about process improvement and operational excellence. One of the main tenets of the continuous improvement paradigm is the principle of "root cause." If there is a product defect, or if there are production errors, the first, and primary, goal of the leader is to discover the source of the defect. He searches for the issue's root cause. Once it is located, he can fix the problem and remove the defect. Those who excel in process improvement understand that energy spent on anything outside of the root cause is wasted and unproductive. To remove the defect (outcome), the core issue (belief) must be resolved. Without addressing the root cause, there is no impact.

Curing diseased tree roots and fixing faulty production lines seems very different than leading people. It is, and it isn't. People are complex—much more complex than an advanced production system or an exotic tree. The principle is the same, but the method is different. Fortunately, your method (behavior) will be influenced and guided by your principle (belief). Don't worry about your surface issues. You can, and will, make an impact with people. To get the right outcome, you must start by focusing on the belief.

Non-Personal Relationships

The "roots" of people (beliefs) are formed and cultivated by all of their life experiences, not just those that occur during work hours. Revisit your "My Leadership Journey" map that you created at the end of Chapter 2. Look at the events that most shaped your "Leadership Philosophy." Were they personal or professional in nature? For most people, they are personal.

The myth of conventional leadership is that you can completely separate personal and professional experiences, interact with people from a distance, and still make an impact. This isn't true. Your professional leadership will be determined, to some degree, by your personal experiences.

Beliefs are always personal.

So to make an impact as a leader, at what level do you need to operate? Behaviors and outcomes (branches, leaves) or beliefs (roots)? Is it any surprise that a conventional leader, focused on changing flexible behaviors, struggles to make a lasting difference? Or that a conscious leader, focused on molding malleable beliefs, creates something of significance?

This is intuitive, but conventional leadership still tries to maintain separation, insisting that the personal and professional be completely divorced. But you know this doesn't work; your own experiences invalidate this myth. Think back to the bosses that had the greatest impact on you. Were your relationships with them merely professional? Or did they have a personal component? We would bet that they had a personal component. Why is this personal component so critical to impactful leadership? Trust.

Trust is personal, not professional.

Trust cannot be created from a distance. Non-personal, courteous, professional communication will never foster trust. If you can't engage in personal communication, you cannot create trust. If you can't create trust, you can't change beliefs.

Trust has an emotional component; it is not purely rational. If I trust you, there is some degree of emotion involved. High-performing teams, as we have stated before, require trust and this emotional element. Their synergistic nature is enabled through the emotional connectivity fueled not by the professional, but by the personal.

It is difficult to have a relationship with a person on a professional pedestal. Yet, when leadership remains purely professional, never crossing into the personal realm, that is exactly what it is expecting—a non-personal relationship. There is no such thing—it is an oxymoron and a myth. Relationships are *personal*. And it is part of the reason why you are frustrated with conventional leadership.

All people, at some level, want to be valued and appreciated. This value and appreciation is best communicated through personal relationships. The conscious leader strives for personal relationships that are professionally appropriate. Professional courtesy can never replace personal communication. To generate impact, a leader doesn't need to become best friends with everyone he leads; but he does need to engage them at a personal level.

Sherlock Holmes

By focusing on the depth of your relationships (and not just expanding their breadth), you provide yourself with more opportunities for pattern recognition within behaviors. If you know the history of those you lead, you can view their behaviors over an extended period of time. This allows you to search for patterns among behaviors that, although seemingly disconnected, are linked by a common belief. History repeats itself.

Let's look at a couple of examples from our friends at Acme Office Supply. It's the end of another quarter, and Julie has some feedback for Todd:

JULIE: And so, Todd, those are the areas in which you have excelled. Nice job! I do have some constructive feedback for you. Over the past two months, I have noticed that you have been turning in your expense reports late and sometimes, incomplete. You need to do a better job with them.
TODD: Yeah, you're right. I have gotten sloppy with them, and I will do a better job going forward.
JULIE: Great, thanks. I knew you would. You always get the job done.

Very straightforward—Julie observed Todd wasn't submitting his expense reports in a timely manner, and confronted this professional behavior in a professional manner. Todd agreed to improve. Done and done. But, could this have been a missed opportunity for Julie? What could have happened if she had been willing to engage on a more personal level?

JULIE: And so, Todd, those are the areas in which you have excelled. Nice Job! I do have some constructive feedback for you. Over the past two months, I have noticed that you have been turning in your expense reports late and sometimes, incomplete. You need to do a better job with this.
TODD: Yeah, you're right. I have gotten sloppy with them, and I will do a better job going forward.

JULIE: I have no doubt you will. You always do a great job. But hey—I need to ask—I have been working with you for over a year and never had any sort of issue with expense reports, until now. I know it's just a blip in the data, but it's also very unlike you. What's up?

TODD: Nothing, just stuff at home. I'll do a better job getting them turned in on time.

JULIE: If you don't mind me asking, is everything okay? Are you okay?

TODD: Sure, I'm fine. It's just that I usually do my expense reports on Saturday mornings, and my son is playing on a traveling baseball team this summer, and I try to make it to all of those games, and it makes it difficult to do expense reports while watching ball games.

JULIE: I'm sure that would be difficult. What position does your son play?

TODD (lighting up): He's a pitcher, and a lefty at that. He's a junior in high school this year, and I think he has a chance to play ball in college. He has a great fastball and is getting better with his other pitches. Two weeks ago, there were four scouts from local colleges that came to the game to watch him play. He has a great attitude...

TODD (10 minutes later): ...and I promise that I will get those expense reports in on time. I know that it makes your life difficult when they are late and incomplete. Don't worry; it won't happen again.

So what was the difference between this interaction and the previous one? Julie risked engaging Todd on a personal level. And by doing that, not only did she discover the real reason (the "why") that his expense reports were late (the "what"), but she grew her relationship with him. Now she can follow up on his son's progress over the summer. She gave him the opportunity to open up and share something personal and meaningful with her. Julie still needs to follow up on the expense report issue, but now she has greater context for the issue. And Todd, feeling a connection with Julie, will be more likely to get those reports submitted so that he doesn't make her life unnecessarily difficult.

The sharing of personal experience results in the growth of professional trust.

When you create relationships that go beyond professional courtesy, you increase your potential to make a meaningful difference in the lives of those you lead. By engaging at a deeper level, the belief level, you can make a significant impact. And that is the crux of conscious leadership.

And that takes us to the final sub-principle of this chapter.

<u>Sub-principle #2:</u> Make a Difference not a Point

"It's not what you tell your players that counts. It's what they hear."
   - Red Auerbach

Relationships characterized by trust, and that contain a personal component, require intentionality. They don't happen by accident. Let's assume that as a conscious leader, you have established these types of relationships—relationships characterized by personal communication. Now what? If you want to create transformational change in the lives of those you lead, what do you do?

You challenge beliefs. Using personal communication, and leveraging the trust which you have created over time, you challenge the beliefs of those you lead. Challenge leads to change, and changing beliefs is impactful. So if you are going to make a sustainable impact in the lives of the people you lead, you have to challenge their beliefs.

That is easier said than done; most people don't like to be challenged. But if you don't challenge people's beliefs, you can't make a difference. With the juxtaposition of these two elements providing our foundation, what does a conscious leader need to believe about communication to be impactful?

You need to believe that the primary beneficiary of the communication is them, not you. This principle will link back to our discussion around motives and mechanics, but it examines communication from a new perspective. Before we go any further, here is a short example:

You discover that your new employee was fired from his previous company after the collection of an "Anonymous Employee Feedback Survey." Trusting the motives of the "leaders" who initiated the survey, he was honest in his feedback. Unfortunately, at some level in the hierarchy, the survey stopped being anonymous. His "leadership" didn't value being challenged. He trusted his old company with his honest feedback, and they broke his trust. What does this mean for him, and you, today?

You should anticipate that he will have a difficult time trusting you, that he might struggle accepting feedback, and that he will definitely struggle giving feedback. He probably believes that no company is trustworthy, and that as an extension of "the company," you are not trustworthy. But, he may not know that he believes that.

As you work together, the predictable behavior issues will probably surface, including communication style and issues with feedback. But as a conscious leader, you can't just stop there. You must go deeper. You have to get to the belief level (which might first consist of making him aware of a belief level). Difficult? Probably. Indispensible? Absolutely!

This is the only way for you to make a significant, positive impact on his life. And this is one of the reasons why conventional leadership is frustrating. It promises impact, but it never delivers.

As a conscious leader, it is your responsibility, and opportunity, to ask the tough questions to penetrate the surface and get down to the belief level. It is your job to observe the branches and leaves (behaviors) and look for patterns that would show issues at the root level (beliefs). You need to be able to understand the personal implications of what he experienced while maintaining professional objectivity.

Impact requires you to ask difficult questions. You will have to challenge and encourage. You will have to critique while maintaining trust. How do you do that? It depends on what you believe about communication.

Start here; ask yourself one simple question, "Am I communicating with this individual to make a difference or to make a point?"

The Question
"Not everything that's true needs to be said."
    - Cassandra Clare

What does this question mean? What is the distinction between a point and a difference? Hold on, we will get there.

This question will allow us to first expose, and then debunk, another myth of conventional leadership—the myth of brutally honest feedback. This myth, once it is exposed, should infuriate you. It should also sadden you. The acceptance of this myth as truth has resulted in not only countless damaged relationships, but also in unrealized potential for impact.

First, let's set up the framework for this myth. Conventional leadership is never more hypocritical than when discussing feedback. It is afraid to enter the really challenging arenas (flawed beliefs), yet it prides itself on honest (or at least transparent) feedback. And so, based on this myth, what does conventional leadership's feedback typically look like? Ugly and worthless. It often makes a point, but it rarely makes a difference.

But the brutally honest feedback myth has lived on. Why? Because making a point is very tempting. It is easy. And sometimes it feels good to make a point. Making a point always includes, "You were wrong." Sometimes, it also includes, "I was right." If you make a point, then you could argue that you "had the difficult conversation." And so you spend your time telling the employee, in essence, that you are better than they are. The focus of the challenge isn't on them, it's on you. You want to feel good about how much you know. But if you are focused on yourself, you will never impact them.

Conventional leadership rarely praises the surface behaviors (because they are never good enough); yet it never critiques the root beliefs (because it doesn't know they exist). The result? The pain of receiving challenging feedback without the benefit of lasting change. This is "making a point." And it is based on the myth of brutally honest feedback.

Sound familiar? Are you mad? You should be. Challenging feedback will cause pain. The pain of challenge should be a means to an end, not an end in itself. To inflict, or receive, pain with no lasting benefit is worthless. Tragically, it is also the conventional method for "coaching."

So let's go back to the question: "Am I communicating to make a difference or a point?"

If this question is not answered correctly, then nothing else matters. If you are trying to make a difference, then your focus will be on the other person. When you are asking these difficult questions and are looking for patterns, your attention will be focused on recognizing opportunities to facilitate growth in someone else, not opportunities to facilitate pride in yourself. You won't waste any pain, and you will challenge only when it can produce positive results—when the challenge can make a difference.

There is no such thing as brutally honest feedback. There is just *honest* feedback. The conscious leader communicates with balance, honestly praising and critiquing. All employees demonstrate behaviors and beliefs worth praising. Pain caused by challenge should never be wasted. It should be used to make a positive difference.

Coaching Sandwich

"Although men are accused of not knowing their own weakness, yet perhaps few know their own strength. It is in men as in soils, where sometimes there is a vein of gold which the owner knows not of."

- Jonathan Swift

How does a conscious leader make a difference instead of a point? Through the "coaching sandwich."

We have spent a good deal of this chapter discussing the personal, emotional, component of relationships. Current research has proven that people require seven positive interactions to balance every negative one. If you want your people to remain emotionally engaged, you have to provide a mountain of positive feedback to emotionally offset the negative feedback. Otherwise, you will destroy trust, and your employees will emotionally detach.

The conscious leader must be aware of how the other person is reacting and responding. You should strive for a balance between challenge and sensitivity. You want to challenge the individual with tough questions, yet be sensitive to not push them over the edge. You want to move fast enough to provoke conflict and growth, and yet slow enough to allow that person to follow. Said differently, you feed your team the coaching sandwich.

The coaching sandwich is a careful balance of praise and critique. The leader/employee interaction always opens up with something positive (the top slice of bread). It should be recent and specific. There should be multiple components to this "praise" layer of the sandwich. After the praise, you then deliver the critique (the middle layer of meat/cheese). Much like the original praise, it should be specific and timely. Finally, you end the interaction on a positive note (the bottom slice of bread). The best way is to create a vision of what tomorrow could look like (positive) if the critique is accepted and implemented. The end must be motivational and positive.

This cannot be overstated. For your critique to really be meaningful, you must balance your critique with praise. Ideally, you need seven praises for each critique. For every employee, this will require work. For some employees, it will require creativity. Yet, if your purpose is to make a difference, then you will find areas to praise (and probably be surprised by your creativity). We will provide some helpful techniques for doing that in the Conscious Leader's Toolbox at the end of this chapter.

It is important to note that the balance between praise and critique doesn't have to be in the same conversation. You can have feedback sessions that are entirely positive. And while we don't recommend it as a standard practice, there is a rare occasion for communication that is purely negative. However, when you step back and observe the communication continuum, there should be a balance between praise and critique that resembles a sandwich.

By now, you should see the importance of asking yourself if you want to make a point or a difference and answering it truthfully—at least to yourself. If your purpose is to make a point (and on certain days it will be), then postpone the conversation until you are in a better place. But if the purpose is really to make a difference and help the employee grow, you can go ahead and have that challenging conversation. But use the coaching sandwich. Don't give brutally honest feedback—just give honest feedback.

Balanced Budget

"A truth that's told with bad intent, beats all the lies you can invent."
- William Blake

This principle is so easy to discuss, yet it is so hard to demonstrate. Let's look at Julie and Todd. In this scenario, they are both having feedback sessions with new employees that they recently hired. Both new employees are deserving of critique, as they need to do a better job staying within budget. As you observe, ask yourself, "Who is making a point, and who is making a difference?"

Julie and New Employee:

JULIE: So, now that your first project is finished, how do you think it went?

NEW EMPLOYEE: I think it went pretty well. I know this is my first real project at Acme, and that I have a lot to learn, but I was pleased with the overall result.

JULIE: Well, you did complete the project, and that is good. But you were way over budget. Remember what I told you when you started? I would give you honest feedback at all times. Your feedback on this project is not good. You were way off budget. You missed your target expenses in six of eight categories.

NEW EMPLOYEE: I know, and I know that needs to get better. But I was trying to serve the customer. And they were happy with the result.

JULIE: They were happy because they got an incredible deal from you. They were thrilled because they were stealing candy from a baby! You gave them everything and charged them nothing. I hired you because you said that you were an expert at managing projects—delivering results while staying within budget. I need you to live up to that.

NEW EMPLOYEE: I will, I'll learn and do better with the budget next time. It was a great experience to work with the new IT system, though.

JULIE: Technology is a tool, not a toy. You need to leverage it to manage costs. I know you think I'm being tough right now, but this is the major leagues, and I expect results. Perfection is the standard, and this project was far from perfect. Let's do better next time, okay?

Todd and New Employee:

TODD: So, now that your first project is finished, how do you think it went?

NEW EMPLOYEE: I think it went pretty well. I know this is my first real project at Acme, and that I have a lot to learn, but I was pleased with the overall result.

TODD: Okay. Good. What were you most pleased with?

NEW EMPLOYEE: Well, the feedback from the customer was very positive. They liked the end result.

TODD: I agree completely. You did a great job of understanding the customer and meeting their needs. And that is so important in a role like yours. Customer service is something that we really embrace as a core value here at Acme. What else were you pleased with?

NEW EMPLOYEE: Well, I learned a lot about how to work with the new IT system.

TODD: Yup. IT (especially this new system) can be very challenging, and I'm thrilled that you got the chance to learn it this quickly in your new role. You can now leverage that learning for future projects. So, what do you think you could have done better?

NEW EMPLOYEE: Well, the obvious one is the budget. I went way over budget.

TODD: Okay. I agree. So let's go there. Why do you think you went over budget?

NEW EMPLOYEE: Well, several reasons. I think the biggest one, however, was my desire to meet the customer's needs no matter what.

TODD: Let's talk about that. I have several thoughts for you. First, you need to recognize that working hard to meet the customer's needs is a great attribute. I'm so pleased that serving the customer comes so naturally to you. But, you need to work to balance that need with the budget. If we run several more projects like this, we will be bankrupt. Our customers will love us because we gave them a dollar for a nickel, but our shareholders might not be so happy. Make sense?

NEW EMPLOYEE: Yeah, it does. And I get it; I just need to be focused on the budget from the start and stick to it.

TODD: This is a big deal. You need to know your priorities and your limitations before you start talking with the customers. That will make it easier to say "No" when you have to. And you will have to. Because as much as I want you to meet the customer's needs, I have to have you staying within budget. The budget is of critical importance, and I can't have you miss it this badly again. Does that make sense?

NEW EMPLOYEE: It does. And you're right. It won't happen again, I promise.

TODD: Great. Think about what an outstanding project manager you will be once you serve your customers while staying within budget. Going forward, I need three things from you in regards to your next project. First, as you said, you have to remain within budget. Second, I need you to bring that same great attitude about serving the customer. And third, I need you to leverage your IT experiences for future projects. Use what you learned this time to help you manage the budget. If you do that, you will knock the next one out of the park.

Identical circumstances, but different conversations. Only one was impactful.

Julie was trying to make a point. She was tough, she demanded perfection, and the employee needed to get the message that it wasn't acceptable to be over budget. Julie never acknowledged any of the positives (outside of completion of the project). There was no sandwich. And to make it worse, while Julie ruthlessly attacked sub-par behaviors, she never addressed any beliefs driving those behaviors. Thus, even though the employee was challenged, it was in vain, because it won't result in a positive, significant difference.

Todd, on the other hand, was trying to make a difference. He wanted the employee to walk away feeling positive and motivated to do better next time. He engaged at a belief level. He challenged the belief that "the customer is always right," not just the behavior of staying within budget. The new employee walked away from that conversation better than he was before he entered. Todd used the coaching sandwich. If you were the new employee, who would you have wanted to interact with? Importantly, which employee do you think will perform at a higher level next time?

Your Story

As you are writing your story, don't try to make a point. It is easy and natural; it's also normal. Making a point can be fun as it makes you look good. But it can't create transformational change. It won't produce anything positive, significant, or meaningful.

Be different. Instead of making a point, have the confidence to make a difference. By doing so, you will be writing a different story.

Be different and engage your employees in personal communication, not just professional courtesy. Be different and create trust by developing relationships that have a personal, not just a professional, component. Be different and be malleable, not flexible.

Be different and stand for the right thing. Be different and stand for something.

Mirror, Mirror on the Wall…Chapter 6

The Conscious Leader's Toolbox

1. **Questions:** By default, we tend to recognize failure patterns within our employees. What if instead of recognizing failure patterns, we searched for and recognized success patterns. How would that change your dialogue with them? How do you think they would respond?

2. **Exercise:** For the next 60 days, begin tracking your employees' positive performance with the same diligence that you track their negative performance. Meet with them just as often, if not more frequently, to deliver positive news as you do critique. You don't always have to buffer the positive feedback. Note their performance over the 60 days; it is better or worse than it was before? Why?

3. **Questions:** Think back to your best manager. What made him/her so great? Was your relationship merely professional, or was it partly personal? Is your relationship with you manager right now purely professional? Why?

4. **Questions:** How would your team describe you as a manager? Would they describe their relationship with you as having a personal component? Do they trust you, or have you placed yourself on a pedestal? What can you do to grow your relationship with them?

5. **Questions:** Think back to your last feedback session as an employee. What were the issues addressed? Was your manager trying to make a point or make a difference? How do you know? Was it impactful?

6. **Questions:** Now think back to your last feedback session as a manager. What were the issues addressed? Were you trying to make a point or make a difference (be honest!)? How do you know? Did you make an impact? What did you do well? What could you do differently next time?

7. **Valuing Exercise:** This exercise will provide a means for you to understand your employees at a deeper level. By merely executing the exercise, it will show them that you are interested in learning what makes them feel valued. If you take what you learn and apply it, truly making each employee feel valuable, then you are on the way to developing a high-performance team.

8. **Coaching Sandwich:** This exercise will provide you with a framework, or a sandwich, as you enter your next feedback session with an employee. It will help you discover how to deliver the top layer (positive), the middle layer (critique), and the bottom layer (positive, vision). You don't need to be brutally honest, just honest.

Valuing Exercise

What Do You Value Most?

- There are 5 factors listed – which ones would make you work harder for your boss and be more engaged?
- Assume that everything else remains the same (no strings attached, no surprises, nothing else changes except for what is stated)
    - **Time** (extra vacation, no "pile of work" waiting for you when you return)
    - **Money** (extra $100k/year for doing the same work)
    - **Challenge** (work will stretch you and grow you, something new every day)
    - **Security** (as long as you show up, you are guaranteed this job indefinitely)
    - **Positive Environment** (friendly, tactful coaching, people are looking out for you)
- These will change over time
    - Your answers today are different than they were 5 years ago, and will change again
- Make sure you understand the "why" behind your ranking

Value Forced Ranking

Category	Rank
Time	____
Money	____
Challenge	____
Security	____
Positive	____

Notes

CONSCIOUS
LEADERSHIP

Valuing Exercise

What Do You Value Most?

- What about your team? Do you know what motivates them?
- Understanding their motivations allows you to communicate your motives

Team Member #1

Category	Rank
Time	____
Money	____
Challenge	____
Security	____
Positive	____

Team Member #2

Category	Rank
Time	____
Money	____
Challenge	____
Security	____
Positive	____

Team Member #3

Category	Rank
Time	____
Money	____
Challenge	____
Security	____
Positive	____

Team Member #4

Category	Rank
Time	____
Money	____
Challenge	____
Security	____
Positive	____

Notes

CONSCIOUS
LEADERSHIP

Coaching Sandwich
Giving Feedback

- Coaching is about changing beliefs and behaviors
  - Reinforce positive and challenge negative
  - When giving feedback, the positive should outweigh the negative
  - Feedback needs to be specific and timely

Positive belief/behavior that you want to reinforce (#1)

- Describe it (specifically):

- Example:

- Why is this important?

Negative belief/behavior that you want to challenge

- Describe it (specifically):

- Example:

- Why is this important?

Creating vision for belief/behavior that you want to reinforce (#2)

- What does the vision look like (specifically):

- Example:

- Why is this important? What are the consequences?

Notes

CONSCIOUS
LEADERSHIP

Reflection Points

- I don't believe in being flexible; I believe in being malleable.
  - o Plastic sword or an iron sword
  - o Flexible
    - Weakness, afraid to commit, unaware of core beliefs
    - Stands for anything, everything, or nothing
    - Behaviors are flexible
  - o Malleable
    - Strength, core ideals and principles guide you, forged in fire
    - Stands for something
    - Creates moral authority
    - Beliefs should be malleable
- Depth, not Breadth
  - o Tree Diagram
    - Observe the leaves/branches, but treat the roots
    - Must address the beliefs, not just the behaviors/outcomes
  - o Life's experiences are interrelated, not compartmentalized
    - The personal and professional overlap
  - o Strive for personal relationships that are professionally appropriate
    - Ask the difficult questions
    - Allow for trust and emotional connection
    - Make people feel valued and appreciated
- Make a Difference, not a Point
  - o What is your purpose of the conversation?
    - Developing their ability or showcasing your ability
  - o Not brutally honest, just honest
    - Balance challenge with sensitivity
  - o Coaching Sandwich
    - People are designed to respond best to a 7:1 ratio of positive/negative reinforcement
    - Sandwich critique in-between praise and encouragement
    - Positive, negative, positive

CHAPTER 7
A LOUSY GOLFER...STILL

"The man who views the world the same at fifty as he did at twenty has wasted thirty years of his life."

- Muhammed Ali

"There is much pleasure to be gained from useless knowledge."

- Bertrand Russell

The popular TV cartoon, G.I. Joe, which was adapted into a movie in 2009, featured a slogan at the end of each episode, "Now you know, and knowing is half the battle." As much as it breaks my heart to publicly rebuff one of my childhood heroes, Duke (G.I. Joe's protagonist) was wrong. Knowing is not half the battle. In fact, knowing may be as little as 10% to 20% of the battle.

Axiom:
I don't believe in knowledge;
I believe in wisdom.

Knowledge is power—at least that is what is said. At some point in our history, at the close of the industrial age and the dawn of the information age, that was probably accurate. And there is some truth in this claim, especially when it is used to support and further childhood education. However, this concept is losing its relevance. Knowledge is no longer the primary prerequisite for power. In fact, unless power is defined as being able to compete on Jeopardy, this once-truth has now been reduced to just another myth. However, this is a myth that is truly entrenched in almost every aspect of our lives.

We live in the twilight of the information age. There has never been another period of time where so much knowledge has been so readily available to so many people. Right now, you could go to the Internet, and within hours, you could have a working knowledge of the history of golf or the physics that govern the operations of the International Space Station. Knowledge and information are everywhere.

This ubiquitous nature of information creates a tremendous pressure for us to learn and assimilate if not all of it, at least as much as we can. Perhaps you get industry updates daily via email. You might get several. Or you might get multiple newspapers delivered to your doorstep, informing you of the latest financial news, key political developments, events around the world, and the local sports page. If you are tech-savvy, you get an electronic version of these newspapers delivered to your computer or Smartphone. You may belong to social networks where you share and receive current information. With all of these sources of knowledge at your fingertips, you probably spend 20 to 30 minutes a day trying to absorb the most critical components.

If this myth—knowledge is power—is true, and today's leaders possess an abundance of information, today's leadership should be much more powerful, and impactful, now than at any other point in history. But it's not!

We are suffering from a deficit, not a surplus, of legendary leaders. And leadership certainly isn't generating advanced levels of impact. Thus, this myth must also be untrue. Knowledge is not power; it's not the key to impact. So what is?

Wisdom. This word isn't used frequently anymore, and when it is, it is often used synonymously with knowledge. But there is a big difference between wisdom and knowledge. That difference, in one word, is application.

Knowledge is a raw ingredient that must be converted into a meaningful output. Wisdom is knowledge applied; and wisdom, not knowledge, leads to impact. Wisdom is power. Wisdom is much more than half the battle.

Pausing for Station Identification

"Knowledge can be communicated, but wisdom cannot."
   - Hermann Hesse

We need to pause here for a couple of reasons. First, it is worth noting that this axiom is different from the previous two. While three of these axioms focus on people, the first two generally focus on *other* people. This one focuses on a special person—*you*. And that makes it a little different.

Second, we need to gain alignment over some definitions. The interpretation of some of the terms in this chapter can be highly variable due to your personal experiences, and so we want to provide you with some concrete definitions. We recognize that this is a leadership book, not a vocabulary book, so this pause will be brief:

- **Information:** Raw data. Although you might think of information as technical or factual data (a triangle has three sides), it doesn't have to be. Information can also be emotional (I feel sad right now) or conceptual (A lack of sleep tonight will generally lead to drowsiness tomorrow). Information is morally agnostic and absent of value judgments about right/wrong. Information is simply a raw ingredient. Information can be accurate or inaccurate (obviously accurate information is much more useful). We use the term "information" both interchangeably and synonymously with "knowledge."

- **Knowledge:** See "information."

- **Action:** Activity. Action is something that you do. Like "information," it is morally agnostic and devoid of value. Action can be good or bad, right or wrong. But action, by itself, is absent of judgment or thought. Action is not to be confused with application. Unlike "information/knowledge," we do not use the terms "action/application" interchangeably.

- **Application:** Right action. Application involves doing the right thing. Application is action with a value component.

- **Wisdom:** The application of knowledge.

That's good enough for now. Although these represent the official definitions of these terms, you will understand them better as you see their descriptions throughout this chapter.

Diet and Exercise

Here is a simple example to illustrate the power of application and the difference between knowledge and wisdom. Let's look at America. Today, more than ever, we are educated on the requirements for good health. We know (through research and common sense) that the human body functions best on eight hours of sleep. We have more information on food than ever before. Fast-food chains are required to post nutritional information conspicuously. Similarly, items you buy at the grocery store have their nutritional information displayed prominently.

We are also educated at a young age on the dangers of smoking. We have seen videos of smokers with lung cancer and damaged respiratory systems. Warning labels are posted on the outside of cigarette cartons, and there are strict regulations in place governing the marketing of tobacco products.

Finally, there is abundant research on the benefits of exercise, both physical and emotional. Exercise has been proven to make you live longer. What more knowledge do we need? More exercise = more days of life.

Yet, America is less healthy today than it was 50 years ago. Americans don't sleep enough. We eat too much junk food. We smoke. We don't exercise, and we are overweight. America's health problems are now not just discussed in the standard medical circles, but they are debated in national political arenas. And both political parties keep championing increased health education as the solution.

But increased knowledge is not the solution. For the vast majority of situations involving an overweight individual, the cure is obvious and simple: eat less and move more. We recognize that there are some rare, serious, medical conditions where this doesn't apply, and we want to be sensitive to those individuals. However, in most cases, this statement holds true.

The gap between the desired result (healthy weight) and the actual result (overweight) is not caused by a lack of knowledge, but by a lack of application of knowledge. Said differently, it is caused by a lack of wisdom. For knowledge to generate an impact, it must be acted upon. We know that eating super-sized value meals for lunch every day is bad for our health. But it doesn't matter what we know. We won't lose weight until we apply that knowledge and order a salad instead.

Nothing we have said so far should shock you; it's intuitive. You impact your health by applying knowledge, not by the knowledge itself. So why do we value information so much?

The Value of a Commodity

Knowledge is a commodity. Think about that for a moment.

Before you challenge us on the truthfulness of this claim, think back to the original definitions. "Knowledge" is defined as "a raw ingredient." Now, think about what generally constitutes commodity trading. Although the original statement is true, it probably bothers you, or at least rubs you the wrong way. Why? That negative feeling is the result of the power of a myth that has penetrated our society.

Yet, what is the difference between corn, oil, copper, soybeans, and information? The only difference is the supply. The supply of traditional commodities is fixed, but the supply of information is infinite. With the advent of technology, it is available to everyone, anywhere, at any time. There is nothing that we can learn that you cannot learn. There is nothing that you know that we cannot know. This wasn't always the case (e.g., back in the agricultural age or industrial age). But in our time, there is an infinite supply of knowledge.

According to the basic economic laws of supply and demand, the increase in supply should have resulted in a decrease in the value of knowledge. So how has information been able to ignore the basic laws of economy? How has a commodity product been able to maintain this much status and prestige?

Knowledge is very seductive. Like many of the myths of conventional leadership, there are several nuances that make the pursuit of knowledge very appealing. And while these nuances may be subtle, they are very powerful and dangerous:

- First, knowledge provides a feeling (however misleading) of progress. If we are learning something new, surely we must be moving forward and progressing. At least it feels as though we should. We think that if we know more tonight than we did this morning, we have grown. With the quantity of information available to us, this is not very difficult to do. An increase in knowledge makes us feel good about ourselves, and we all like to feel good about ourselves.

- Second, knowledge provides us with a sense of superiority. Let's be truthful with each other for a moment. When you are engaged in a conversation with a group of people, and you know something that everyone else doesn't (including the latest corporate gossip), you feel slightly more important than everyone else. Your knowledge generates feelings of superiority (relax—we aren't judging you—we are relating to you). It is very appealing when people come to you for help or advice because they know that you possess information that they don't.

- The final nuance that makes knowledge so attractive is its necessity. Although you can't make a significant impact with knowledge alone, you can't make a significant impact without it. Knowledge isn't worthless; its value is just as a raw ingredient, not a finished product. Commodities have certain value, but value as an input, not as an output.

- To further illustrate this input/output relationship between knowledge and wisdom, think about a cake. If you go to a birthday party, you might bring a cake (wisdom). You would never show up with a platter containing the cake's raw ingredients (knowledge)—flour, eggs, milk, and sugar. You would convert those ingredients, flour, eggs, milk and sugar, into something more valuable. You would bake a cake. So while the raw ingredients (knowledge) are of little value alone, they are required in the creation of the final product—the cake (wisdom).

Wisdom is the application of knowledge. Before anything can be applied, knowledge must be obtained. Fortunately, now it's not difficult to obtain information. This leads us to a pivotal difference between conventional leadership and conscious leadership.

Conventional leadership believes that the value is in the commodity (the raw ingredient—knowledge). Conscious leadership, acknowledging the role of the raw ingredients, believes that the value is in the application of knowledge (the cake—wisdom).

After all, would you rather eat raw eggs or a chocolate cake?

But what does this belief in knowledge or wisdom have to do with people? A lot. It doesn't just drive your behavior towards other people. It has a tremendous impact on a very important person—*you*. This principle, and this myth, will determine your personal growth, development, and impact as a leader.

Conscious leadership, and this book, is nothing more than information. By itself, it is incapable of generating impact. But, if applied, it will provide the wisdom to allow conscious leaders to create impact. You don't want to be well-informed; you want to be wise.

Experienced Applicants Only

"Experience is not what happens to a man; it is what a man does with what happens to him."
    - Aldous Huxley

The confusion between the true value of knowledge and wisdom is never more readily apparent than in the hiring process. This is one area where the corporate world pays dearly for believing the myths of conventional leadership. We would wager that the following scene at Acme Office Supply is strikingly familiar:

Todd's marketing group has just received extra headcount. Acme's finances are in better shape than they were last year, and they are trying to focus more on innovation and have created a new position dedicated to innovation. The role of the successful applicant will be to leverage creativity and innovation to market existing products into new channels. Todd and Julie are reviewing some resumes to decide who to bring in for an interview.

JULIE: Look at the amount of experience that Candidate #1 has. He has done this exact job for the past 12 years. He could do this job right now. This should be an easy interview process.

TODD: What do you think about Candidate #2? True, she hasn't done this exact role before, but she has been promoted four times over the past 6 years at her current company. And, at least from the resume, it looks as though she has a history of high performance and innovation—exactly what we need.

JULIE: Sure. But she has never marketed existing products into new channels. She has no experience here. It would take valuable time to get her up to speed. Candidate #1 could be ready from his first day on the job. He has done this before. Let's interview him, and get this over with.

TODD: I know he has done this before, but has he done it well? His resume is very vague, and if he did perform at a high level, why has he not been promoted? I am not saying that he is a slacker, but by no means do I think he has an edge on Candidate #2. From the timing on Candidate #2's resume, she has taken on four roles in which she had no previous experience and was extremely successful in all of them. She is obviously a good learner, and possesses high levels of learning agility. Why would this time be different?

JULIE: I'm just concerned that she has never done this job before. That's a big risk.

TODD: Not as big of a risk as hiring a candidate who is the poster child for mediocrity. I don't want my team to be mediocre, and I know you don't, either. He could be an anchor for our entire department. I'm not saying his experience is a negative. I just don't think it is as meaningful as you do...

There are many different variations of the above dialogue, but the theme is constant and happens all the time. Why? Why are we so naturally attracted to experience? For the same reason that we are naturally drawn to knowledge. The myth of conventional leadership, the critical value of knowledge, drives the allure of experience. Like knowledge, experience isn't worthless. It has value; we are not discounting it completely. Experience alone is nothing more than action. Just because you have done something doesn't mean that you can do it well.

Familiarity is not synonymous with proficiency.

What matters is not your experience, but what you have *done* with your experience. What have you learned? How have you grown? How have you changed? What have you done differently based on that experience? The conscious leader (as we discussed in Chapter 2) reflects on his experiences. He takes those learnings and then applies them. This is the picture of wisdom. The conventional leader just keeps on trucking, doing the same thing again and again, having one year of experience 20 times over.

Do you play golf? If so, for how long? Are you good? Here is my golfing story; I have played golf for over 20 years. I have a lot of experience. And I am bad. Even worse, I am just as bad now as I was 20 years ago. Can anyone relate to me? There have to be some of you out there who also are just as bad now as you were 20 years ago. What is the take-home lesson from this (besides the need to practice our putting)?

Our experience playing golf didn't necessarily impact our ability to perform. We didn't apply lessons that we learned. While this is intuitive, we don't make this connection when we hire. Why? Our beliefs and values.

Conventional leadership values the role a person is in. Conscious leadership values the person in a role.

It's not that experience is worthless; it's just not worth as much as conventional leadership assumes. Ultimately, it's a value judgment. Conscious leadership doesn't value the raw amount of time spent in a role; it values the transferable skills gained from spending time in a role. It's a simple as the difference between quantity and quality. You can either focus on the quantity of activities performed or the quality of transferable capabilities developed. More doesn't always mean better.

Safety Blankets

Experience feels like a safety blanket. If someone has done this job before (and he wasn't fired by his previous employer), he probably is not going to be a train wreck in the position. But, if he has done the same role for a long period of time, then he is probably not a rock star, either. If he were, most likely he would have been promoted. So although there is a good chance that this is a safe hire, there is also a good chance that this is a mediocre hire. It is low risk and low reward.

If the experienced candidate turns out to be a bust, no one can accuse you of being a bad interviewer. The candidate had plenty of experience, so of course it was a logical hire. When you hire someone without experience, you take a risk. While there is the potential for greatness, there is also the potential for the candidate to fail (reflecting poorly on you and your interviewing skills).

The conventional leader believes in the value of stability, normalcy, and a "cover-your-back" policy. As a result, experience is the driving factor in hiring decisions. The conscious leader believes in the value of past performance and high capacity. They are drawn to candidates who have demonstrated excellent performance in previous roles, as this will often be a good predictor of future performance. This type of hire offers higher reward. It also carries higher risk, but as we will explain, that risk can be mitigated.

A candidate lacking experience will require development and training—the less experience in a role, the more development required. This is where the risk (of having less experience) can be mitigated. The conscious leader embraces the opportunity to coach, train, and develop another person. The success of the coaching is determined partially by expertise, but mostly by effort.

Conventional leadership claims that people are valuable. But the conventional leader either cannot, or will not, invest the time and energy to develop a non-experienced candidate. This behavior is rationalized by lack of time, importance of short-term results, or an environment where failure is unacceptable. Regardless of the excuse, this behavior reveals the true belief of the conventional leader: "People are not most valuable to me."

The conscious leader, however, looks at what the candidate has done in his previous roles. Has there been progress? Has the individual grown, learned, and developed? We all start somewhere; no one is born with experience. If the candidate demonstrates a high capacity, lots of potential, and some transferable skills, the conscious leader will hire a less-experienced candidate. He will train, coach, and develop him. Why?

The conscious leader really does believe that people are the most important part of an organization. And because his behaviors flow from that belief, he doesn't mind spending the time and effort training a high-capacity individual. In fact, he enjoys it. If a leader really values people above all else, there is nothing more impactful—and more rewarding—than developing another person.

Wisdom, the application of knowledge, manifests itself in several other areas of conscious leadership. And wisdom, not experience, will prove to be critical for the conscious leader as we explore other domains. It is essential for the conscious leader to be wise. The core issue is not what you know, but what you do with what you know.

Sub-principle #1:
Chess, not Checkers

You should be noticing a pattern within conventional leadership. Most of its myths are expressed in a manner that is completely opposite from truth. For example, "transparency" implies manipulation. "Brutally honest feedback" has nothing to do with giving useful feedback to someone. "Being fair" is typically anything but.

So, consider the usage of the following terms that are "hot" within conventional leadership today: "Big-picture thinking"; "Thirty-thousand foot view"; "Get out of the weeds and see the forest"; "Strategic"; "Bird's-eye view." What do you suppose the fixation on these terms reveals about conventional leadership? Right; its thought process is anything but strategic or big-picture.

Consider two popular board games: chess and checkers. Which one do you think is more popular? Definitely checkers. Why? Ask around. You will find (as did we when we conducted our own market research on this topic) that the number one reason people prefer checkers over chess is that it is easier to learn and easier to play.

Chess requires lots of focus, practice, effort, and work. There are complexities, subtleties, and nuances that you must master even as a novice. This is a major deterrent for most people. Chess is difficult because it requires not just long-term, but also short-term, thinking and focus. You must be able to think several moves ahead while not jeopardizing your immediate position. You must engage in game theory (if I do "X," my opponent will do "Y"). This degree of difficulty is why the conventional leader will talk about big-picture thinking while "kinging" his red checker.

Although chess isn't as popular—nor as conventional—as checkers, which one do you think more closely resembles leadership? Probably chess.

The key difference between checkers and chess is relationship—specifically, your relationship with the environment. Think back to our DTR talk from Chapter 4. A conscious leader is constantly aware of his environment, importing ideas and exporting influence. This push/pull relationship is the key differentiation between checkers and chess. By understanding the context of the game, he can understand the consequences of his moves as well as anticipate his opponent's reaction.

By understanding his relationship with the environment, the conscious leader can see both the big picture as well as the details. He can envision his future moves while making his next move.

This brings us to another myth of conventional leadership: you must focus on either the forest (big picture) or the trees (details of the here and now). Not true. Conscious leadership, like chess, demands awareness of both. Like a camera, you must be able to zoom in and understand enough of the details to create relevant ideas, and then zoom out and see where those details fit within the context of the overall environment.

Leadership is a game of chess. If you don't learn its rules and principles, you will end up in checkmate.

Strategic Mechanics

"The person who can combine frames of reference and draw connections between ostensibly unrelated points of view is likely to be the one who makes the creative breakthrough."
   - Denise Shekerjian

Consider another analogy. You get into your car on a Tuesday morning and insert the key in the ignition. But it won't start; nothing happens. So you call a mechanic, and he inspects your car. The issue is the ignition, right? Your key won't start the car. However, he doesn't really spend much time actually looking at the key and ignition. Instead, he opens the hood and begins examining and testing different sections of the automobile.

Here is where the mechanic, much like the chess-player, reflects the beliefs of conscious leadership. The mechanic has to apply wisdom to understand how seemingly unrelated components of the automobile are actually interconnected. To fix your car, he has to understand each component individually as well as collectively. The mechanic must understand the independent function of each part (the trees), how they connect with each other, and the aggregate function of the engine (the forest). The mechanic must "play chess" with your automobile to make it operational again.

This is conscious leadership (at the automobile level). The conscious leader is always aware of the environment and the context in which he is leading. You have to know how one piece of the puzzle connects with the others. Application increases your awareness of these interconnections.

You need to have the wisdom to see the real value of understanding the big picture. Most conventional leaders don't exert the effort required to understand the big picture because they don't understand its value. Application increases your self-awareness of its value. But just like most people steer away from chess, very few leaders exert the effort to see both the forest and the trees, because it requires constant intentionality, application, discipline, and focus. Through application of knowledge, you will increase your understanding of the big picture and become increasingly aware that leadership is a game of chess.

The Rules of Chess

"Nothing has such power to broaden the mind as the ability to investigate systematically and truly all that comes under thy observation in life."

    - Marcus Aurelius

Most people, even conventional leaders, would agree in principle with what we have discussed so far: leaders need to understand a situation on both the micro and macro levels. Keep in mind, however, that chess appeals in principle to most conventional leaders as well. And yet they play checkers. In order to play chess, you must exert effort and discipline as you study the game. This is no different. While every conscious leader is unique, there are three universal principles that all chess players apply:

- **Pause and reflect:** Reflection is required. Reflection requires stillness. Motion makes observation very difficult. It is almost impossible to accurately analyze the situation and discover interconnectivity while you are busy.

  Conventional leadership loves activity, and resists stillness at all cost. The conscious leader has the wisdom to know that if he doesn't pause, he will make a bad move. Please don't gloss over this. We are conscious that this seems rudimentary and simple; it is so simple that most people don't do it. This is why we're revisiting it again from Chapter 2.

  Yet, pausing is absolutely necessary. It allows you to reflect, de-clutter your mind, and assess a situation. It allows to you to figure out which beliefs are driving your behavior, and potentially identify which beliefs are driving the behavior of others.

- **Reframe the situation (forest level):** This happens after you have stopped moving. As we have discussed, this involves your relationship with the environment. Specifically, try to go up (seeing things as a bigger picture) before you go down. Try to view your situation from a perspective where you can see more than just your world. You "see" other parts of the environment by learning about them, and this requires gathering information. As information is so plentiful, this should be easy.

The difficult part, which requires wisdom, is discerning which information is important and which isn't. You don't need to know everything about everything. The 80/20 rule applies. Learn the 20 percent that you need to know about the areas that affect you and your specific situation. This learning, combined with reflection and observation, will allow you to see how the pieces fit together.

The different, and higher, perspective will increase your line-of-sight. You cannot prepare for what you cannot see. Without this high-level perspective, it is difficult to see anything except for that which is directly in front of you.

- **Engage those on the front lines (tree level):** The conscious leader cannot spend all of his time observing and reflecting. The conscious leader must spend time in the action with his people, relating to them, understanding their world and their perspectives, and working alongside them. You need to understand the details—not all of the details, but the important ones.

  Here, you will discover what really matters and what doesn't. If you are in a war, and you want to learn the status of a particular battle, don't rely on the generals in the office for information. Ask the troops on the ground!

We are now going to introduce you to a process that will help you play chess.

Sub-principle #2:
The 5i's

"Creativity is the ability to see relationships where none exist."
- Thomas Disch

The 5i's process is a framework by which knowledge is converted into wisdom. We said that the primary difference between knowledge and wisdom is application. The conversion process contains five unique parts; each is designed to help you apply the knowledge that you have acquired.

You will do better not to think of the phases of the process not as linear stages, but instead as guiding spaces. The 5i's can occur either sequentially or simultaneously.

Regardless of order, information passes through these spaces as it's converted into wisdom. This process will help the conscious leader be wiser, more strategic, and a better chess player. Here is an overview of the 5i's process:

Information → Insights → Ideation → Innovation → Impact

The Conscious Leader's Toolbox at the end of this chapter contains a breakdown of the 5i's process. This breakdown includes both tips and questions to guide you through each stage of the process. As the details are contained in the Toolbox, we will only provide a brief overview here:

- **Information:** Information is the starting point for wisdom. As we have previously discussed, think of information as your base ingredients in the process. Once you have acquired the raw data, you can start applying it. You don't need all of the information, just the important information.

- **Insights:** Insights are the interpretation of the information you gathered. What do the data mean? Are they related? During the insight process, it is critical that you look for interconnections within the data. Understanding the relationships within the system is more important than understanding how each part of the system works.

- **Ideation:** Ideation is the creation phase of the 5i's process. This is where, based off insights gleaned through your interpretation of the information, you generate new ideas. Don't limit yourself to what is logical; allow intuition to take over. Ask yourself what is perfect, not what is possible.

- **Innovation:** Innovation is the implementation phase of the 5i's process. Think of it as the commercialization of creativity. It involves considering all of the material that you generated during the ideation phase, optimizing it, and making it come to life with limited resources. During the ideation phase, you want to question the impossible. Once you have moved on to this phase, you want to qualify and quantify the costs of the impractical. This is the portion of the process that scares away most conventional leaders. It often requires difficult decisions and tough choices, some of which are mutually exclusive.

- **Impact:** The 5i's process results in impact. Although your impact will serve as inspiration to others, it is critical to note that inspiration is a by-product of impact. Without impact, there is no inspiration. Impact needs to be communicated clearly, specifically, and frequently. Specific impact provides you and your team with meaning and motivation.

Your Story

Wisdom is unique, and it is one of the defining characteristics of a conscious leader. Without wisdom, it is difficult to train, coach, and develop others. Without wisdom, it is difficult for your leadership to make a meaningful difference. Without wisdom, it is difficult to generate impact in the lives of other people.

Checkers is easy. So is behavior change. So is conventional leadership. Because it's easy, everyone else is doing it. If everyone is doing it, by definition, it is the status quo.

Don't settle for being an average Joe. Don't be content with winning half the battle. Commit yourself to doing what it takes to win the war.

Chess is challenging. So is belief change. So is conscious leadership. But it provides you the opportunity to generate sustainable impact and create transformational change. Impact is what makes your story unique and enables it to inspire others.

Mirror, Mirror on the Wall...Chapter 7

The Conscious Leader's Toolbox

1. **Questions:** What do you do to stay abreast of current trends within your industry? How much time do you spend each day gathering new information? How much time do you spend reflecting on your experiences? How much time do you spend thinking about how to apply that new knowledge?

2. **Questions:** Can you identify, within the last six months, two or three new ideas that you have applied/implemented based on the new information you acquired? What were they? If you can't identify examples where you have applied the knowledge you gained, maybe you need to spend less time focusing on obtaining new knowledge and more time applying what you already know.

3. **Questions:** How much impact does experience play in your hiring decisions? Who was the last person you hired? How much relative importance did you place on experience? Was it a good hire? Was it an impactful hire? Are you a good golfer?

4. **Questions:** How often do you stop moving and reflect? What does that look like for you? It should be at least every two to three weeks. What did you learn from your last "stillness session?" What interconnectivities did you discover? What relationships did you define?

5. **5i's Process:** Following is a breakdown of the 5i's process by phase. It contains hints and questions to facilitate your progress through each phase. Use it as you convert knowledge into wisdom.

5i's Process

Converting Knowledge Into Wisdom

- This is a process/framework by which you can convert wisdom into knowledge
- The 5i process can apply to any situation—professional or personal, business or leadership
- Process is not 100% linear
  - Phases of the process can overlap but will generally begin with iNFORMATION and end with iMPACT
  - Think of the categories as spaces, not steps
- Process is continual and repeating

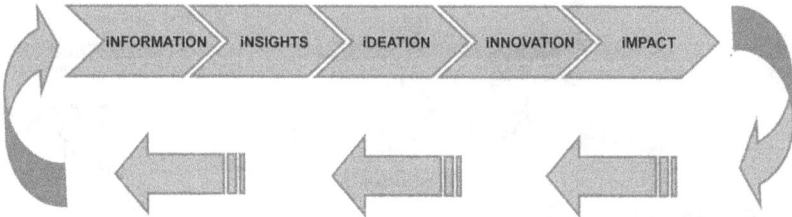

iNFORMATION iNSIGHTS iDEATION iNNOVATION iMPACT

5is Process
iNFORMATION

5i

- iNFORMATION, or knowledge, is the starting point for wisdom
- iNFORMATION is a key **ingredient** in the process, but its true value will be in what you do with it

iNFORMATION Hints

- Quality, not quantity
- Data versus assumptions
- Look both ways
  - Context within your current environment
  - Historic analogs for your current situation
- Look where no one else is looking
  - What are the questions that no one else is asking?
  - Assume that the consensus thought is wrong
- Look for the obvious
  - Often, the most relevant data is right in front of our eyes
- Look for the simple
  - Are you overcomplicating the situation?
- Explain the situation to a 5-year-old

iNFORMATION Checklist

- Where did you look?
- Where did everyone else look?
- What did you learn from history?
- Where did the group consensus start?
- What was right in front of you?
- How would you explain the situation to a 5-year-old?
- What data seem to be unrelated?

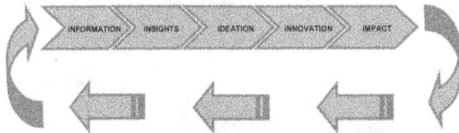

INFORMATION → INSIGHTS → IDEATION → INNOVATION → IMPACT

CONSCIOUS LEADERSHIP

5i's Process
iNSIGHTS

5i

- iNSIGHTS are the result of the **interpretation** of the iNFORMATION
- Seek to understand the relationships within the data; where are they interconnected?

iNSIGHT Hints

- Synthesize, don't analyze, the information
  - Discover relationships within the data
- Define those relationships (associative or causal)
  - Look for multiple interconnections
  - Context (environment) over actual text (information)
- iNSIGHTS can be obvious or subtle
  - Power is not related to conspicuousness
- Look for deviations/aberrations
  - Identify inconsistencies (the exception, not the rule)
  - Look for points of contrast, not similarity
- Don't make assumptions about the iNSIGHTS
- Question everything (including yourself)
  - Assume the consensus is wrong

iNSIGHT Checklist

- What interconnections did you discover within the data?
- List examples of relationships within the data:
- Were the relationships causal or associative?
- Why is the context important in this situation?
- Which assumptions about the data did you question?
- What assumptions about the data did the consensus hold?
- What deviations did you observe?

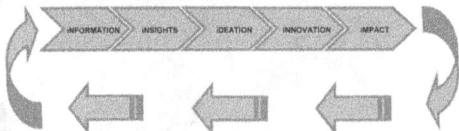

INFORMATION → INSIGHTS → IDEATION → INNOVATION → IMPACT

CONSCIOUS LEADERSHIP

5i's Process

iDEATION

- iDEATION is the creation phase of the process, where new ideas are generated based on iNSIGHTS
- iDEATION, when it's most effective, is driven primarily by **intuition** instead of logic

iDEATION Hints

- Redefine the situation/opportunity
  - Develop a new framework to view the scenario
  - Ask different questions to change the perspective
- Connection is more important than function
  - Understand details and big-picture
  - Connectional expertise vs. functional expertise
- Describe the ideal situation
  - Differences between ideal and current
  - Identify why the ideal is not reality
- Impossible ideas
  - Do not discount based on "practicality"
- How can you leverage current strengths?
  - Identify and build on what is going well
  - Leverage patterns of success, not failure

iDEATION Checklist

- Describe the current situation in terms of iNSIGHTS:

- What is the ideal situation? What would be perfect?

- Is the ideal your current goal? Why or why not?

- What ideas are you discounting as impossible? Why?

- What resources would you need to make the ideal a reality?

- What is currently working well?

- How can you leverage those strengths?

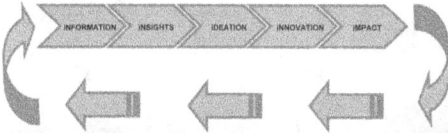

5i's Process

iNNOVATION

- iNNOVATION is the **implementation**, or commercialization, of the your ideas and creativity
- iNNOVATION is about optimizing your ideas, making them come to life, quantifying the costs

iNNOVATION Hints

- Identify the idea that excites you the most
  - Less is more – keep it simple
  - Listen to your intuition and passion
  - Why (specifically) are you excited?
- Estimate costs and identify needed resources
  - Which ones are scarce/plentiful
- Other people need to be involved
  - Leverage their expertise and relationships
- Embrace the difficult decisions
  - Resource allocation
  - Hallmark of a meaningful innovation
- Saying "Yes" to one idea often means "no" to another
  - Identify what is most important
  - Over-commit your resources (including yourself)

iNNOVATION Checklist

- What idea excites you the most? Why?

- Have you overcomplicated the original idea?

- What resources do you need to make it happen?

- Who do you need to get involved? Why?

- What do you need to say "No" to?

- Where will the necessary resources come from?

- Describe over-commitment:

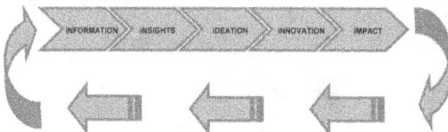

5i's Process

iMPACT

- iMPACT is the end result, the "why" driving the entire process (and driving your leadership)
- The level of iMPACT will **inspire** others (inspiration cannot exist without iMPACT)

iMPACT Hints

- Know the specifics of the "why"
  - Provides meaning for you and your team
  - Clarify the win in clear terms
- Make it personal
  - Describe the end before you begin
- Frequently communicate the iMPACT
  - Easy to get lost in the weeds
  - Ensures that activities stay aligned
- Communicate differently to different stakeholders
- Quantify the iMPACT
  - Measure creates meaning
  - Develop credible metrics
- Your iMPACT will serve as inspiration for others

iMPACT Checklist

- Articulate the iMPACT in clear, concise terms:
- Why is this important to you? Your team? Stakeholders?
- How can you make the iMPACT personal?
- Describe ways to frequently communicate the iMPACT:
- Can you quantifiably measure your level of iMPACT?
- What metrics can you develop?
- Who will you inspire? Why will they be inspired?

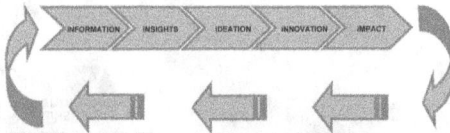

INFORMATION → INSIGHTS → IDEATION → INNOVATION → IMPACT

CONSCIOUS LEADERSHIP

5i's Process

Putting It All Together

iNFORMATION (ingredients):

iNSIGHTS (interpretation):

iDEATION (intuition):

iNNOVATION (implementation):

iMPACT (inspiration):

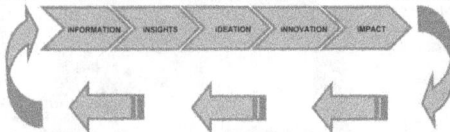

INFORMATION → INSIGHTS → IDEATION → INNOVATION → IMPACT

CONSCIOUS LEADERSHIP

Reflection Points

- I don't believe in knowledge; I believe in wisdom.
  - o The difference between knowledge and wisdom is application
    - Application leads to impact
    - Knowledge is easy to obtain and provides the illusion of progress
  - o Information is a commodity
    - Knowledge is a raw ingredient of wisdom
  - o Experience does not necessarily equate to wisdom
    - Experience is a safety blanket during the hiring process
    - Hire people with high potential and develop them
    - Look for transferable capabilities
- Chess, not Checkers
  - o See the forest and the trees
    - Pause and reflect
    - Reframe the situation from a different perspective
    - Engage those on the front lines
  - o Don't bring checkers to a chess tournament
- 5i's Process
  - o Framework for converting knowledge into wisdom:
    - Information
    - Insights
    - Ideation
    - Innovation
    - Impact

CONSCIOUS
LEADERSHIP

CHAPTER 8
SAVING LIVES

"Things which matter most must never be at the mercy of things which matter least."
  - Goethe

"It is not enough to be busy; so are the ants. The question is: what are we busy about?"
  - Henry David Thoreau

Introduction—Process Domain

We have finished our exploration of the first, and most important, domain of conscious leadership, people. We now turn our attention to the second domain, process. Process is the link between people and performance, and it deals with engagement and interaction.

Specifically, the process interactions can be either personal (people interacting with other people) or they can be non-personal (people interacting with their work). Generally speaking, people, interacting through process, create performance. There is a causal relationship between these three domains, although it lacks the linearity to warrant an "➔." Each of the domains can be viewed as its own entity.

In regards to process, we will explore how you view your work and your relationship with that work. How do you organize and categorize your work? How do you work most efficiently and effectively? Improved process can lead to improved performance.

How do you generate significant process improvement? How do you impact process in a manner that is positive and substantial? The same way you impact every other facet of conscious leadership—through belief change.

So, what does the conscious leader believe about process?

<h2 style="text-align:center"><u>Axiom:</u>
I don't believe in prioritization;
I believe in triage.</h2>

What? Who doesn't believe in prioritization? After all, there are thousands of time-management courses offered today preaching the gospel of prioritization. Acme Office Supply (and your local office supply store) sells multiple versions of calendars and customized planners. They are all designed for your specific prioritization needs, the goal is to help you better organize your time. And if you don't like bulky calendars, you can go digital.

The business world has recognized that time management is a big deal. You have been asked to do more work with fewer resources. To help you squeeze the "more" into the "less," there is a renewed focus on time and time management. How do you stretch time and pack more "stuff" in there? Here are some of the conventional techniques:

- **Formal Time-management Training:** The idea is that if you can learn to be more efficient with your time, you can do more with less. So, your company tries to provide you with as much information and knowledge as possible pertaining to time.

  Your organization might have offered time-management courses through a company such as Franklin Covey®. Or, in testament to the power of moral authority and "walking the walk," they might have cut the two-day formal training down to a one- or two-hour online course. They didn't want you to spend all that time in training. They are leading by example—trying to do "more" with "less." Why? They wanted to save time in their attempt to help you learn how to save time. Inspiring?

- **Technology:** Technology promises to increase your ability to efficiently manage time. The idea is that as technology improves, you will be able to cram greater amounts of "more" into smaller amounts of "less." And so, every year brings about more gadgets and trinkets. Phones get not only smaller but also smarter. Your phone is so smart that it doesn't even need you to use the keypad anymore—you can just talk to it. You can write, type, or dictate your words into your Smartphone, and they can be translated into a different language before being sent to the other side of the world, all in a matter of seconds.

  The shimmer and glitz of technology have seduced organizations into believing that improved technology is always the solution, regardless of the problem. This is especially true when the problem is considered to be time management. Unfortunately, this is a myth. But when myths are accepted as truth, the resulting behavior and outcome are rarely good.

- **Energy Drinks:** How do these fit? The promise is that energy drinks will give you more time. If you can reduce the time previously allotted to sleep, you can use that time elsewhere. You will be more effective, not because you are more efficient with your time, but because you have more of it.

  As a result, you can now go to the convenience store, or the grocery store, and find an entire aisle full of drinks, potions, and elixirs that are designed to reduce your body's dependence on sleep. You can enjoy various flavors, consistencies, and potencies of these drinks. "Time" in a bottle...or jitters in a bottle?

The outcome? When you combine our trainings and certifications in time management, upgraded and improved technology, and our higher energy levels, you would think that we would display a complete mastery over time. We should be more productive than ever, spending the majority of our time on activities that are impactful. But are we? More importantly, are you?

Almost a rhetorical question, right? You are probably busier and engaged in more activities than ever before. However, you are probably not highly productive, spending the majority of your time engaged in impact-generating activities.

So what's the real issue? The problem isn't an imperfect behavior (inefficient time management). The core, or root, problem, as is often the case, is a faulty belief—the myth of prioritization.

Everyone is busy. With the exception of those who recently retired (to whom we extend a hearty "congratulations"), everyone is busier today than they were yesterday. Conventional leadership promises that by engaging in more effective prioritization, you will be able to solve your busyness problem. The myth claims that by improving your ability to prioritize, you will experience increased effectiveness and efficiency with your time. But it hasn't worked. And unless the next version of the Smartphone can increase the number of hours in the day, it isn't going to work. Your experience, as well as the experiences of those all around you, prove this myth to be false.

By prioritizing, conventional leaders are simultaneously busier and less impactful. Why doesn't prioritization work?

Addition

"There is nothing so useless as doing efficiently that which shouldn't be done at all."
- Peter Drucker

The myth of prioritization is simply this: You will get everything done. The truth is just as simple: No, you won't.

Conventional leadership's time management is based on the idea of prioritization. Prioritization infers that you will complete everything. You have made a list of the things that you have to do. This is a cornerstone of most time-management courses. If you don't write it down (preferably in a list), it isn't real. So, we all have our "to-do" lists. Prioritization subtlety suggests that you will get everything on that list done. All that is required from you is re-ordering based on priority. You need to re-arrange the order of the items on the list to make sure that you get the most urgent items taken care of first. Once those items are completed, you can take care of the rest of the list.

Prioritization teaches addition. You continually add items to your list, and then re-arrange them. How do you remove an item? You remove an item through completion.

You remove some items once they are completed. You add other items, and you re-arrange your list again.

And so we keep adding more items, more jobs, more projects, and more tasks to our list. And we keep re-arranging them. And the list is never finished. In fact, it keeps on growing. This didn't used to be the case, but now it is unmanageable. Why?

Increased pressure. The intensity of the pressures that we mentioned in the beginning of the book is greater now than it has ever been. And prioritization isn't capable of dealing with this level of intensity. Here is how those pressures affect the "do more with less" equation:

- Size/Scope of Work: Increases the "More"
- Globalization: Increases the "More"
- Economic Downturn: Decreases the "Less"
- Pace/Cadence: Faster

The result? There is too much "more" to fit into too little "less." It doesn't matter how effective your planner is at helping you make a list, how smart your phone is, or how many energy drinks you consume. By adding projects and items to your "to-do" list at a faster pace than you can complete them, you ensure that the list continues to get longer and longer.

Conventional leadership offers a fairly normal solution—prioritization. Just re-arrange the list. So you move things around, and shuffle their order, but ultimately, you are left with a re-arranged list that still has too much "more" than you can complete with your "less."

Why doesn't prioritization work anymore? It worked in the past. That is one of the problems with conventional leadership—what worked yesterday often doesn't work today.

Prioritization's recent failure can be mostly explained through a single principle. It ignores a basic concept of economics: scarcity of resources. Economics teaches that resources are limited. In any given environment, the amount of resources is finite (e.g., oil, water, farmland, iron, etc.). Those who live in that specific environment must be conscious that those resources are set; and then make difficult decisions on where to selectively allocate those resources.

As a leader, your resources are finite and limited. This includes your time. Regardless of how many energy drinks you consume, you only have 24 hours in a day. So do we. There is merit in attempting to use these resources as effectively and efficiently as possible. But we need to be conscious of the truth that because resources are fixed, they require selection allocation.

Prioritization doesn't believe in scarcity of resources. It never explicitly claims that we have unlimited amounts of time. But, in a very subtle manner, by suggesting that we keep adding and adding items to our list, it infers that our resources are infinite. But based on economic principles, if you really believe that the "less" is a fixed amount, you know that you can't keep adding "more." The numbers don't add up; it won't work.

Conventional leadership has tried. And as recently as five years ago, with less intensity resulting from fewer pressures, the myth of prioritization wasn't fully exposed. It is today, because you know the outcome. You are busier now than ever before. Your level of activity has increased; but your level of impact hasn't (or at least it hasn't increased in proportion to your level of activity).

What is the solution for the conscious leader? By now, you shouldn't be surprised—a belief change.

Gettysburg and Smallville

Believe in triage.

Depending on your background, especially if it includes either health care or military service, this word connotes one of two distinct pictures. And both are relevant for our process discussion. Webster's Dictionary defines triage as: "the process of sorting victims, as of a battle or disaster, to determine medical priority in order to increase the number of survivors."

For conscious leaders in today's world, triage involves the selection of some tasks and the intentional neglect of others. You will not get everything done. Tasks cannot be re-arranged; they must be deleted.

Why? To generate impact. Let's examine the concept of triage as it relates to both a battlefield and a community hospital.

Battlefield

Imagine that you are a Union medic walking the fields of Gettysburg in early July, 1863. The last three days of war have produced some 50,000 casualties (Union and Confederacy). The fighting has moved on, and with the cannons finally silent, you can hear the cries of fallen soldiers who need medical attention. You have a few medical kits and about four hours of daylight at your disposal. Your goal is to save as many lives as possible.

Considering your scarcity of resources, and your goal of saving as many lives as possible, how do you organize your work? What is your process? You identify and focus on those soldiers whose lives can be saved, and intentionally neglect those whose lives cannot. Think about that, and let it set in. It should jar you.

This means that although there is a young man in his early twenties lying in front of you—screaming and writhing in pain as he's lost multiple limbs and is bleeding profusely—you must step over him. You must intentionally neglect him to attend to another soldier who is less severely wounded. This sounds heartless, but it is necessary. Why?

Because your job is to save as many lives as possible.

The odds of the severely wounded soldier surviving are very slim. Even if you could rescue him, it would require the expenditure of all your resources (medical supplies and hours of daylight). By intentionally neglecting him, leaving him there alone on the battlefield, you create for yourself the opportunity to attend to a dozen other fallen men whom you have a better chance of saving. You can now impact multiple lives.

What are the consequences of investing all your resources in this one man? The loss of not one man's life, but of a dozen lives you could have saved. By intentionally neglecting one, you are able to save many.

What about triage in a hospital? Although triage behavior may look different at a rural, community hospital than on a battlefield, the belief is the same.

Rural, Community Hospital

Let's change the scene. Imagine that you are in Smallville, USA—a town of about 30,000 people. You are the triage nurse at the community hospital. You are staffed with one doctor at the hospital, and another doctor on call. Most of your patients suffer from minor wounds; typical examples include a boy who needs stitches because he fell out of a tree, a girl who broke her arm, or a woman with an infection.

Today, you have two such patients in your waiting room, and one such patient back with the doctor. Suddenly, you hear the wail of an ambulance's siren. The paramedic wheels the victim of a motorcycle accident. There is a man in his early twenties lying in front of you—screaming and writhing in pain as he's lost multiple limbs and is bleeding profusely.

This young man is wheeled through the waiting room, cutting in front of the two people who were already waiting for the doctor. You interrupt the attending doctor, who is stitching up a small gash on the arm of a young boy. Barging in, you insist that he come with you immediately and leave the boy with stitches only halfway complete. Together, you race to attend to the young man who was in the accident. As the triage nurse, you channel all the resources of this rural community hospital to focus on this young man. Why?

Because your job is to save as many lives as possible.

The behavior is different, but the belief is the same. The hospital staff, under the direction of the triage nurse, intentionally neglects the patients who need stitches, splints, and antibiotics and chooses to expend all of their resources on this severely wounded young man. The young man might die if not immediately attended to. The other patients, although they will be uncomfortable for a couple of hours, are not in danger of losing their lives.

We saw the same young man in two different situations. And although we saw two very distinct behaviors, we saw only one belief.

On the battlefield, the medic chose to ignore this young man and spend his resources on others. At the rural, community hospital, the nurse chose to ignore the less-severe patients, knowing that he could get to them later, and focus all available resources on this one man. Both the medic and the doctor were governed by the same belief—triage: the intentional neglect of some and choosing of others in order to save as many as possible.

As a conscious leader, triage, not prioritization, needs to be the belief that drives your behavior as you interact with your work. Like the battlefield medic or the community physician, your resources are scarce. Depending on your profession, your job might not be to save as many lives as possible. But, as a leader, you have the potential and opportunity to generate as much impact as possible.

Location, Location, Location

Prioritization asserts that you will get everything done; you just need to reorder your list. Triage acknowledges that you won't get everything done, and that you must intentionally delete items on your list.

Triage makes sense. It is intuitive. Even the most stubborn conventional leader would admit that resources are scarce. Once you are conscious of your finite resources, triage is the only belief that makes sense. Embracing this belief will lead to the behavior of intentionally neglecting some tasks and choosing others.

So you now share something in common with the battlefield medic and the community hospital nurse: you now believe in triage.

Although we now share a common belief with the medic and the nurse, there is something that we don't share in common with them. We need to wrestle with a question that didn't apply to them and with a belief that is unique to us. The question is this: "Where do you believe you are?"

Huh? Consider our previous examples of the medic and the nurse. The medic didn't have to be conscious of his belief regarding his location. Through observation, he saw that he was on the battlefield; the same situation applies to the nurse. He looked and saw that he was in a community hospital. Their belief in their locations was on a subconscious level because of the obvious and apparent nature of the truth.

We aren't so fortunate. We have to be conscious of what we believe regarding our location. What you believe about your location will determine what type (battlefield or rural, community hospital) of triage behavior you display, not whether or not you should triage. This is much more difficult than it seems.

We want to believe that our work, and our life, is like the community hospital—friendly, slow-paced, and laid back. There are not many difficult decisions to make, and when you do have to make a hard decision, you get praised for doing the right thing. At the community hospital, most of the items on your list will get done.

In addition, when you do have to make a decision to intentionally neglect some items, the neglect is usually easy and temporary. It is not difficult deciding to neglect stitching up a boy's small gash to attend to a man minutes away from death. In fact, the boy's mom probably encouraged the physician to neglect her son for the time being and go attend the young man. The mom and boy were content to be momentarily neglected for the sake of the greater good—saving as many lives as possible. If this picture accurately describes your daily environment, then we wish you "congratulations." You must be retired. For the rest of us, however, the battlefield is the more accurate depiction of work.

What happens when the neglect isn't temporary? What happens when serving the greater good means stepping over the young man on the battlefield? The consequences of this type of neglect are permanent.

There are no cheers and pats on the back. Outsiders, with only a partial view of the situation, might call us cruel or hard-hearted. Eventually, we might end up second-guessing ourselves, suffering re-occurring nightmares. On the battlefield, neglect has painful and often negative consequences, even when it saves others.

As a result, we really want to believe that our work resembles the Smallville community hospital, where doing the right thing is easy, obvious, rewarded, and gratifying. But deep down inside, we know that our work bears a striking resemblance to the Gettysburg battlefield.

Dismissing the Evidence

"Reason guides but a small part of man, and the rest obeys feeling, true or false, and passion, good or bad."
      - Joseph Roux

Battlefield triage is hard for everyone, including the conscious leader. At work, it can mean letting people down. It can mean walking away from a project that isn't complete. It can appear as rude and selfish. It will disappoint others.

When we choose to save as many lives as possible, we are doing the right thing. We are generating impact and creating a positive, meaningful difference. But there are consequences; and they can be painful.

For some, the cost of the consequences outweighs the value of the impact (conventional leaders don't value impact as much as they value maintaining the status quo). So what is the alternative to believing that your work, and your triage, resembles a battlefield? There are two options available to the conventional leader:

- You can believe that your workplace is like a slow-paced, rural, community hospital. You will triage accordingly.
- You can continue to believe in the myth of prioritization.

These are the two primary options available for the conventional leader who doesn't want to believe that his work resembles a battlefield. Let's examine the first option. What would it look like if conventional leadership believed that their location resembled Smallville?

Fortunately for us, the CEO of Acme Office Supply is a great case study. He is a conventional leader who believes (albeit subconsciously) that Acme resembles a rural, community hospital (option one above). And he is giving an interview this morning following the release of Acme's quarterly earnings report. Let's listen in as he communicates Acme's corporate culture and belief in community-hospital triage. Afterwards, we will get to observe the reaction of the investment community:

INTERVIEWER: This morning Acme announced that it hit its forecasted earnings, and re-iterated its guidance of double-digit growth through the end of the year. The stock price is up 12% in pre-market trading. Congratulations Mr. CEO! In this type of environment, in the face of the incredible external pressures, that type of performance is rare. And your forecast is astounding in light of yesterday's breaking news: the entrance of three giant, multi-national competitors into the office supply market. You don't seem daunted by their entry into your space at all. What is Acme's secret?

CEO: Thank you for the kind words. Life is good right now at Acme. We keep moving at a nice, easy pace. The secret to our success really is driven by our culture. In fact, we have tried to maintain the same culture and pace of work at Acme today that existed 25 years ago. And I am sure we will be doing the same things, at the same relaxed pace, 25 years from now. It is part of who we are, and we aren't going to change what has been working so well. Being transparent, I must take exception to your reference to those 3 multi-national companies as "competitors." We work in a very friendly environment. We expect to collaborate with those companies, not compete with them. There is a lot we can teach them, and a lot they can teach us. There is enough business for everyone, and we expect that everyone will win as we work with them and share best practices...

INTERVIEWER: Umm....thank you Mr. CEO. It is now time for a commercial break.

INTERVIEWER (after the break): This just in. Breaking news: Despite the tremendous quarterly earnings report and forecast released by Acme Office Supply earlier this morning, in pre-market trading, the stock has plunged 22%...wait...26%...no, I'm wrong again...29%....

Your investors and customers would not just lose respect for you, but would flat out ridicule you, if they found out you believed your business resembled the Smallville hospital. You could never admit that your organization resembles a rural, community hospital; conventional leadership can't admit it either.

Conventional leaders are afraid to believe in battlefield triage because it is hard, and unwilling to believe in rural, community hospital triage because it is embarrassing. As a result, they have no choice but to continue to believe in the myth of prioritization. Although they know our resources are scarce, they would rather prioritize than triage. And so, their "to-do" lists keep on growing.

Make no mistake—battlefield triage is difficult. Even after you choose to believe in it, you are faced with new challenges. Specifically, what behaviors flow from that belief? How do you engage in battlefield triage?

The next sub-principle will help answer that question. This principle won't make the decision to triage less frightening, but it will make it simpler. By understanding the "why" behind the "how," you will have increased clarity in choosing what to save and what to intentionally neglect.

Sub-Principle #1:
Important, not Urgent

The important versus the urgent. On the surface, this seems like a simple concept; it is. Invest your resources in the important; don't spend them on the urgent. Although this concept might be simple, it is far from easy. However, if you can master this principle and the associated nuances, triage becomes much less complicated.

Intuitively, it makes sense to pursue that which is important over that which is urgent. Yet, most of the time this is a struggle. We aren't being critical; we recognize that this is extremely challenging. This concept is easy to discuss, but it's difficult to execute. Both of our friends at Acme Office Supply, Julie and Todd, struggle with this as well:

Nearing completion of his second full year on the job, Todd has been working with Julie on a large project over the past six months named "StarGate." Derived from Project Sandstorm (which was placed on indefinite hold), StarGate is a new digital platform that is the first in its class for all of Acme—a multi-purpose web portal. This portal has the ability to serve as an ordering system, a new marketing channel, and a customer relationship database. They are to give a live demonstration of StarGate to senior management in two weeks, with a soft launch to follow four weeks later. Although neither the demo nor the system is ready today, both dates are achievable if all resources are channeled into the project. Julie and Todd are discussing the current situation during their Friday morning meeting:

TODD: If we go hard at this, we will make our deadlines. I think we're in good shape for both the presentation and the soft launch.

JULIE: I agree. Oh, I forgot to tell you. I called the communications team today, and they want us to host this quarter's company get-together. It's in six weeks.

TODD: I don't think we have time to do that, not with all of this going on.

JULIE: We can't say "no." You know the visibility that these types of events bring to our department. It would really make us look good with senior management, and it would be a great platform to unveil StarGate to the entire company. Did I mention that it is very important to senior management?

TODD: If this event is supposed to be in six weeks, who is going to lead it from our group? I have my entire team focused on this portal.

JULIE: We will figure something out.

TODD: Oh, that reminds me, with everything else going on, I forgot to tell you that earlier this week, I talked with PaperClips (The 2nd largest office-supply retailer, who currently does very little business with Acme). They loved our latest campaign and finally want to do some more business with us—in the form of some exclusive projects. They agreed to bring their leadership team up to our office and meet with our leadership team. If you don't mind, I need you, as the leader of this department, to spend a lot of time with them when they visit and make them feel important.

JULIE: I'm thrilled that they are finally interested, but when do they want to come up? I don't know if we have the time to do that, not with all of this going on. I really want to see them, and I know this is very important, but do you think that we can push it back a couple of months or have a conference call?

TODD: We can't say "no." You know the potential business that we could gain from a visit of a customer like Paperclips. It would be a great platform for StarGate, and you know how important these customer visits are for team morale. We can find time; they said they can make anything work within the next six weeks.

JULIE: If they are supposed to visit within the next six weeks, who is going to coordinate everything?

TODD: We will figure something out.

JULIE: Agreed. We just need to manage our time well and prioritize.

TODD: I'll start on that now. We'll get it all done.

No they won't. Todd and Julie are both wrong. They won't get everything done. They will re-arrange their list and prioritize, but they won't get everything done. If they triage, they will intentionally neglect some items, permanently, and so they still won't get everything done. But they will have the power to be able to choose what gets done, the important, and what gets neglected.

Unfortunately, they will spend their resources on the urgent, not the important. Guaranteed. If they triage, at times the urgent will still take precedence over the important. If they prioritize, the urgent will always take precedence over the important. Why is that? Why is the urgent always so alluring as compared to the important? Why is it so difficult to neglect?

A lot of myths and a little truth. There are several myths, coupled with one truth, regarding the urgent that explain its appeal. Let's discuss the one truth first.

The Urgent Truth

"The really important things are said over cocktails and never done."
    - Peter Drucker

Here it is—the one truth about urgent items: they are urgent. Breakthrough idea, huh? Did you write that down? Okay, we get it. But, stop and reflect on this for a moment.

By their very nature and definition, urgent items will always clamor for your immediate attention. That is what makes them urgent. You are familiar with this, whether it is an email that reads, "URGENT ACTION REQUIRED," in the subject line, or a red light blinking for eight voicemails from the same number, or the loud knock on your office door. Urgent items don't request your attention; urgent items *demand* your attention—immediately! If they didn't, they wouldn't be urgent.

What happens if we ignore something urgent? Most of the time, if we don't give those items our immediate attention, we feel terrible. Saying, "No," creates an immediate, unpleasant feeling.

So what should a conscious leader do? Or better, what should a conscious leader believe?

- **Belief:** Embrace the fact that urgent items will always clamor for your attention—this is their nature. If you are conscious that all urgent items look identical in this regard, you will view the clamoring of any particular urgent item as less unique. You will improve your ability to decipher what really deserves your attention. It will be easier to determine whether an item is urgent and important or if it's just urgent.

- **Belief:** Embrace the fact that saying "no" to an urgent request will be unpleasant in the short-term. However, saying "yes" to a non-important request will be unpleasant in the long-term. By expecting and anticipating that temporary feeling of pain, you weaken it. If you believe that the pain is typical, temporary, and predictable, it becomes less powerful, and you will strengthen your ability to say "no."

We said there was one truth that we would discuss regarding urgent items. We have: urgent items are urgent. How does a conscious leader respond to truth? Believe it and embrace it. However, there are myths about urgent items that we shouldn't embrace. As a conscious leader, you should debunk these myths and replace them with truth.

Firefighting Arsonist

This term appears to be an oxymoron, but it's really not. It's an uncommon term but a familiar concept, applicable to a multitude of scenarios, and it's very useful at explaining the allure of the urgent. We like to be busy. We like to feel that we are accomplishing something. The firefighting arsonist will set his own fires, or at least intentionally allow them to be set, so that he can experience the thrill of accomplishment as he extinguishes them.

Think back to the last time at work when multiple fires went off simultaneously (maybe this was yesterday). You attacked them, one by one, and at the end of the day, you extinguished all of them, and everything was calm again. How did you feel (besides tired)? You probably felt a sense of accomplishment; this positive feeling is typical and should be expected.

Unfortunately, there is a good chance that even though you experienced a positive feeling, you didn't accomplish anything meaningful. You didn't generate any impact. And that sense of accomplishment you feel? It is based on a myth.

Completing urgent tasks provides a false sense of accomplishment that can be seductive. Have you ever noticed that the prevalence and frequency of fire-drills? They are common for certain individuals while rare for others. For some people, the fire-drill is the rule, not the exception. Somehow for these select individuals, everything is an emergency, and there are always urgent fires that must be attended to immediately.

How is it that these fires follow some individuals and not others? The answer is simple— some people are firefighting arsonists. They set their own fires. And then they rush to put them out.

Fires follow those who are addicted to the rush of extinguishment. Fire-fighting is exciting! It is so exciting that these individuals intentionally set fires just so they can put them out. Unfortunately, extinguishing self-lit fires is not meaningful and creates no impact. It is a myth that there is value in putting out these types of fires.

The number one cause of organizational fires is prioritization. It leads to fires that are not only started intentionally but also to those that are started accidentally. How does that happen? Trying to do everything, we prioritize, and in doing so, we neglect some important items. We discover our neglect when the fire breaks out, and then we have to scramble to extinguish it.

Here is another myth of the urgent, "Things will slow down after [XXX]..." This is almost never true. If it were, time management would be much simpler, and we wouldn't have to triage. Our "to-do" list would become shorter without any triage. An honest view of our environment reveals that this isn't the case. The intensity of pressures will continue to increase. We will continue to be asked to do more with less and do it faster. Although things won't slow down, conventional leadership accepts this myth as truth. It allows them to avoid making difficult triage decisions by perpetuating the urgent.

If the number of fires is limited, you need to be a better fire-fighter with a bigger fire engine and more water. If the number of fires is infinite, however, you need to be fireproof.

If the only thing preventing you from focusing on the important was extinguishing a finite number of fires, then *of course* you should sacrifice the important for the urgent. If you extinguished all of the urgent fires today, you would have the remaining four days in the week to focus on the important. However, this never happens.

There is an infinite supply of urgent matters and fires, especially if you are the arsonist responsible for creating those fires. If you try to put all of them out, you never get to the important.

We Believe...

"It seems essential, in relationships and all tasks, that we concentrate only on what is most significant and important."

    - Søren Kierkegaard

At this point, you might be a little aggravated with us. We have stated truths that are obvious and intuitive. Triage makes sense. Neglecting the urgent for the sake of the important also makes sense. You probably already knew that. But it just isn't that easy.

Right now, we are just as guilty as the financial consultants who inform you that the solution to your poverty problem is to make more money. Our solution to the time-management problem is to triage and invest in the important. Okay, that's fine, but the "how" is missing. We are getting there now. The good news is that triage isn't magic or myth. Like the 5is process used to convert knowledge into wisdom, there is a tangible mental process for triage that you can walk through.

This process is a behavior, and before we discuss it further, we want to ensure your beliefs are correct. You must believe that you cannot continue to prioritize (or you will lack the motivation to triage effectively). And once you commit to triage, you must believe that you will be involved in battlefield triage. You must believe that urgent items will always clamor for your attention, and that saying "No" will always produce short-term discomfort. You must believe that although urgent items are urgent, they are not always important. You must believe that putting out fires that you start isn't impactful or productive, it's wasteful. You must also believe that there is an endless supply of these fires.

The rest of this chapter is about the behaviors that stem from those beliefs. If your beliefs haven't been forged into the above descriptions, any flexibility demonstrated with regard to the following behaviors will be undone when something more convenient arises.

Assuming we are aligned at the belief-level, let's move on to three behaviors that can help you triage effectively:

- **Define Importance:** The first question you need to ask yourself is not, "What items are truly important?" but rather, "How do I define importance?" Answer truthfully. Think like a chess player. Be idealistic and pragmatic. If a key factor in your definition of importance is keeping your boss from being upset, many of your urgent emails from him will also become important.

This is a personal judgment that will change. Your definition of important will be different than ours. And your definition of important today will be different from your definition of important this time next year. There are times where keeping your boss placated might be—and *should* be—the most important factor. But you need to know that.

So how do you define importance? Ask and answer this question often. Write those answers down. You will need wisdom—not just knowledge—to arrive at an adequate definition. And you will need wisdom to know when that definition needs to change.

- **Clarify Relative Importance:** Once you have defined importance, you can start to look at the items on your list. What is truly important, based on your definition, and what is not important? Why? Do your best to factor out urgency altogether. Allow importance, and the definition that you have assigned to it, to drive your decision-making. This takes discipline and effort. If possible, try to force-rank the items. This will help you understand the value of each item on the list. Every time you change your definition of important, re-rank your items.

- **Create Buckets:** Once you have defined importance, and assigned a relative level of importance to the different tasks on your list, you can then classify them into one of three buckets. We aren't going to tell you to neglect all jobs that don't reach a certain "importance threshold." That is neither realistic nor intelligent. The three bucket approach is going to keep triage from being a binary process with only black and white as your options.

Bucket Lists

Bucket One (The Important Bucket)

Your first bucket, as you might guess, is filled with those projects that are truly important. They might be urgent, but they probably aren't. However, they are impactful. Most truly important projects are not urgent, because they tend to be the long-term, large-scale projects that you work on for an extended period of time. These projects' extended time frames keep them from being urgent.

The ironic part about conventional leadership is although these tasks are the most important, the lack of urgency surrounding them (due to the long time frame required to complete) often leads to these projects getting triaged or de-prioritized first. Don't let that happen.

These projects are how you leave a legacy. You probably won't have many jobs in this bucket at any point in time. You will have one or two large-sized jobs, and two or three medium-sized jobs. Place these in the first bucket.

If you don't have projects of this scale that meet these definitions on your list, we would encourage you to stop moving and reflect for a moment. Are there current projects fitting these definitions that you could join? Are there projects like this that you could start?

Make sure that you are devoting regular, consistent time to the items in this bucket. Ideally, you would spend time on something in this bucket daily, but we realize that might not be realistic. However, it is realistic—and imperative—that you devote some time to these projects each week.

Bucket Two (The Not-Important Bucket)
Your second bucket is not as intuitive as the first one. It is filled with those items on your list that lack importance. These items have no importance at all! Do not let urgency factor into the decision to put an item in this bucket. The only criterion that matters is importance. Who cares how urgent an item is if it's not important?

Urgency is not important. If you neglect a non-important, urgent item or if you neglect a non-important, non-urgent item, the result is the same—*nothing*.

Let importance, or the lack thereof, drive your bucket classification. For this bucket, we are looking for things that are not important. These items need to be neglected. Delegate them if you can. Ignore them if you cannot. But regardless, through the process of triage, ensure that you neglect them. They are not important, so why spend time on these at all?

Surprisingly, at any given point in time, you probably have several, maybe a dozen, items on your list that could fit into this bucket. The items in this bucket tend to be smaller, but they can be large. It is important to note that the degree of urgency will vary tremendously. Some will be extremely urgent and some will not be urgent at all.

The secret is to intentionally put those items in this bucket—now! This takes discipline. Avoid the temptation to prioritize them to the bottom of your list—cross them off altogether!

A note of caution: although these jobs are not important, if they are urgent, there's a good chance you will disappoint someone else by neglecting them. These jobs are most likely important to someone. This is hard, but it's also unavoidable. Remember, you must intentionally neglect some to save as many as possible. Intentionally neglect these. It's okay to disappoint others occasionally. Your resources are scarce.

Bucket Three (The "Good Enough" Bucket)

The third bucket is even less intuitive than the second. This is the "good-enough" bucket. The first two buckets were black or white. This bucket contains shades of gray. These are the jobs that are semi-important, and they are often urgent. Their importance, or partial importance, arises from the consequences of neglect.

If you neglected these items, you would create negative impact. Perhaps neglect would draw negative attention to yourself or someone else, or it would hinder someone else's important work. As a result, total neglect of these jobs isn't the right thing to do. For a variety of reasons, these jobs are those that you either cannot, or should not, completely neglect. But you don't want to expend all of your resources on them, either.

Unfortunately, these jobs often get prioritized to the top of our list. Fear, in this case stemming from the consequences of neglect, is a powerful motivator. So, although you don't want these items to be at the top of your list, consuming the bulk of your resources (that spot is reserved for your truly important jobs), you can't completely neglect them, either.

Execute these jobs with a "good enough" mentality. The importance of these jobs arises from the consequences of neglect. So perform these jobs at a level just "good enough" to get them past that threshold. They should be performed at a level where they avoid the consequences of neglect, but no better—just good enough to stay out of trouble. Save your resources for the impactful work.

It's okay to pause and read that again. Yes, we are advocating performing certain jobs at a "good enough" level. Why? Your resources are limited. Focus your attention and resources where they will yield the highest return.

Your Story

A conscious leader is aware that resources are scarce and finite. Don't prioritize—you will end up squandering them on the urgent. Instead, make the difficult decision and triage—investing them in the important.

A conventional leader might be satisfied with the rush that comes from extinguishing fires he lit. You aren't. You want to make an impact.

The setting for your story is not a rural, community hospital. The story you are writing is set in a battlefield. Battlefields are where stories become legends. Battles transform leaders into heroes. The hero of your story resembles the Union medic. His responsibility, and your opportunity, is to save as many lives as possible.

Mirror, Mirror on the Wall...Chapter 8

The Conscious Leader's Toolbox

1. **Questions:** How would you define your time-management skills? Are you busier today than you were five years ago? Why?

2. **Questions:** Is your natural tendency to prioritize or triage? Why? What are the pros/cons to doing this? Have you ever completed all of the items on your prioritization list?

3. **Questions:** What scares you most about triage? Do you think that your current situation resembles a rural community hospital or a battlefield? Why?

4. **Questions:** Is the fear of disappointing someone else preventing you from neglecting some items that you need to neglect? What is the task? Who are you afraid of disappointing? Why?

5. **Importance List:** This is a template that can help ensure that you are investing regular time into items that are really important. You can fill this out every day or every week.

6. **Three Buckets:** This exercise was described at the end of the chapter. This tool is designed to help you implement that exercise. It will help you classify your work as "important," "not important," or "good enough."

The "Important" List

Documenting Daily

- To ensure the important isn't sacrificed for the urgent, you need documentation
  - At the beginning of each week, write down the 5 most important tasks of the week
    - Track them throughout the week
    - Forces you to clarify what is really important
    - Provides you a mechanism for tracking your progress
    - Creates accountability

Important Job Name	Description (Why Important?)	Progress Tracker (Did you invest productive time?)				
		Mon	Tues	Wed	Thurs	Fri
#1						
#2						
#3						
#4						
#5						

Notes

CONSCIOUS
LEADERSHIP

3 Buckets

Triage

- Define "importance" (be specific) – be truthful with yourself
  - If in doubt, look at your actions; they will reveal your true beliefs
- Make a list of all of the jobs/projects in which you are involved
- Rank them based ONLY on importance

Definition of "Importance":

Job	Importance Rank	Job	Importance Rank

Notes

CONSCIOUS
LEADERSHIP

3 Buckets

Triage

- Categorize your jobs (from the previous exercise) into 3 buckets:
  - **Important:** Work that is meaningful and impactful (urgency is irrelevant)
    - You should give this work 100% effort (do it well)
  - **Not Important:** Work that is not important but demands your time
    - Remove/delete these jobs (delegate or ignore); urgency/lack of urgency is not a factor
  - **Good Enough:** Only importance is derived from the negative consequences of neglect;
    - Give this work limited effort (just enough to avoid consequences)

Important:

Not Important:

Good Enough:

Notes

3 Buckets

Triage

- Review your previous exercises (Importance Ranking and Bucket Classification)
- Answer these questions to gain insights into your current beliefs about triage:

Triage Questions

- Where do you need to allocate more resources and spend more time?

- Why aren't you allocating resources to those projects/areas now?

- What activities do you need to delete altogether? How will you remove them?

- Why haven't you already removed these projects?

- What projects do you need to reduce your effort and perform at levels that are just "good enough"? What would that look like?

- Do you have any hesitations about doing some work "good enough"? Why?

- If you could spend an entire week working on any project you desired, what would it be? Why? What insights can you glean from your answer?

Notes

CONSCIOUS
LEADERSHIP

Reflection Points

- I don't believe in prioritization; I believe in triage.
  - o Prioritization: the re-ordering of tasks
    - Attempts to do "more" with "less" indefinitely
    - Implies you will get everything done
    - Advocates for addition
    - Removal of tasks by completion
  - o Triage: the intentional neglect of some in order to save as many lives as possible
    - Scarcity of resources
    - Your job is to save as many lives as possible
    - Battlefield triage or rural, community hospital triage
    - Location matters
- Important, not Urgent
  - o Urgent jobs are urgent
    - Urgent jobs always clamor for our attention
    - There will always be more urgent jobs, things will never slow down
    - Firefighting arsonist
      - Extinguishing fires provides a false sense of productivity
  - o Important
    - Often neglected because of extended time frame
  - o How do I triage?
    - Define importance—requires wisdom
    - Clarify relative importance
    - Create three buckets
      - Bucket one: Jobs that are truly important—focus your resources here
      - Bucket two: Jobs that are not important—neglect these
      - Bucket three: Jobs that are semi-important owing to consequences of neglect—perform these at levels of "good enough"

CHAPTER 9
CONSENSUS TO DO NOTHING

"A consensus means everyone agrees to say collectively what no one believes individually."
   - Abba Eban

"The greater thing in this world is not so much where we stand as in what direction we are going."
   - Oliver Wendell Holmes

Axiom:
I don't believe in agreement;
I believe in alignment

What impact does conflict have on you and your organization? Is it positive or negative, constructive or destructive, harnessed or avoided?

The goal is not to resolve conflict peaceably; the goal is to leverage conflict *powerfully*. Does conflict have that type of impact within your organization? Probably not. Why can we say that confidently?

Conventional leadership doesn't know to manage conflict. Conscious leadership does.

Rearview Mirror

This axiom builds on some previously introduced beliefs. So, before we address conflict management, we are going to pause and reflect for a moment. If we are not aligned on some foundational beliefs with regards to conflict, you won't realize the maximum impact this axiom can provide.

Conscious leadership is about generating impact by changing beliefs, and the only way to change beliefs is through challenge and conflict. Conflict is an absolute necessity for creating meaningful change (see Chapter 3). Not only do you have to believe this principle, you have to know you believe it. Why? Your behavior, especially as it relates to conflict management, depends on it.

If you believe that conflict is a necessity, you will embrace it, not just tolerate it. You will welcome it, encourage it, and intentionally orchestrate it. You will be pleased when conflict arises. When conflict appears, you will dive into it and explore it boldly. You won't be concerned about conflict's presence; you will be concerned about its *absence*. Smooth sailing terrifies the conscious leader.

If you don't believe that conflict is a necessity, at best, you will endure it, and at worst, you will evade it. You will tolerate it under certain conditions, but will avoid it if at all possible. And when conflict does arise, you will try to extinguish it as quickly as possible. Unfortunately, these beliefs are typical, normal, and the status quo of most organizations today.

Conventional leadership believes conflict is a *cost* of doing business. Conscious leadership believes conflict is *critical* to doing business.

This doesn't necessarily mean that the conscious leader experiences more routine conflict than the conventional leader. The conventional leader experiences conflict as a result of poor leadership. His inability to generate impact on a consistent basis attracts disappointment, discord, and discontentment from those around him. Conflict arises from his external environment. The conflict that a conscious leader experiences comes from a different place—himself. He invites and orchestrates conflict; and as a result, he makes a meaningful difference.

When it comes to managing conflict, the approach of a conscious leader is to be proactive, intentionally embracing and leveraging the conflict. The approach of a conventional leader is to be reactive, avoiding and ignoring the challenge. If it is ignored, maybe it will go away…

Think back to the original model: "Belief ➜ Behavior ➜ Outcome." The conscious leader intentionally *invites* conflict at the belief phase of the model. The conventional leader inevitably *attracts* conflict at the outcome phase of the model.

So what do you believe about conflict? Do you believe it is necessary? Or do you believe it is a necessary evil?

Conventional leadership seeks to resolve the pain of conflict though the process of agreement. Conscious leadership seeks to leverage the power of conflict through the process of alignment. We will explore agreement first.

Power Drain

"A committee is a cul-de-sac down which ideas are lured and then quietly strangled."
    - Sir Barnett Cocks

When conflict arises, a conventional leader labors to reach agreement. He works with all involved parties until a group consensus is reached. On the surface, this seems to make sense. If a certain issue creates conflict, conventional leadership recommends you get everyone involved in the same room and work together to resolve the issue.

The conventional leader believes that resolution dictates that everyone needs to be involved, everyone needs to have a say, and most importantly, everyone needs to reach agreement with regard to the final decision. Ideally, everyone walks out of the room feeling good because a unanimous consensus was reached. So the question facing the conventional leader now becomes, "How do you get people to agree?"

First, they have to be flexible. There are many different points-of-view involved, so all parties need to be willing to compromise. If everyone gives a little, we all should meet in the middle. The conventional leader believes this will resolve the issue.

But what happens when everyone has compromised, and the issue is still not resolved? What do you do when everyone has given a little, but there is still disagreement? What is the standard reaction of conventional leadership?

Unwilling to make a decision (even if he knows the right thing to do), the conventional leader will abdicate responsibility and do what is fair. He will poll the audience and determine what the majority deem to be the fairest option. Hoping to avoid accountability, he will invoke the fairness doctrine. Why? Although everyone will be unhappy and no impact will be generated, he can't be held responsible. He can claim that he was just being fair.

This is why it is so important for a conventional leader to reach agreement— preferably unanimous agreement—on the proper resolution to conflict. It has been said that consensus decisions are often at odds with intelligent ones. Instinctively and experientially, you know this is the case. But conventional leadership pursues consensus and agreement anyway.

Need more proof? Let's look at an illustration of some flexible conventional leaders who are trying to reach agreement and be fair:

It is 2:00 a.m., and Julie is awake. She has insomnia (she is stressed about the web-portal system). She has exhausted her prerecorded DVR options, having watched all saved episodes of reality-dating shows. Trying to avoid commercials, she flips through her channels and inadvertently lands on C-SPAN®. Observing a busy room full of suits, she correctly concludes that the politicians have been putting in long hours. It turns out that tonight/today is an important deadline, as a bill must be passed addressing national finances. The Republicans, Democrats, and Independents have been discussing this piece of legislation for many months. At 2:14 a.m., she hears the following announcement, "The Senate has reached a consensus on the long-debated bill..."

Irrespective of her political preference, upon hearing those words, what do you think Julie immediately assumes will happen? Nothing! She assumes the bill is powerless to generate impact or create meaningful change. This is Julie's immediate reaction to Congressional consensus. It's also our reaction, and it's probably your natural reaction as well. Unfortunately, our assumptions probably reflect reality. If this is the reality that agreement generates, why is there so much time and energy spent pursuing it?

Lose – Lose

"The compromise will always be more expensive than either of the suggestions it is compromising."
       - Arthur Bloch

Agreement is a myth not because of blatant errors and shocking lies; it is a myth because of subtleties. Just like the term "transparency," the term "agreement" contains several dangerous nuances.

Agreement creates a "win – lose" environment because it has an implicit "me" focus. What does this mean? If conflict must be resolved through agreement then there must be compromise. When engaged in compromise, we think in terms of "giving in." Either you are going to give in, or I am going to give in. Whoever gives in more, loses; whoever gives in less, wins. Well, not really.

The word "compromise" evokes negative feelings more often than positive ones. Why? If you give in more than the other guy, you lose. The negative feeling in this situation is obvious because we all hate losing, But why do you still not feel so great about yourself if you win by giving in less than the other guy? This isn't so obvious. You don't feel good about yourself because despite winning, you still gave in. Giving in doesn't feel good because giving in is losing.

This is the nature of agreement. Upon resolution of the conflict, all parties must be on a level playing field. They must be standing in the exact same location. If you're not there now, you have to compromise to get to that location. You will have to give in and the other guy will have to give in. Someone will lose; and someone will win…but still lose.

By striving for agreement, conflict becomes a contest defined by winning and losing, by winners and losers. This is how agreement converts conflict from a good thing into a bad thing. Ironically, under the guise of agreement, conflict management is transformed from collaboration into competition. This is why (at least one of the reasons) that there is so little progress in politics. Both sides are so concerned with winning and losing they forget the original intent of the debated issues. They also lose sight of their original purpose as elected representatives as both sides become further polarized and embittered. Agreement creates no winners; everyone loses.

Battle Lines

There is something else dangerous about agreement. When the terms of engagement are defined by winning and losing, the process gets ugly. No longer is the issue viewed in terms of my perspective and your perspective on a given situation. Instead, the issue is viewed in terms of who owns the truth. When truth is viewed as something that is owned instead of something to be discovered, conflict escalates into battle. No wonder conventional leaders try to avoid conflict. Who wants a constant battle?

As consensus becomes combat, other changes also occur. Although we are unable to identify a specific place or time when it happened, the conflict is now personal. It is no longer about the issue; it is about me versus you. If you attack me personally, I will consider my viewpoint as "being right" and your viewpoint as "being wrong." Anytime conflict is personal, regardless of resolution or compromise or consensus, there are wounds and scars. And there is a loser and a there is a winner…who feels like a loser.

Ironically, conventional leadership confuses conflict with relationship. Conflict is personal, and relationships are professional. Perhaps conflict is personal *because* relationships are professional.

Conventional leadership is incapable of managing conflict. It can neither leverage it nor resolve it. Why? Conventional leadership believes in agreement. Conscious leadership doesn't; it believes in alignment—and what you believe makes all the difference.

Location or Direction

What makes alignment so special? Alignment is professional and non-personal; it has no "me." Alignment doesn't "give in" as it doesn't compromise. Why not? Alignment doesn't seek to reach consensus. By not seeking consensus, alignment removes the "win – lose" element from conflict, and replaces it with "win – win." Sound too good to be true?

If conscious leadership is to be as powerful as we've suggested, and if it is as transformational as we've claimed, this must be true! If conflict cannot produce results characterized as "win – win," then conflict isn't something to intentionally pursue. Why would you embrace something that results in losing at least 50% of the time?

You wouldn't. As the pursuit of agreement almost guarantees losing, conventional leadership avoids and ignores conflict. What is the fundamental shift that allows alignment to change the odds and produce "win – win" outcomes?

The goal of agreement is for everyone to *finish standing* in the same location. The goal of alignment is for everyone to *start moving* in the same direction.

Alignment is broader than agreement. By this, we mean that agreement focuses on details more so than alignment. When trying to reach agreement, we focus on how much we are giving in, and the discussion becomes a negotiation. Compromise is about bartering. As the process of giving in requires concession, I start by conceding something small. You respond by giving in and offering up something equally small. The process has become a negotiation, and we behave in ways typical of bartering. Specifically, we exaggerate. We inflate the value of our token offerings in an attempt to change your perception of their true value.

Eventually, both parties begin suspecting, and eventually accusing, the other side of bending the truth. Although both sides claim transparency, trust is lost. Blame has entered the negotiation.

As the tension continues to escalate and become more personal, both sides claim rightful ownership of the truth. They defend their stance as "being right," attack their opponent as "being wrong," and clash over the value of their concessions. The relative importance of details dramatically increases. Details are much more important in a personal negotiation regarding truth than in an objective discussion regarding issues. As details afford many opportunities to "be right" or "be wrong," they become the focus, and all parties lose sight of what really matters.

Alignment is not concerned with the granular details of the conflict. Disagreement and alignment are not mutually exclusive. We can disagree and still align. How is that possible?

Alignment focuses on the ultimate, big-picture outcome instead of the in-between steps. When conflict arises, an alignment discussion begins at the end. Alignment first seeks clarity on the ultimate desired outcome. It doesn't worry about the details of the starting point or the in-between steps until absolutely necessary. This change in perspective is transformational.

The initial requirement of alignment is that both parties face the same direction as they view their desired outcome. Often, the preferred outcome of both parties is similar. Consider politicians: both Republicans and Democrats want international peace and domestic progress while being fiscally responsible. The power of alignment is realized when both parties, facing the same direction, viewing the same outcome, simply start moving even though the details haven't been worked out! Here's the magic: when both parties start moving together in alignment, the degree of conflict in the remaining details vanishes.

Forward motion in the same direction causes insignificant conflict to disappear. The conflict that really matters rises to the surface.

Now, you are really focused on the two or three key issues that really matter instead of myriads of insignificant and meaningless details. The conflict is no longer personal. "Being right" and "being wrong" have been replaced with issue-based discussions. You are no longer looking to compromise, and you don't have to give in as there is freedom to disagree. You don't have to artificially inflate the value of your concessions through transparent negotiations. Best of all, you have made forward progress with unresolved disagreement about details.

Forward motion does not require agreement; unfortunately, agreement will not move forward without consensus.

By refusing to move forward from your current location, the degree of conflict is magnified. Often, the conflict regarding the details and in-between steps doesn't even matter; the pace of change within the environment renders the original interpretation of those details moot. But you can't see that until you start moving together.

Alignment allows the parties to focus on similarities—what's going right. Agreement forces the parties to focus on differences—what's going wrong. Whatever you focus on, you magnify.

Owning the Truth

Let's see how the differences between agreement and alignment could play out at Acme Office Supply:

Julie and Todd finally presented StarGate, the new multi-purpose web-ordering portal, to senior management, and they received approval to proceed. In fact, senior management was so impressed with the estimated value of this portal that they revised their budget for Julie's department—upward! The new budget now forecasted Julie's department to deliver an annual increase in net income of 14% (up from the original 10%) over the next 12 months. Julie and Todd were now accountable to deliver more to the organization's bottom line. Missing this revised budget would have disastrous consequences for both of their careers. After the meeting with senior management, they sat down to discuss their next steps.

This is a conversation focused on *agreement*:

TODD: As you know, I have been working on my flipchart project for almost one-and-a-half years now. Originally, I didn't think we would see significant revenue for another 18 months, but I think that we could narrow that window to 6-8 months using StarGate. Its customer-relationship management component, combined with its ordering capability, could really reduce that timeline. But that would require additional funding right now.
JULIE: Todd, come on! How many discussions have we had about controlling spending? StarGate is supposed to reduce our expenses, not increase them. We need this portal to replace our

traditional ordering system immediately to reduce our processing costs. We could also reduce our spend on traditional printing costs of order forms and catalogs. And I think we can cut costs by reducing headcount as soon as StarGate is operationalized. Leveraging this low-cost position, we can reduce our prices and generate the extra revenue we need. Actually, Todd, in light of this meeting, your flipchart project may have to get put on the back burner and the funding re-allocated to make us more profitable. We definitely can't spend more money on it!

TODD: What?! You said yourself, as have other members of the management team, that the flipchart market-development program was one of the best and most innovative ideas at Acme in a long time!! I have not only spent my time and energy on this project, but I have hired and trained others to do the same. We could be capable of launching within a few months, and you want to pull back now?

JULIE: Todd, I understand you are frustrated...

TODD: I'm very frustrated! And I'm confused. StarGate is supposed to be a tool to better integrate Acme with our customers and create a marketplace reputation of innovation. That's part of our strategic map [see Acme's Strategic Map, Chapter 4, CSF #2 and #3]. You want to use the web-based portal to lower prices further, which is in direct violation of our long-term strategy [see CSF #1]. And on top of that, you are going to use it to immediately lay people off? What kind of message does that send to your team about the effect of innovation at Acme? Those that stay will know that you don't care about them and that they could be next. How hard do you think they will work to make StarGate successful?

JULIE: Todd, stop. We need to get on the same page here, and fast. I am not discounting your flipchart program, nor am I trying to axe my entire department. But reality is that we need to increase profitability now. You need to start thinking like a businessman and be willing to make the difficult decisions. This isn't personal.

You have probably experienced something like this before. The myths of conventional leadership are both subtle and insidious. The word "agreement" was never used in this conversation. Yet, the entire discussion revolved around the principle of agreement.

Immediately, Todd and Julie both started discussing their individual viewpoints. They jumped into the details without first discussing the final outcome. They never set a direction; they just tried to get in the same location. Without either Todd or Julie being conscious of the agreement trap, the conflict became personal.

Somehow, during the course of this discussion, Julie assumed full ownership of the entire department (Todd using "your" and Julie using "my" to describe the team). Paradoxically, even though Julie owned the entire department, Todd somehow assumed full ownership of the flipchart program (Todd referring to the time that he has invested and Julie using "your" to describe the program). They both thought that they had full ownership of the truth.

Any time the words "This isn't personal..." are spoken, you can be assured that something personal is being discussed. In this conversation, the conflict became personal as neither Julie nor Todd wanted to give in. The conflict then escalated into battle, with both Julie and Todd concerned about "being right" and "being wrong." Todd accused Julie of not knowing (or understanding) Acme's Strategic Map. Julie accused Todd of being a poor businessman afraid of making hard decisions.

What is the result of this agreement-based conversation? Two losers, zero winners, strained relationships, and a poor outcome that made no progress towards delivering a 14% increase in net income.

Win – Win

This is a conversation focused on *alignment*:

TODD: This isn't a pleasant place to be, but we need to dig in. So starting with the basics, we need to increase net income by a lot, right?

JULIE: Yup. I agree. And so that gives us two fundamental choices.

TODD: We can either increase our revenue or decrease our costs...

JULIE: Hopefully, StarGate will allow us to do both.

TODD: You know where I will land on this, Julie. I am in favor of using this portal to help drive multiple CSFs from our Strategic Map. StarGate could really decrease the timeline needed for the flipchart initiative to produce results. This will increase costs some initially, but the revenue increase should outpace the associated cost increase. What do you think?

JULIE: And you probably aren't surprised by where I land on this. I would much rather fall on the side of reducing costs. We can use StarGate to eliminate many costs associated with traditional order processing (including printing costs and inefficient headcount utilization), and then have it evolve into its CRM role next year. Do you agree?

TODD: Not really. But I think we are closer than might appear. We want the same thing—to increase our net income. And I understand the need to balance reducing costs while also striving to take market share from our competitors. We just fall on different sides of that middle fence. I have a compromise.

JULIE: Okay, I'm all ears.

TODD: Before today, you knew there was a good chance that my department would overspend with the launch of the flipchart program. I know that spending must be offset. What if I promise to maintain the currently allocated spending budget at its current level while driving new business? I will identify cost-savings generated by the portal implementation, and I will use those savings to fund the market development the flipchart program needs to grow. Then, any extra revenue that we obtain (and I think we will find a lot of business within 6-8 months) will go straight to the bottom line.

JULIE: Hmmm. Not what I initially envisioned. But I agree that it makes sense. And if anyone can pull it off, it would be you.

Okay, go forward with that idea. But remember—it has to be cost neutral. And, Todd, you own this part of the portal. I will work to identify cost-savings elsewhere, but I am holding you accountable for a cost-neutral, net-income-positive, flipchart launch.

TODD: I'm all in!

Unfortunately, you might not have experienced something like this before. This alignment-driven conversation is ironic as the word "alignment" was never used. Instead, the word "agree" was used three times, and the word "compromise" was used once. In addition, there seemed to be compromise at the end of the discussion. Don't allow yourself to draw conclusions based only observing blossoms and branches; get to the roots. In spite of surface-level appearances, this was undoubtedly and unequivocally an alignment-focused conversation.

Note that Todd and Julie started at the end, discussing the final outcome. They gained alignment around the end goal, focusing first on the direction they needed to face. Although there was still divergence and disagreement on some details, the conversation remained non-personal, focusing on objective issues not personal viewpoints.

Facing the same direction, Julie and Todd then moved forward without having all the details worked out. Much of the conflict caused by these details will disappear as they continue to move forward, as they weren't really that important in the first place. The truly important issues will resurface, and Julie and Todd will start the process all over again. The net result?

"Win – win." Both sides got what they originally wanted. Todd was able to launch his flipchart program, and Julie controlled her costs. This outcome is often the result of alignment-focused conflict management. It creates a positive, engaging, accountable atmosphere. Neither individual is focused on giving in, winning, losing, being right, or being wrong. Instead, they are focused on moving forward.

But Wait, There's More…

"The ability to accept responsibility is the measure of the man."
   - Roy L. Hunt

Did you notice that Julie gave Todd ownership of his program? She let him figure out how to make the numbers work. This is often the result of alignment. Alignment leads to empowerment. Empowerment results in accountability. Accountability increases engagement.

In stark contrast, a consensus decision removes accountability by distributing ownership. Numbers provide anonymity and safety, as no one on owns a unique portion of the decision. By allowing the right to disagree, alignment assigns the responsibility to deliver.

Alignment is about unity, not uniformity. Conscious leadership is not about creating indistinguishable people or identical systems. Uniqueness is a source of competitive advantage; difference enables excellence.

Choosing alignment over agreement requires courage. To a degree, you will have to let go and empower others. It requires the confidence to resist the temptation to be right, to fight, and to win. And it demands the humility to focus the discussion on the outcome and the direction, not your personal viewpoint about the right location.

Conflict is powerful; its power can be constructive or destructive. Alignment allows you to harness and control the power of conflict, channeling that power into growth and transformational change. If you can control the power of conflict, you have the potential to generate impact.

Although alignment requires a large amount of confidence and courage, the following sub-principle requires even more.

<u>Sub-Principle #1:</u>
Contrarian, not Complementary

Does your department have any yes-men? Picture one of them in your mind right now. Think back to the last conversation you observed this yes-man having with a superior. Did he agree that the reduction in bonus payout would not affect employee engagement? The yes-man might have pointed out that the money saved would be distributed to shareholders via dividends; after all, many of the employees have company stock in their 401(k).

Or did he tell the VP that her idea to implement a fully computerized and automated call center—offshore—was a great way to improve customer satisfaction ratings? He pointed out that the customers will really appreciate the speed and precision of the computerized system. After all, if the offshore representatives introduce themselves with aliases, most customers wont even notice the call center is now offshore. These stories should be comical, but they're actually sad because they're true.

Think about how you felt when you pictured your department's number one yes-man. What emotions did you sense? Indifference? Anger? Disgust? Revulsion? Were these emotions a result of the yes-man, or were they a result of the executive receiving the "feedback"? Most likely, both. The yes-man because he lacks the courage to call a spade a spade, and the executive because he lacked the awareness to see through the charade.

It is easy to see the faults of others in this arena, but it is very difficult to see these tendencies in the mirror. Being truthful, we all possess the tendency to be both the spineless yes-man and the disillusioned executive. Everyone wants to win the approval of those in high-powered positions, and everyone wants to hear that their ideas are excellent, ground-breaking, and novel. Thus, conventional leadership encourages us to surround ourselves with people who provide complementary viewpoints.

In doing so, we miss one of the biggest sources of true innovation and new ideas—the contrarian.

A contrarian—also known as an outlier, antagonizer, or non-conformist—is frequently the best source and purest supplier of creative thought. The contrarian has a different perspective than the rest of the team, and his vantage point allows him to view problems (and solutions) differently. Difference enables excellence. Yet, as discussed earlier, we are taught at an early age that we must go along to get along. Unfortunately, the voice of these contrarians is often never heard.

A conscious leader needs to learn to take "no" for an answer. In fact, if as a leader, you aren't hearing "no," or if you aren't hearing "no" enough, then demand it. Seek out "no" with diligence and persistence.

Historical Value

"Whoever wishes to foresee the future must consult the past; for human events ever resemble those of preceding times. This arises from the fact that they are produced by men who ever have been, and ever shall be, animated by the same passions, and thus they necessarily have the same results."
 - Niccolo Machiavelli

The stories of history's great conscious leaders tell of their appreciation for and insistence on the contrarian viewpoint. Recognizing its value, they often invited, and sometimes demanded, its presence.

General John Marshall, during World War II, would often yell at his men; this seems normal, especially for military generals during times of war. But what is not normal is why and when he yelled at his men. He yelled at them not for challenging him, but for agreeing with him.

He would present his officers with a strategic initiative, and occasionally they would "yes" him. When this happened, instead of taking their "feedback" at face value, Marhsall would yell at his men and abruptly end the session, ordering it to reconvene the next day. He made it clear that during the next session he expected them to challenge him instead of placate him. Why did he do this? He was conscious both of what he knew and of what he didn't know.

Marshall knew enough to know it was impossible that his initial plan was flawless. In order to make it better and more impactful, it had to be challenged, not blindly supported.

Winston Churchill, employed a different behavior than Marshall, but he shared the same belief. During World War II, Churchill intentionally surrounded himself with a group of individuals whose primary purpose was to present him with the truth about the state of the war and challenge his perspective. To qualify as a member of this group, an individual must have had no political ties to Churchill, nor could he have been in

Churchill's direct reporting line. Churchill knew that the natural tendency of others would be to tell him what they thought he wanted to hear. Thus, they would be tempted to sugarcoat the harsh realities of the war. He wanted the truth, and he wanted challenge. He employed this group of individuals to ensure that he received both.

The result? Churchill thwarted Nazi plans of world conquest and domination. Marshall authored and implemented the Marshall plan, which rebuilt Europe after the Nazi's defeat. The stories written by these legendary leaders not only shaped the world of yesterday, but continue to shape the world today. And the world will undoubtedly feel their impact tomorrow.

Spot Me

The conscious leader seeks contrarian challenge, not complementary consensus. As we discussed earlier, biological muscle growth is a result of stress and strain. Belief growth is no different; it requires challenge. If beliefs are not challenged, they will not change. Without belief change, a leader is ineffective and irrelevant.

At this point in our journey, the importance of challenge for a conscious leader has been established. Let's make the contrarian concept personal. How do you orchestrate meaningful conflict in your life? You start here:

Howdy Pardner!

It has been proven that partner-based fitness programs are more successful than individual programs. Workouts are more frequent, more intense, and more likely to produce lasting change when you have a partner than when you workout alone. Why?

A partner will encourage you when you are getting tired. A partner will cheer for you when you reach a new personal best. A partner will correct you when your form is incorrect. A partner will challenge you when you become complacent. A partner will make you less likely to hit the snooze button. Importantly, your partner will "spot" you when the weight becomes too heavy or difficult.

For those of you unfamiliar with this term, a "spotter" is a specific type of fitness partner. When someone is lifting a weight, the spotter will stand behind him, informing the lifter of his form, and encouraging him, often by shouting, to finish the final repetition. If the lifter begins to struggle or shows signs of dropping the weight, the spotter will physically assist the lifter, picking up the weight to prevent injury.

What is the benefit of a partner? A partner increases your impact.

Whether you are referring to a workout program or a war strategy, a partner will make you more impactful. Regardless of how good, smart, or charismatic you are alone, you will be better—exponentially better—with a partner. Especially a contrarian partner. Why?

Looking in the mirror can be challenging. You need someone who can identify your blind spots. You need someone who can be a protective hedge against self-deception (a skill we all possess). You need someone who can challenge your beliefs, your ideas, your systems, and your status quo. You need someone who can pressure-test your best thoughts. The ability and willingness to challenge are characteristics of a great partner.

Your partner is not your best friend. Right now, picture your best friend. Now ask yourself, "Why is that person my best friend?" Chances are, you are best friends because of all you share in common. Frequently, friendships are determined by similarities and commonalities. You share mutual interests, hobbies, work, sports, and perhaps personalities. You might share some similar life experiences. You have probably been best friends for a long time. There is probably agreement—tacit or explicit— between you and your best friend with regard to many of your core beliefs.

While these qualities and this level of agreement make a great friend, they make a lousy partner. Alignment, not agreement, is the defining characteristic of a great partner.

Your partner should be someone who is different than you, someone who has a different perspective and viewpoint. Ideally, your partner will have slightly different beliefs than you. Your partner needs to feel comfortable getting in your face from time to time. This type of partner, a contrarian, can challenge you and be a catalyst for growth. You can have multiple partners in a lifetime. Unlike great friendships, great partnerships usually only last for a season or two.

A partnership is between individuals, as this type of relationship is too difficult to create or sustain within a large group of people. Even with only one individual, it is difficult and time intensive to create an atmosphere of trust where challenge can flourish. A partner should be able to challenge you safely—meaning that it is often behind closed doors and away from the view of the public.

Enhancing Challenge

"The human understanding is like a false mirror, which, receiving rays irregularly, distorts and discolors the nature of things by mingling its own nature with it."
   - Francis Bacon

Seeking contrarian viewpoints is tough. It requires a healthy dose of courage. No one likes being confronted with the fact that they are wrong, but contrarian viewpoints are critical. The contrarian viewpoint is the cure for complacency and the catalyst for impact.

Without challenge, the best ideas will never emerge. Initial ideas will never be pressure-tested. Contrarians provide the opportunity for others' knowledge to be converted into your wisdom. You can apply their learnings to your ideas and systems, and avoid making predictable mistakes.

Think back to Chapter 2 about the defining characteristics of a leader: humility, self-awareness, and confidence. It should come as no surprise that the value of contrarian viewpoints is enhanced in the presence of the following:

- **Humility/Vulnerability:** This has been a constant theme throughout the book, and it is a constant theme within the story of conscious leadership. You must be humble enough to look in the mirror and realize there is room for improvement. You must be humble enough to admit to yourself your idea might not be perfect; it could be better. This allows you to ask others for feedback. Once you receive that feedback, you must be humble enough to admit that the refinements or changes to your idea could represent improvements. Your vulnerability opens your eyes to the reality that the refined version is better than your original idea.

- **Confidence:** As we have said, the confidence of a conscious leader is different than the cockiness typically displayed by conventional leader. Confidence is not complete assurance that I am right; it is assurance that if I am wrong, I am not worth any less as a person. I am still capable of producing excellence. The continual exposure of your ideas to challenge and critique from others requires extreme confidence. You be able to realize the refinement of your original idea is a good thing that increases impact, not a negative thing that decreases your value. Confidence means your self-worth is not defined by the agreement of others.

- **Externalization:** You must be able to externalize criticism and critique. You must make it non-personal. You cannot confuse the challenge of your idea with the challenge of your person. You must be wise enough to keep challenge professional. This is difficult and requires practice.

- **Intentionality:** You must seek out contrarian viewpoints; you won't accidentally stumble upon them. Conflict is not enjoyable, either for the giver or the receiver. You must make others feel comfortable challenging you. You must proactively seek, dig, and push so that they reveal their true thoughts. We have been programmed and coded to avoid conflict. Thus, you must make others feel comfortable being truthful with you, and then you must thank them for their truthfulness on the back-end, regardless of how much the challenge might sting.

Notice that self-awareness was not listed above. Self-awareness is one of the primary reasons for pursuing a contrarian partnership. Your partner will be able to see things that you miss in the mirror. A contrarian partner will force you to clarify what you believe and why you believe it. In doing so, your self-awareness will increase. Self-awareness isn't a prerequisite for a contrarian partnership; it is a result of that partnership.

Your Story

If you shine light into a piece of concave or convex glass the light will either scatter, dancing across the room, or it will come together into a focused beam of energy. If you are like us, the idea of light converging into a laser is the more appealing of those two images.

Appealing as it might be, resist the urge to converge too quickly. The most impactful stories are written by legendary leaders who sought divergence before convergence, and who sought alignment instead of agreement.

Focus on your direction, not your location. Be courageous and empower others. Show discipline, and seek contrarian viewpoints that scatter your beliefs and create divergence within your ideas. Once you gain clarity, you can begin to filter and align the streams of light. Some of the rays will be strengthened, and others will be discarded. Only now should you focus the light rays and converge them into a powerful beam of energy.

The impact of the focused light, having been initially refracted through the filter of contrarians, will be much greater than had you simply sought convergence and consensus from the start.

Leverage contrarians and alignment to amplify the power of your story.

Mirror, Mirror on the Wall...Chapter 9

The Conscious Leader's Toolbox

1. **Questions:** What are the two biggest conflicts facing you at work right now? Are you seeking alignment or agreement over them? Has the conflict become personal? How can you tell?

2. **Questions:** Within the last six months, when has another person challenged you the most? How did you respond? When did you most intentionally challenge another individual? How did they respond? What steps are you taking to make those around you comfortable challenging you?

3. **Questions:** When was the last time that you empowered someone as a result of reaching alignment around conflict? What were the details of that situation? When was the last time you were empowered as a result of someone reaching alignment around conflict? What were the details of that situation?

4. **Questions:** Name two "yes-men" in your department. Now, name the two most susceptible, highly ranked managers in your department who listen to (and prefer the "feedback" of) "yes-men." If your department was surveyed anonymously, would you be identified as a "yes-man"?

5. **Questions:** Do you have a partner? Who? How did you discover this partner? Describe your relationship. Give two examples of ideas that your partner helped refine, blind spots that he alerted you to, or times when he called you out and challenged you. What were the circumstances?

6. **Partner/Mentor:** A mentor can serve as a great partner. You should always strive to have a mentor, as well as to be a mentor for someone else. A mentor isn't forever, and it also isn't for everything. It is specific. This exercise will help you identify some potential partners/mentors as well as increase the value of those relationships.

7. **Harnessing Conflict:** This exercise will help you identify what steps are needed to move the focus of a conflict from agreement to alignment.

Mentors

Partners You Admire

- Learn leadership from great leaders
- Examine the lives of leaders you want to emulate
- Pick 2 people whom you admire and analyze them:

Leader #1

- Name:

- Relationship Details:

- Personal Brand:

- Professional Brand:

- What do you admire most about this individual? Why?

- Strengths:

- Weaknesses:

- If you could "steal" 1 character trait from this person, what would it be?

- What trait of yours could this person benefit the most from?

Notes

CONSCIOUS
LEADERSHIP

Mentors

Partners You Admire

- Learn leadership from great leaders
- Examine the lives of leaders you want to emulate
- Pick 2 people whom you admire and analyze them:

Leader #2

- Name:

- Relationship Details:

- Personal Brand:

- Professional Brand:

- What do you admire most about this individual? Why?

- Strengths:

- Weaknesses:

- If you could "steal" 1 character trait from this person, what would it be?

- What trait of yours could this person benefit the most from?

Notes

CONSCIOUS
LEADERSHIP

Mentors

Partners You Admire

• The following questions will help you draw insights from the leaders you admire:

• What are the similarities between Leader #1 and #2?

• What are the differences between Leader #1 and #2?

• How have they developed their brand? Have they done it intentionally?

• What does your assessment of their strengths/weaknesses say about you?

• What could you learn from them?

• What could they learn from you?

• Do you have an official "mentor" or partner relationship with either of them? Could you? Have you asked?

• Are you acting as a mentor for someone else? Could you?

Notes

CONSCIOUS
LEADERSHIP

Harnessing Conflict

Win-Win

- Don't make conflict a negotiation with a winner and a loser
  - Work to see the issue from the other party's perspective
- Direction, not location – find areas where you can progress
  - Forward motion resolves many issues

Directional Questions

- How do you define the issue?

- How would the other party define the issue?

- What do you want as your ultimate outcome?

- What does the other party want as the ultimate outcome?

- What are the irreconcilable differences between the parties?

- Do those differences involve the final outcome or the in-between details?

- Are there any areas where you could move forward right now?

Notes

CONSCIOUS
LEADERSHIP

Reflection Points

- I don't believe in agreement; I believe in alignment.
  - Conventional leadership seeks to resolve the pain of conflict through agreement
  - Conscious leadership seeks to leverage the power of conflict through alignment
  - Agreement
    - Consensus decisions involve compromise and giving in
    - Personal, me-centric
    - Focus on the location
    - Concerned with "being right" and "being wrong"
    - Turns into negotiations over details
    - Lose – lose, highlights differences
    - Safety in numbers, lacks empowerment and accountability
  - Alignment
    - Begins by discussing the end
    - Non-personal, issue-centric, professional
    - Focus on the direction
      - Face the same direction first
      - Begin moving forward without details worked out
      - Movement together diminishes conflict
    - Win – win, highlights similarities
    - Results in empowerment, accountability, and engagement
    - Allows the right to disagree and assigns the responsibility to deliver
- Contrarian, not complementary
  - Take "no" for an answer
  - Unity, not uniformity
  - Contrarians are the source of many innovative ideas
  - Howdy Pardner!
    - Not your best friend
    - Align but don't agree
    - Hedge against self-deception
    - Alert to blind spots
    - Pressure-test new ideas

CONSENSUS TO DO NOTHING

- Convert their knowledge into your wisdom
o Seek out contrarian viewpoints
  - Requirements:
    - Humility
    - Confidence
    - Externalization of conflict
    - Intentionality
  - Results in increased self-awareness

CONSCIOUS
LEADERSHIP

CHAPTER 10

OUTPUTS AND INPUTS

"Do or do not. There is no try."
  - Jedi Master Yoda

"Never tell people how to do things. Tell them what to do and they will surprise you with their ingenuity."
  - General George Patton

Introduction—Performance

Finally—performance. This is what really counts; this is what it's all about.

Both conventional leadership and conscious leadership observe performance first. This makes sense, as it is often tangible and measurable. It is also capable of creating pain very quickly. The pain created from poor performance is felt quicker, and often with more force, than pain caused by people or process. For example, if the efficiency of your meetings is grinding to a halt, owing to transparent conversations focused on agreement, you will feel some pain eventually. But, if a shipment of product to one of your key customers is delayed as a result of this inefficiency, you will feel lots of pain immediately.

Performance generates the income and pays the bills, and thus it is incredibly important to both the conventional and conscious leader. Performance wins awards and causes terminations. Performance is almost magical. If performance is good, cash magically appears in a company's bank account; if performance is poor, whatever cash was left magically disappears. Conventional leadership and conscious leadership are both aligned on the importance of performance.

However, this is where the similarities end. Conventional leadership doesn't just observe performance first, it addresses it first. Conscious leadership, although it observes performance first, actually addresses it last. Does this should mean that conventional leadership values performance more than conscious leadership? No. Does this mean that conventional leaders will outperform conscious leaders? Absolutely not! Conscious leaders outperform conventional leaders—often in the short term, and always in the long term.

A conventional leader's performance often reflects incremental improvement. These types of performance gains are normal and expected; they satisfy the status quo. A conscious leader's performance, on the other hand, often reflects exponential progress, as he generates transformational change capable of redefining a category or impacting an entire market.

What is ultimately responsible for the difference between the incremental and the exponential? It's not only different behaviors, but more importantly, different beliefs.

It's a truth that performance should be observed first. It's a myth, however, that it should be addressed first. The behavior of addressing performance first reflects a faulty belief system. It also explains why conscious leaders outperform conventional leaders.

Why do we consider this belief (performance should be addressed first) a myth? Two primary reasons: Cause-and-effect and time delay.

Performance has a cause-and-effect type relationship with people and process. The link between people/process and performance is causal, not associative. Although this link is not as strong as those in the "Belief ➙ Behavior ➙ Outcome" model, it does exist. For those of you who like math, think:

- Great People + Great Process = Great Performance (most of the time)

This doesn't necessarily work in reverse, however. Performance is the output. People and process are the inputs. If you want to change the output, you must first address the inputs. Only by first improving people and process (the inputs) will you be able to impact performance (the output).

Although its own domain, performance does not stand alone—this is a myth. You have to understand the inputs before you can make any sense of the output. Conscious leaders observe performance first, but explore and address it last. This isn't because we don't value performance; it's because we understand it.

A time delay exists between people/process and performance. Just as this relationship is only partially causal, it is also only partially time-sensitive. It is rarely immediate. Just because you improve your people and process today doesn't mean that you will you will improve your performance today. In fact, you might not even notice an improvement in performance tomorrow—it might take months, or even years.

The time delay works in the opposite direction as well. If the quality of your people and process declines today, it is unlikely that the quality of your performance will also decline today. It might not reflect those negative changes for a long time. But it will decline eventually; the quality of your performance is always tied to the quality of your people and your process. Recognizing this time delay allows us to rewrite the previous equation:

- Great People + Great Process + Time = Great Performance

Conventional leadership lacks the wisdom to see and understand this time lag, and it lacks the discipline to execute against it. Ironically, in its attempts to create immediate performance improvement, it renders that performance improvement unattainable.

Ultimately, conventional leadership is underperforming because of faulty beliefs. The performance domain is no different than the people domain or the process domain.

Your beliefs will drive your behaviors which will influence your outcomes. You can't generate breakthrough performance if your beliefs are based on myths. So what does a conscious leader believe about performance?

Axiom:
I don't believe in objectives;
I believe in outcomes.

With the introduction of this axiom, we are conscious of two potential points of confusion that we want to clarify:

First, in this chapter, we will be discussing the "outcome" from a slightly different perspective than we have previously in the "Belief → Behavior → Outcome" model. Previously, we examined "outcomes" in regards to its position relative to "beliefs" and "behaviors." Here, we will be exploring the form and function of the "outcome" independently (i.e., what do you believe about outcomes?). We will use the core model to understand the third component of that model. To simplify, the above axiom could have been written in this manner:

Axiom:
I don't believe in "Belief → Behavior → *Objectives*;"
I believe in "Belief → Behavior → *Outcomes*."

We will be comparing and contrasting "objectives" and "outcomes," uncovering myths that need to be debunked and truths that need to be embraced. This means we will be exploring "outcome" and "objective" with regard to each one's unique set of beliefs and behaviors.

This leads us to our second clarification. Those of you who have developed your inner contrarian—which we applaud—should have all sorts of flashing red lights going off right now. Your challenge to us: "Aren't we just playing with semantics right here? How can objectives and outcomes be that different?"

This is far from trivial word play. These words could be replaced with different words, but the ideas represented by those words are not interchangeable. In this chapter, you will see that objectives and outcomes will represent two entirely different belief systems, and your beliefs will determine your performance.

Late one Saturday afternoon, with his older son now pitching at college, Todd is at the local park with his younger son who's playing Little League baseball. The game was over, and Todd's son was playing with his friends. Todd's back was turned, and the next thing he knew, his son was screaming and crying. Apparently, one of his friends had inadvertently thrown his glove on the top of a small building (the concession stand). Although afraid of heights, Todd, like any good father, sets out to find a ladder so that he can climb to the roof and retrieve his son's glove. After asking around, Todd finally finds an old, rickety, rusted ladder.

He places the ladder against the north side of the building, ensuring that he wouldn't be staring into the sunset. After retying his shoes and securing the ladder, Todd begins to climb. Halfway up, a gust of wind whooshes by, and the ladder wobbles. Todd steadies the ladder and continues his ascent. Finally, he reaches the top of the ladder and stands on the roof. But, there is no glove. He surveys the entire roof and finds nothing but dried leaves and spider webs.

Todd calls down to his boy. Shouting over the wind, Todd discovers that his son isn't exactly sure his glove is on the top of *that* building; but he thinks that his glove is on the top of *a* building. The park had a row of several buildings, and Todd's son never actually saw the glove get thrown—he was just telling his dad what he heard a friend say. Todd walks to the corner of his building, peers over the edge, and sees the silhouette of his son's glove on the next building over. He can't reach it from where he is. Now, he will have to climb down the rickety deathtrap, reset the ladder, and do it all again.

This story illustrates the difference between outcomes and objectives. The outcome is the desired end result—the "what." In this case, the desired end result is the retrieval of the glove. The objectives are the steps along the way—the "how." In this story, the objectives included: locating a ladder, setting it up so that he wasn't looking into the sun, stabilizing the ladder during a stiff breeze, climbing the rungs until the roof was reached, and descending the ladder.

Todd accomplished his objectives without achieving his outcome; he just climbed a ladder. This simple story should make us pause and ask ourselves a critical question:

What if your ladder is against the wrong building?

Conventional leadership has blurred the lines between long-term business planning/ mission (objectives) and long-range direction setting/vision (outcomes). Like mission and vision, objectives and outcomes are designed to complement each other and work together. But they are not interchangeable.

An objective is a reality check against an outcome, not a replacement for an outcome. You can test the progress of your desired outcome through the use of objectives. But objectives and outcomes are not interchangeable. An objective is a component of, not a substitute for, an outcome.

Although this outcome focus seems intuitive, a commonly accepted myth of conventional leadership is that objectives, not outcomes, should be our focal point. Think about your current appraisal system/scorecard and the associated annual objectives, key performance indicators, and/or its driving metrics. How many of them are truly outcome-based, focused on retrieving the glove, aligned to the "what"? How many of them are objective-based, focused on climbing the rungs of the ladder, aligned to the "how"?

We are not completely discounting objectives. They have their role and provide some value (which we will discuss in a moment). However, their role is not to serve as a leader's central focal point. Yet, conventional leadership insists that performance should be centered on objectives, instead of outcomes. Why?

Bad Math...

"Math is like love—a simple idea, but it can get complicated."
  - R. Drabek

Just like with most of the myths of conventional leadership, this fable is fueled by subtleties that are both deceptive and dangerous. Let's examine objectives closely.

An objective is a subset of an outcome that is specifically tailored to one group of people. For example, a marketing objective might be to generate a 30% increase in brand awareness, whereas a business outcome would be to increase profitability by 12%. The myth asserts that if *different* objectives are assigned to *different* groups of people working in *different* departments, the organization will work together towards the *same* outcome.

Right away, this doesn't make much sense. Further extrapolation of this myth reveals that it makes no sense. Objective-based performance asserts the following: If the marketing department creates the right amount of brand awareness; the supply chain provides the right amount of material transit time; the sales force makes the right amount of calls; the production team prevents the right amount of defects; and the finance team controls the right amount of borrowing; the company will achieve its overall outcome. This myth can be expressed as another mathematical equation:

Marketing (Objective):	1
Supply Chain (Objective):	1
Sales (Objective):	1
Production (Objective):	1
Finance (Objective)	1
Total (Outcome):	**5**

On the surface, this math expression seems to make sense. Objectives try to create business success by ensuring that each piece of the organization contributes appropriately. This is one of the appeals of the myth.

Another appeal of objective-based performance is that it keeps employees from being penalized for events outside of their control. Assume the marketing team increases brand awareness, but the company missed its profit goals due to an economic downturn that reduced the average consumer's disposable income. Although the company did not achieve its desired outcome, technically, the marketing team did its job and should be rewarded. Objective-based performance insulates individuals from unforeseen external events.

It also insulates them from unforeseen internal events. Suppose a recall limits the availability of your product during the holiday season. Even though the marketing team delivered its objective by raising brand awareness to appropriate levels, a defect caused by production will keep the product off the shelves this year, lowering net revenue. Objective-based performance keeps the marketing team from being penalized for the mistakes of the production team.

Is this the fair thing to do? Perhaps—but we won't engage that topic here. Is this the right thing to do? Perhaps not—at least not all of the time; and that topic is one we will explore.

...Equals Less Impact

An objective is safe, both for the employee and for the manager. Typically, they are simple, trackable, and measureable—all of which are good things. But how do you know that you are tracking the right objectives?

Consider this statement as it relates to leadership and performance evaluation: "If something is not measureable, it is not meaningful." Most of the time, this statement holds true. Most of the time, a successful performance evaluation depends on your ability to quantify its quality. Said differently, to meaningfully access performance, you must measure its value.

Now consider the converse of that statement: "If something is measureable, it is meaningful." Most of the time, this statement is false. There are many different aspects of performance you can measure. However, just because something can be counted does not make it valuable.

Even if you devise objectives that are measureable, you are faced with another dilemma. How do you define "meaningful?" Is the objective meaningful for the individual? The team? The department? The company? Meaning is relative and is influenced by your perspective. Meaning will be defined differently by different people at different levels in different departments across the organization.

For the individual employee, an objective-based focus promotes a narrow view of the organization. It encourages an employee to focus on a narrow portion of the business, and it rewards mastery of that function. The employee is concerned only about the performance of his particular portion of the business. The attainment of these siloed objectives becomes each individual's highest priority. What does this do to the organization holistically?

It creates intra-departmental competition—in a bad way. Different departments will do what is necessary to achieve their individual objectives, sometimes at the expense of other departments. Because each department is hyper-focused on its objectives, it is oblivious to the objectives of other departments. Sight is lost of the company's desired outcome and vision, and different divisions begin to compete with each other.

Objective-based performance does provide individuals with insulation from that which is undesirable and unforeseen, such as an economic downturn or new governmental legislation. Unfortunately, it also creates isolation from that which is desirable and needs to be seen, such as the company vision and the function of different departments.

Communication breaks down as collaboration gives way to competition. As departments and employees lose alignment, motives are questioned, and trust is eroded. Without trust, conflict and challenge are now used to weaken others—tearing them down—instead of strengthening others—building them up. For an organization which strongly believes in objectives, the mathematical equation really looks like this:

Marketing (Objective):	1
Supply Chain (Objective):	1
Sales (Objective):	1
Production (Objective):	1
Finance (Objective):	1
Total (Outcome):	**3**

This equation only captures the losses of objective-focused performance caused by intra-department competition. Unfortunately, there are additional sources of loss.

Whatcha Doin?

"Above all be of single aim, have a legitimate and useful purpose, and devote yourself unreservedly to it."

- James Allen

Objectives will fail to motivate, inspire, and engage your people. People—all people—want to be a part of something bigger than themselves. This is one of the reasons that teams are so powerful—a person now belongs to a group larger than himself. This is why a bold vision statement is impactful. It calls people into a story bigger than themselves. An outcome has the potential to inspire; an objective can only instruct. . Here is a story you may have heard before but is worth retelling, as it illustrates this point perfectly:

In the middle ages, a king hired some workers to complete a project. One afternoon, he stopped to assess the progress. As he explored the site, he saw three workers, all hitting a large stone with a piece of iron. The king asked each one of them individually what they were doing. The first man replied, "I'm chiseling a stone." The second man replied, "I'm constructing a wall." The third man replied, "I'm building a cathedral."

Which one of those workers do you think was the most engaged? Which one was the least engaged? Which one was focused on outcomes, and which one was focused on objectives? Which one do you think cared the most, and would work the hardest, to ensure that the cathedral is perfect? The story is familiar, but the principle is timeless—an objective-based focus limits inspiration.

Equally damaging, a focus on objectives also limits *innovation*. The myopic nature of objectives (climbing the rungs of the ladder) tends to lead managers to create control systems. These control systems are used to monitor performance and behavior. The manager will then look for his employee's performance and behavior compared to the standard plan and take corrective action on any deviations. An objective-based focus controls deviations and ensures consistent, normal, and predictable results.

But, isn't deviation a major source of new ideas and innovation for a company? And if a leader creates these control systems ensuring the achievement of siloed objectives, where does innovation come from? Where do new ideas come from? There are none. Those organizations don't have any meaningful new ideas or real innovation. What does this do to the company's ultimate desired outcome? It reduces its impact— significantly!

Show us an organization who is highly focused on objectives, and we will show you an organization with compartmentalized teams capable of making lots of points, but unable of making a difference. Lacking trust, they will lack innovation as they compete against each other for the same resources, leveraging the power of challenge as a control factor instead of a creative force. Every. Single. Time. What's the alternative?

Direction Setting

The conscious leader will focus on outcomes. He won't make long-term granular plans, focusing on the objectives—the "how." Instead, he will engage in long-range direction setting, focusing on the outcomes—the "what."

There may be many different versions of "how," but there will be very few variations of "what." The company really has only a couple critical outcomes essential to success. Those outcomes should act as the compass for the company's various departments.

Note that when a conscious leader sets the direction instead of building the plans, he empowers his people. He gives them a map and provides them with the final destination. Although he is more than willing to coach his people, he gives them the freedom to determine the best way to travel. This form of outcome-based leadership is only possible if you have hired high-capacity people working in an environment characterized by high levels of trust.

The conventional leader, through his objective-laden plans, gathers control to himself. He is a "micromanager." Instead of a map, he gives his people a GPS and then tracks their every move. It doesn't really matter who he hired, or how talented they are, because he removes all autonomy and freedom to think or act independently.

Outcome centricity fosters empowerment and keeps everyone aligned, moving in the same direction. Objectives demand tight controls and detailed plans. Why? Objectives might vary wildly between different departments; outcomes won't. By nature, a singular, outcome-based focus removes intra-organizational sabotage and wasteful competition over resources. If everyone is motivated and engaged, moving in the same direction, fueled by the same inspiration, performance should improve. Although this might be intuitive, it is rarely implemented. Why?

Focusing on outcomes is difficult. Outcomes are much less tangible than objectives. They are hard to define and measure. To harness the power of outcome centricity successfully, you are required to understand both the big picture (forest) perspective of the organization as well as your department's role within that picture (trees). You must be able to recognize the interconnections between different business functions. You must be able to play chess. How many "leaders" do you know that are capable of doing that? Could Julie? Could your boss? Could you? Could your team?

Chess players are extremely effective. They create a single, unifying outcome aligning the entire organization. Their teams rally around this desired outcome and are empowered to make decisions that will transform that vision into reality. These are the leaders who generate impact; they know where to place their ladder.

So, how does a leader best define the outcome? That leads us into our first sub-principle of this chapter:

Sub-principle #1:
Diagnosis, not Development
"The problem is we don't understand the problem."
- Paul MacCready

Conventional leadership loves to develop solutions to problems and create action plans. And conventional leadership, through catchy acronyms and good marketing, has made those action plans exciting and memorable.

The myth is that these quickly developed, solution-focused action plans will make a difference. Believing this myth, when initially encountering a problem, conventional leaders begin mass-producing solutions. Lots of time is spent developing solutions; very little time is spent understanding the problem. We are left executing multiple action plans and solution diagrams without generating any meaningful results—except personal frustration.

This sub-principle, although in the performance domain, is related to the "Depth, not Breadth" sub-principle within the people domain. There are some similarities, but there are also many differences. The fundamental, shared belief is that in order to accurately diagnose a problem—people or performance—you must really understand it at a root level. When dealing with people, the nuances involve communication and connection. This section is dedicated to those nuances related to performance.

When faced with a problem, the conscious leader will not immediately rush to provide a solution. Instead, he will ask difficult questions required to identify the core issue, knowing that some of these questions might actually inflame and provoke the situation even further. The conscious leader often devotes more time to understanding the problem and framing the issue than to actually developing the solution. Why? More value is created in understanding and framing the problem than in developing the solution. Without an accurate diagnosis, impact is impossible.

For example, consider a typical visit to a doctor's office. To illustrate this principle, we have categorized the visit into two sections: problem diagnosis and solution development. As you read through this example, identify exactly where the value was created:

- **Background:** Your throat is sore and red; you are coughing; your body aches; and you are running a high fever.

- **Problem Diagnosis:** You fill out a mountain of paperwork in the lobby, documenting your past medical history and current symptoms. The nurse calls you back to a room, asks you a battery of questions, takes samples of blood and urine, and then leaves. After 10 games of Solitaire, the doctor walks in. She reads your paperwork and the notes taken by the nurse. She asks you some clarifying questions regarding your symptoms and examines the results of your blood/ urine analysis. She then looks at your throat, listens to your lungs, and inspects your lymph nodes. After taking some more notes, she pronounces that you have strep throat.

- **Solution Development:** The doctor then pulls a pad of paper from her drawer and writes you a prescription for an antibiotic. You take that prescription to the pharmacy and get it filled. You start taking the medicine, and within 24 hours, you feel noticeably better.

In this example, where was the value created? You might have felt better once you started taking the medicine, but that isn't where the value was created. Remember the principle of time delay with regard to performance. The value was created through the accurate diagnosis of the problem (the doctor's determination of the illness), not the development of the solution (writing a prescription and having it filled at the pharmacy).

Once a proper diagnosis was made, anyone could go to the Internet, find a current Physicians' Desk Reference, and identify the appropriate medication. The solution to strep throat is an antibiotic. Once the problem has been accurately defined, even a 12 year-old, armed only with the Internet and her seventh-grade life science education, could develop an a appropriate and satisfactory action plan.

We visit the doctor and pay her money to accurately diagnose the problem. She didn't need to go to school for 15 years to learn that the solution to strep throat was an antibiotic. She went to school for 15 years to learn how to differentially and accurately diagnose strep throat. If she had made a mistake and misdiagnosed your illness (you really had a viral flu), the antibiotic would have been worthless.

Without proper diagnosis, the solution is irrelevant. So, what's required to accurately diagnose the problem? Accurate beliefs.

You need to believe in the critical importance of diagnosis. If you believe that the diagnosis is more important than the solution, your behaviors will change. You will ask more questions, probe at a deeper level, and look for additional interconnections. You will spend the extra time, effort, and energy because you believe in the value of the diagnosis. Only once you have accurately diagnosed the problem will you begin developing the solution.

Conventional leadership doesn't believe in the value of diagnosis. It believes in the value of the action plan. And if one action plan is good, then seven action plans must be great!

The Conventional Achievement Awards

You don't have to look very far into corporations today to uncover the focus placed on developing viable solutions. These solutions often present themselves in the form of action plans. The rush to develop solutions, however, without accurately diagnosing the problem, has led to many action plans that are nothing short of comical. Yet, conventional leadership, through fancy names, acronyms, guerilla marketing, and peer pressure, has gained significant recognition for some of these terms to a degree nothing short of remarkable.

Thus, it is only fitting that we pause for a moment of transparency. We want to ensure that you fully grasp the magnitude of conventional leadership's contribution to the action plan. We think that the fair thing to do is to celebrate these "meaningful" contributions. Let's begin the program:

It is our honor to recognize conventional leadership's achievement in the category of action plans. We are fortunate to have been given so many meaningful and memorable action plans throughout the years. Tonight's celebration is dedicated to recognizing the best of those plans. Many plans were nominated, and we have chosen to honor four plans for their contribution to conventional leadership.

4th place: The Performance Improvement Plan (PIP)

This action plan is used with employees whose performance has been poor for an extended period of time. The PIP masquerades as a tool capable of reversing this trend of underperformance. With complete transparency, it allows the employee to regain good standing with the company. A PIP consists of the following: establishment of lofty goals never previously considered attainable, allocation of a short time period in which the employee must reach those goals, and managerial disengagement in the employee's pursuit of these goals. If the employee can deliver on these objectives, he can regain his good status within the company. If not, termination of employment is the probable next step.

The PIP is remarkable because it sees only outcomes, ignoring not only beliefs but also behaviors. So, where is the value in the PIP? Under the guise of partnership, the PIP provides a method of terminating employment while reducing the probability of a pending lawsuit. This plan makes the top four because, despite its name, it has nothing to do with improving performance.

3rd place: The Long-Range Business Plan (LRBP)

The LRBP is the fastest mover this year, gaining considerable traction in current corporate circles. The standard LRBP is a 60 page document—not including the appendix—devoted to mapping out detailed business plans over the next several years. Lots of time, effort, and money are invested into this plan annually. Despite its name, within 180 days post-launch, the LRBP frequently has become meaningless. Why? The dynamic environment.

The marketplace continues to change consistently, quickly, and dramatically. As the external and internal landscapes evolve, they significantly change the business assumptions upon which the LRBP was founded. For example, the introduction of electricity immediately rendered the candle makers' LRBPs worthless! Should the pace of change slow, the plan would still be worthless within 180 days post-launch. Why? No one can remember 60 pages worth of material for that long. Regardless, at the beginning of next year, in an effort to demonstrate commitment and preparedness, the team will march right back into those meetings and begin creating a new LRBP. Unless your definition of "long-range" is 180 days, the LRBP can't plan for anything. The use of irony gets it a third-place finish.

2nd place: The 30-60-90 Day Plan

Conventional leadership has made this a requirement for interviewing. The candidate, interviewing for a new position either internally or externally, creates and presents a thorough list of what he will do and achieve within the first 30, 60, and 90 days of starting his new position—should he get the job. Displaying creativity that was inspiration to the LRBP, the 30-60-90 document should be named the "Seven-Day Plan." After the first seven days (which always include meeting stakeholders, meeting the team, getting set up with IT, etc.), nothing else on this plan ever materializes. Why?

The actual content of the plan, outside of the first seven days, is inaccurate. The only person capable of creating a workable 30-60-90 day plan for that role is the one either currently in the role or the one hiring for the role. The interviewee, lacking perspective, takes his best shot, but he creates the plan while he is at stage one of the Adult Learning Model (Unconscious Incompetence). Although he doesn't know what he doesn't know, he is still asked for a plan. But…the 30-60-90 has more to offer. After making a strong run at the gold, the 30-60-90 takes second place this year.

Its brilliance is not just its seven-day lifespan, but its ability to induce hypocrisy. Presented during an interview, both the candidate and interviewer know the plan is meaningless. They both know that by the eighth day, the plan will be in a garbage can. And they know that the other person also knows this. But, as lots of time and effort is expended developing this plan, they both pretend it is useful, and it is thoroughly discussed in the interview. Sometimes, it is even used as justification for decisions made during the hiring process (either positive or negative). Impressive!

1st place: The "Solution-Based" Plan

This plan wins top prize due to outstanding marketing! Today, you can find solution-based dialogue, solution-based selling, solution-based service, and even solution-based leadership. Our competitive intelligence department reports that conventional leadership is working on developing something even bigger…the *solution-based solution*!

The original premise driving the solution-based campaign is legitimate. It focuses on solving the needs and problems of the issue at hand, instead of just promoting an unrelated agenda. And, we are aligned with this premise! The marketing genius here, however, is the complete divorce of the "what" from the "how." The solution-based system suggests they operate independently from each other. Advising someone to engage in solution-based anything is like telling someone who is poor to make more money. Of course they want more money, just like you want solutions to your problems—the "what." The missing pieces are the previous steps in the equation (i.e., the "how" of making more money). This is where the challenge lies. A person is not poor because they lacked the knowledge that money was the solution to poverty. They are poor because they lacked the wisdom to know how to make more money.

Conventional leadership's complete and utter disregard for common sense, its boldness to continue to offer the "what" without the "how" as a viable choice, and its marketing ability allow the "solution-based" plan to stand above the competition this year. Our solution? First place!

We hope you enjoyed the award ceremony.

Questions or Answers

"A prudent question is one-half of wisdom."
          - Francis Bacon

Becoming serious once again, we need to ask why we so naturally drawn towards developing solutions. Solution development is appealing for the same reason that focusing on behaviors/outcomes is appealing: it is tangible and easy.

But leadership isn't about developing solutions, it is about defining problems. This is difficult, because as a leader, you feel pressure to have the answers and provide the solutions. But remember, the primary role of a leader is not to answer questions, but to ask them. Leaders ask new questions; managers answer questions that have already been asked. It is much more difficult to define an unknown problem than it is to solve a known problem. Diagnosis requires asking questions, not providing answers.

Conventional leadership can apply knowledge to a problem and develop a solution that might be somewhat effective. But you probably aren't satisfied with solutions that are somewhat effective. If you aren't satisfied with somewhat effective, mediocre, normal solutions, you must do the difficult work.

The difficult work, which is most-often neglected, is diagnosing the problem. The conscious leader will apply wisdom to discover the root issue by asking the right questions and looking for the right information. Once the problem is correctly diagnosed, the development of the correct solution will occur naturally. Focus your resources on diagnosing the problem.

As leaders, we shouldn't fear developing the wrong solution to a problem. We should fear developing the right solution to the wrong problem.

The LRBP is a great example of what can happen when you jump to developing solutions without first diagnosing problems—it is neither effective nor efficient. Accurate diagnosis of a problem is one of the best cures for inefficiency, and this brings us to our next sub-principle:

Sub-principle #2:
Productivity, not Activity

This sub-principle is frequently quoted—often by the same conventional leaders who are focused on objectives. This is either comical or hypocritical—or sometimes both. You cannot simultaneously be objective-focused and productivity-focused. The concepts are mutually exclusive. Focusing on objectives (instead of outcomes) will always limit productivity.

The result of this confusion is activity and busyness. Conventional leadership loves to be busy. The lure of activity is strong. Why?

Activity is placing a television in front of a treadmill, running while watching a show about natural parks. You see scenery changing; you hear birds chirping; you are breathing heavily, and your legs are moving. Although you might feel like you are running through mountains and valleys, you're not. You are completely stationary. Activity provides the illusion of impact. You feel like you are getting something done. But, remember the firefighting arsonist. Often, you are busy putting out fires you helped create.

This sub-principle takes the fire-fighting arsonist idea a step further. Activity doesn't just seduce the employee into thinking he is making an impact; it also seduces the manager of that employee. A heavy focus on activity provides even the weakest manager the ability to track the progress of his employee and hold him "accountable." Conventional leadership loves activity as it provides them feelings of power and control. Although these conventional leaders are holding their employees accountable to activities that contribute nothing towards the desired outcome, they can masquerade as leaders who know what they're doing.

Busted

"To know how to disguise is the knowledge of kings."
   - Cardinal De Richelieu

Productivity exposes frauds. Productivity demands results. You either move the organization forward towards its desired outcome, or you don't. You either generate impact, or you don't. Productivity exposes treadmills—those belonging to both the employee and the manager.

Activity can mask incompetence. But ineptitude cannot hide when you are asked to really produce. Productivity makes it immediately apparent which leaders are playing checkers and which leaders are playing chess. Productivity demands decisions that are right, not decisions that are fair and easy. It creates real accountability for both the employee and the manager.

But when this concept (productivity instead of activity) is truly "walked" and not just "talked," the difference can be staggering. Once you define the outcome, and get your team aligned around that outcome, you are free to truly engage in triage, neglecting the urgent activities that don't move you in that direction. You produce the "what's" that lead you towards tomorrow's vision, and don't worry about the "how's" along the way. You don't check the clock, you check the numbers. It is a very liberating principle. How can you spot an activity-focused leader? There are two tell-tale signs: Change for the sake of change and control for the sake of control.

Change for the Sake of Change

Conscious leadership is about impactful change—change that makes a positive difference. This means that change is purposeful and intentional. And it means that change is initially internal; you change the world by first changing yourself. But if impact is the ultimate outcome, it also means that there are times when you shouldn't change.

Change is a means to an end, not an end in itself. In isolation, change is an activity. The result of the change will define its effectiveness. Conscious leadership is about changing beliefs to generate impact.

Conventional leaders, especially those who are activity-focused, use change to avoid accountability. If they can create a situation where the goalposts are constantly moving, they never have to face true responsibility. Why do you think companies are constantly in a state of restructuring (a large, organizational change)? Sure, some of it's due to the dynamic environment. And it's a good thing when it's done right, and when it's done for the right reasons; motives matter.

A large restructuring effort removes accountability. When performance drops, a conventional leader blames others and announces the need for change. Then, through company write-offs and departmental re-organization, both the organization and the individual avoid responsibility. The organization is not accountable to the investors, and an individual is not accountable to the organization. Conventional leaders fondly refer to this as taking one step backwards to take two steps forwards. Change for the sake of change allows the conventional leader to avoid responsibility.

Control for the Sake of Control

One word: Micromanager. Pause for a moment and think back to the most notorious micromanager you have ever worked for. He loved administrative work and details. He would ask you to complete multiple checklists, reformat the same material into 12 different documents, and assign you tasks worded to sound important, but incapable of producing an impact.

He used those activities and objectives to maintain control over his employees, his department, and sometime, himself. Often, the micromanager is threatened by high performing employees. Their productivity has the potential to expose his ineptitude. By micro-managing every granular detail of their work, both the "how" and the "what," he controls and caps their performance. Intentionally (although perhaps subconsciously), he levels them down, and this gives him a feeling of security.

The micromanager creates unnecessary work for you to do (activity) for the sake of control. He, and his employees, will tend to be very busy; but they will rarely produce anything truly meaningful.

Ironically, the volume of meaningless work created by these micromanagers has inspired the creation of some hugely successful comedies. Are you familiar with the movie "Office Space," the TV series "The Office," or the comic strip "Dilbert"? These are all funny because we can relate them to real life—which is actually pretty sad.

Based on a True Story

Let's drop in on Julie and Todd again:

Three months have passed since senior management signed off on StarGate, and the web-portal system has launched. It isn't 100% functional yet, but it is operational. Julie and Todd have been working to deliver the desired outcome—increased net income of 14% (instead of the original 10%). Todd and Julie are meeting today to discuss StarGate—their progress to date as well as next steps:

JULIE: I need you to give me an update of your progress with StarGate, because I am very concerned. I presented an overview to senior management last week, and they are questioning our performance and our ability to deliver. They are not happy, and bottom line, several things need to happen immediately. Here is what I need you to do...

TODD: Okay, so before we get into what we need to do, can you tell me about the meeting?

JULIE: It was simple. I gave them a presentation containing our current progress with StarGate. And they weren't happy with it.

TODD: What did that update look like? What did you show them?

JULIE: I showed them the weekly goal tracker that I created (although it wasn't populated with real data yet due to design issues with the vendor). And I showed them the long-term communication plan developed to share our best practices and new capabilities with Acme's other divisions. I also shared my forecast about the additional ROI that the second and third generation versions of StarGate could produce. Finally, I showed them the five different cost-saving options that our vendor has provided and let them know that we were assembling a cross-functional team to discuss those options.

TODD: And what did they say?

JULIE: They asked why our costs were increasing, specifically in your department. You have spent more money in the last 90 days than you did in the last six months! At this pace, we won't even hit our original 10% budget. They also asked why the customer service score is down and why our inventory levels have increased.

TODD: So did you tell them why? As they are all strategic business people, I would think that they should have at least been satisfied, if not impressed, with the rationale.

JULIE: Impressed about what? I don't know what I could have told them that would have impressed them.

TODD: Well, the ordering portal has gone live, and we have introduced it to our customers through an innovative program that is new to the industry—it combines training and marketing! While we train them on how to use the system, we are simultaneously marketing the additional benefits of the portal (and our products) to their business. In addition, we are leveraging our time with an engaged audience to communicate our flipchart campaign with them. That's 3 in 1! It's never been done before, and it's reducing the time-to-market for the flipchart campaign by over 12 months! Think about the impact that this could have for the other divisions and their products. How were they not impressed?

JULIE: But that program costs extra money. And our customer service score has suffered.

TODD: Of course it has...what did they think would happen initially? We overspent in the last 3 months with this training, but now that our customers are using the system, we will be able to greatly reduce our investment in our outsourced customer call center. This will offset those extra costs. The savings over the next nine months will exceed the additional expenditures of the past three months. And the decline in customer service is only temporary as we are currently making adjustments to the outsourced call center. It should return to its normal rates within the next two months. Again, this is to be expected. We are on track to produce some solid performance results. So I'm just really confused as to how they weren't impressed.

JULIE: Well, I hope you are correct. Right now it just looks bad. So here is what has to change immediately as a result of that meeting...

TODD: Wait! We still haven't discussed their reaction to the most exciting part of the update. What about the new business?

Julie, like many conventional leaders, excels at activity. She was very active, creating plenty of documentation for senior management—including reports explaining other reports. But she struggled to produce performance. And when Todd, like senior management, begins to question her productivity, her pretense is removed. Ineptitude can be concealed with activity but is revealed though productivity.

JULIE: Can you be more specific?

TODD: So you know the customers loved StarGate and were blown away with our innovation. We are beginning to move away from our current commodity brand status. And, three of the five biggest players in the market wanted to sign exclusive deals with Acme for the flipchart program (now launching within the next 90 days). That is why I had to begin to order the extra inventory. Surely you told senior management all of that...and they still weren't impressed?

JULIE (flustered, confused): Of course I did. Why wouldn't I have? I told you I gave them a status update and overview. And to reiterate, they were concerned about our performance. We are not producing desired results.

TODD (not believing her): Their reaction doesn't make any sense. But I guess we can deal with that.

JULIE: We will have to. So before we talk about what I need from you, do you have any questions for me?

TODD: Actually, I do have some important business questions for you. I need your advice. What are the ramifications, legally and logistically, of exclusivity deals with customers of this size? What is Acme's private-label branding policy? I want to make sure that we get it right, because the business from those three big players will generate more than enough revenue for us to hit our 14%.

JULIE: I have no idea, and why does that matter? Obviously we can't be exclusive with three customers at the same time, just one. That's just common sense. Is this really part of your plan?

TODD: Sure we can. We alter the flipchart slightly—in three different ways. This will create three different sets of SKU's for use within each customer's own private-label brand. We can do this while simultaneously selling Acme-branded flipcharts (at a higher price/quality to improve our brand's perceived value). The customers now have exclusivity with their own unique flipchart that is private labeled. I know this is complex, and I am not sure that I have it 100% correct—that is why I need your advice.

JULIE (confused and frustrated): So why would these customers want their own private-label brand on products that are almost identical to ours with Acme branding? That makes no sense.

TODD: Sure it does, that's one of the big benefits of private labeling. Think about your local grocery store and all the different brands of laundry detergent that you can buy—store brand and name brand. It allows the private-label brand to benefit with good products (sold cheaply). It allows our brand to benefit (being seen as higher-end products). And it allows both us and them to further define and segment the market—all while selling more product!

JULIE (arrogantly): Todd, if you are "exclusive" with one particular customer, then obviously you can't sell your products to other customers. And I don't know why a customer would want to buy almost two identical products. If this is your big plan, then we really are in trouble...

TODD: Huh? I don't understand. Maybe I'm not explaining this well. Let me start from the top.

JULIE: No, don't. I can't waste any more time on these crazy ideas. Here is what we are going to do: 1. I need you to provide me with detailed updates—weekly. Use the template that I created. I want each section broken out and filled in completely.

2. Provide me with a long-range plan detailing the effect of your decision to reduce our investment in the outsourced call center. 3. Before any customer visits, I want you to send me a copy of your final proposal for them, along with this customer-analysis template filled out. 4. After each call, I want you to fill out this call note template that includes the individuals you contacted, as well as a forecast for their business with Acme for the rest of the year. I would like that forecast to go to the product-category level. 5. Send me your calendar two months in advance with a list of customers that you plan on visiting.

TODD: What?!? This mak   es no sense. I'm not going to have time to visit any more potential customers because I will be spending all my time filling out reports.

JULIE: Todd, at the end of our last meeting you agreed that you would be accountable for delivering these results. And so I'm just holding you accountable to produce. That's what leadership is all about.

Natural Reaction

Okay, that might have been a little over the top. But unfortunately, it was probably not a lot over the top. This dialogue provides a good comparison between activity and productivity. It is okay for management to question and examine progress within key programs. In fact, it is a good thing. Never be afraid to inspect what you expect. Yet these interactions exposed Julie and her true beliefs, specifically regarding activity and productivity.

Julie had been very busy, and had prepared lots of reports and plans to show management. Unfortunately, her activity had made very little impact. We can assume that senior management was underwhelmed with what she said, and as a result, they began asking her questions regarding not her activity, but her productivity. These were difficult questions that were tough to answer.

Remember, focusing on outcomes and productivity requires chess, not checkers. You must have a thorough mastery of the big picture as well as an understanding of the important details. Unfortunately, Julie was playing checkers. She didn't understand the impact that Todd's initiatives would have on the overall business results. She hadn't accurately diagnosed the problem, and she didn't understand the context and her environment.

A focus on productivity and outcomes revealed her ineptitude—both to senior management and to Todd.

In this situation, the reaction of a conscious leader, being self-aware and humble, would have been to wisely stop, reflect, and ask some questions. He would have sought to diagnose the problem accurately, which would have resulted in his increased comprehension of the entire situation.

What was her natural reaction? The same as any other conventional leaders—more control and micromanagement. She developed activity-based solutions. But she didn't make an impact.

Your Story

Performance is a hallmark of conscious leadership. It is difficult, if not impossible, to generate impact without performance.

Performing with excellence should be a constant theme throughout your story as a conscious leader. It should be intertwined throughout each chapter. But performance should not be the plot of your story. Performance, although it is observed first, is best addressed by taking action in the domains of people and process. High-quality inputs yield a high-quality output.

To generate high-quality on a consistent basis, you need to believe that the output is an outcome, not an objective. Spend your energy diagnosing the problem, asking the difficult questions. Once you have created the proper framework, then you are in a place to develop the proper solution. Neglecting this step will result in leadership that is active but not productive.

Supported by a solid foundation of people and process, performance is the pinnacle of conscious leadership. The performance of a conscious leader is not normal or standard; it is different. Quality performance is always noticed. Impact can't be hidden.

Impact is the ultimate output. You have the potential to consistently generate impact, but you have to change the inputs. High-quality beliefs yield powerful impact.

Mirror, Mirror on the Wall...Chapter 10

The Conscious Leader's Toolbox

1. **Questions:** Are you currently evaluated by objectives or outcomes? Why? Do you assess the performance of your team by objectives or outcomes? Why? If we asked your team the same question, would their answers align with yours?

2. **Questions:** Do you find it easier to diagnose problems or develop solutions? Why?

3. **Questions:** Think of an example over the past six months where you developed a solution without having accurately diagnosed the problem. What did you think the problem was? What was your solution? What was the result? What was the real problem? What would you have done differently?

4. **Questions:** Think of an example over the past six months where you spent time accurately diagnosing the problem before you developed a solution. What was the final framework of the problem? How was the problem different than it appeared at first glance? What was the subsequent solution you developed? What was the result?

5. **Questions:** What were the differences between Question #3 and Question #4? How can you respond like you did in Question #4 more frequently?

6. **Questions:** Where do you feel that you are most productive at work? What makes that area so productive? How could you replicate that level of productivity in other areas of your work?

7. **Strategic Map:** Revisit the following portions of your strategic map. If you haven't already, fill out the following sections. If these are already completed, revisit them and determine if there is anything that you want to change.
   - **B.** Tomorrow Statement
   - **C.** Vision
   - **D.** Mission
   - **E.F.** (Doesn't have to be fully completed) Belief, Behavior

8. **Value Identifier:** Complete the following exercises to help you define your output and distinguish between activity and productivity.

Value Identifier

Defining the Output

- All work (goods or services) have inputs and outputs
- Intellectual work involves making decisions or solving problems
    - Input: What is our starting point? What product/material/information do we receive?
        - Easy to define
    - Output: What is the finished product? What value have we added? What do we sell?
        - Very difficult to define

Input (specifically):

- What is your starting point?
- What material/information do you receive?
- What problem are you being asked to solve?
- What are you being given? What are you asked to do with it?

Output (specifically):

- Who are your customers?
- What is most important to them?
- How would your customers define your output?
- What do you make/create?
- How do you change the input you receive?
- What problems have you solved or decisions have you made?

Notes

CONSCIOUS
LEADERSHIP

Value Identifier

Activity or Productivity

- All activities can be classified into 1 of 3 categories:
  - Value: Activity that changes shape/nature of product, increases worth
    - Example: Machining sheet metal into curved tubes
  - Non-Value: Activity required to perform value-adding process
    - Example: Transporting sheet metal from the receiving dock to the workstation
  - Waste: Loss of time, energy, resources
    - Example: Sheet metal was shaped incorrectly and material had to be scrapped

Activity	Classification (Value, Non-Value, Waste)	Reason	Potential for Improvement

Notes

CONSCIOUS
LEADERSHIP

Reflection Points

- High performance is critically important—the hallmark of conscious leadership
- Performance is observed first, but addressed last
  - o Cause-and-effect
    - Performance is the output, people and process are the inputs
  - o Time-delay
- I don't believe in objectives; I believe in outcomes.
  - o Make sure your ladder is leaning against the right building
  - o Objectives
    - Safe, trackable, easy, measurable (but not always meaningful)
    - Result in intra-department competition for resources
    - Reduce potential for creativity and innovation
  - o Outcomes
    - Difficult to define and measure (multiple factors)
    - Creates alignment and focus within team
    - Leader must be capable of playing chess
- Diagnosis, not Development
  - o Value is created by understanding the real issue
  - o Once problem is accurately defined, solution will often be self-evident
  - o Ask questions before you provide answers
  - o Create a framework for the problem
  - o Solve for the right problem
- Productivity, not Activity
  - o Activity
    - Illusion of making a difference, getting things done
    - Managers can track and hold accountable
    - Change for the sake of change
    - Control for the sake of control
  - o Productivity
    - Exposes ineptitude
    - Requires wisdom
    - Creates accountability and leads to difficult decisions

CONSCIOUS
LEADERSHIP

CHAPTER 11

UNAVOIDABLE AND INDISPENSABLE

"Lord, deliver me from the man who never makes a mistake, and also from the man who makes the same mistake twice."
- Dr. William J. Mayo

"You can always pitch better."
- Sandy Koufax

<u>Axiom:</u>
**I don't believe in best practices;
I believe in better practices.**

If we were sitting across the table from you in Las Vegas, right now we would place our wallet on the table and make a bet with you. The wager: at some point within the last six months you have been challenged to embrace a best practice. Would you take that bet? If you countered, and changed the time frame from six months to six weeks, we wouldn't blink. Our wallet remains on the table. Six days? We would hesitate, but we would probably still keep our wallet on the table (although we might take some cash out of it just in case).

Chances are, you are most likely confronted with the idea of best practices every six *hours*.

Here is the problem: there is no such thing as a best practice. They don't exist. They are a myth of conventional leadership. And if you believe in best practices, you will have a hard time generating new ideas that can truly create impact.

A best practice assumes that there is no room for improvement. The word "best" is superlative. Best, by design, cannot be advanced or progressed. The myth of best practices assumes that the environment is static—like a photograph. Unfortunately, we are asked to spend a sizable portion of our resources—including time, money, and energy—communicating, standardizing, and enforcing best practices. So we issue a new best practice, but as soon as it is implemented, it becomes obsolete, and we have to begin again with a new "best" practice. Why?

Your world isn't static; it's dynamic. Your environment doesn't resemble a photograph, it resembles a video. What is best today will not be best tomorrow.

A brief glance through the history of business will validate this principle. This concept explains why blue-chip companies that attain market dominance and for a period of time appear invincible, eventually fail. The collapse of these renowned giants often comes at the hands of companies previously unheard of and unrecognized. The juggernaut killers don't just dethrone the incumbent and take over the market; they create an entirely new market.

The 8-track, vinyl record, cassette tape, and compact disc were all best practices within the music industry. The telegraph, the fixed-line telephone, and the long-distance telephone service were all best practices within the communications industry. The candle was the best practice—for centuries—in the lighting industry. Yet all of these "best practices" were replaced by…wait for it…*better practices*.

The idea of best practices encourages complacency. If you are already implementing the best method of doing a job, there is no need to search for potential improvements. Importantly, there is no reason to consider other new ideas. Why should you? If you are currently implementing best practices, there is no need to invite challenge or intentionally orchestrate conflict.

The "Best Practice" Best Practice

Does this conversation sound familiar?

In addition to holding weekly one-on-one meetings with her direct reports, Julie also conducts bi-weekly meetings with her leadership team (including Todd). One of the goals of these meetings is the sharing of best practices. The intention is that during these meetings, her team will share their best practices with the rest of the group, and then each leader will distribute them to their respective teams. Julie is meeting with Todd (his one-on-one) after the most recent leadership team meeting:

JULIE: I have an idea I want to run by you. I am frustrated with our lack of ability to effectively communicate and implement best practices across the division. We have these great ideas, and we keep them to ourselves. So, I think we need a standardized approach that guarantees the deployment of these best practices across the division.
TODD: So...you want to create a best practice...for sharing best practices?
JULIE: I guess that's right.
TODD: Maybe, but I don't know. I think we do a decent job of sharing best practices right now. Not every new idea applies to every department. I think you are doing a good job right now orchestrating the sharing of these ideas between leaders. Every other week, your entire leadership team gets a high-level overview of what everyone else is doing. When someone

shares an idea that might impact my department, I follow up with that person after the meeting. This allows me to make sure I understand it completely and get clarity on the aspects that might apply to my team.

JULIE: But how many best practices do you miss because you think they don't apply to your department?

TODD: Um...I don't know. I don't think many.

JULIE: Right, you don't know for sure. That means that you could be missing some. So here is the plan: every month, each member of your team will send you five best practices they discovered. From that list, you select the top five you think would be applicable to the broader audience. Then you, along with the rest of my leadership team, will each post the best practices you chose to our company's intranet. Each month, the entire division, including you and your team, will go to that intranet site and comment on each best practice. This ensures that they are seen by all, and nothing is missed. Then, during our bi-weekly meetings, we can discuss those comments.

TODD: I don't know. I'm a little worried. Specifically, I guess I have two concerns. First, I am afraid that people will spend their time commenting on best practices that are not applicable to them. Second, it seems like we will be spending a lot of time talking about best practices instead of actually implementing them.

JULIE: What do you mean?

TODD: I'm just afraid that it won't be the most productive use of everyone's time. You have six reports on your leadership team, and we each have a team of reports, so that means that there will be a total of around 30-40 best practices posted each month. Do you really want every person in your entire division to comment on all of them each month?

JULIE: Isn't that the idea? It will ensure that we don't miss anything. Once this gets up and rolling, and people get comfortable with it, then we could create another section on the site. People could use that section to post success they experienced by implementing newly learned best practices. I think everyone should be able to post at least one new success each month, don't you? Think of all of the cross-functional collaboration and innovation this communication system of best practices will create.

TODD (Silent...still silent...finally): So, can I challenge you a little bit here?

This scene, and all of its ridiculousness, is probably being acted out right now in some organization today. Hopefully not yours...

The Costume Party

"Don't worry about people stealing an idea. If it's original, you will have to ram it down their throats."

    - Howard Aiken

Make no mistake; we are not claiming that a leader shouldn't learn new ideas from others. In fact, the concept of importing new ideas from external sources is one of the core tenets of conscious leadership. What we are asserting, however, is that the resources and energy required to import the new idea should be proportionate to its potential impact. Conventional leadership tends to overestimate this potential because it is not well-connected with the environment and underestimates the pace of change.

The real potential impact of most of the "best" practices is not equal to the resources required to successfully export/import them. You know this is true. So does the leader who created the system and is currently championing its value. So, why does conventional leadership spend all this effort communicating "best" practices knowing there is limited potential for impact?

Think back to our original discussion about the difference between a manager and a true leader. A manager wants to create systems that provide control. His desired outcome is normal—normal people executing normal jobs in a normal fashion producing normal results. The institutionalization of best practices affords him the opportunity to establish control and normalize results under the guise of a bastion of impact.

A hyper-focus on best-practice standardization is symptomatic of a manager masquerading as a leader, or a conventional leader impersonating a conscious leader. A conscious leader recognizes that questions are more important than answers. A leader sets a new direction by asking questions that challenge the status quo. A manager is driven to provide answers that reinforce the status quo. The concept of best practices is all about providing answers. The concept of better practices is all about asking questions.

Belief in better practices allows us to acknowledge that not all ideas are equal. Some ideas have limited value, and limited resources should be allocated towards their importation/exportation. This belief also acknowledges that the rapidly changing environment reduces the lifespan of new ideas. An idea that is novel today can be obsolete tomorrow. If you are a believer in better practices, it is very difficult to become complacent with normal and content with the status quo. A belief in better practices invites challenge and change.

But doesn't the idea of best practices do all of this as well? Not really. Think about the last time your department launched a new initiative that was based on a best practice. As this best practice was exported from another department and imported into your department, was it customized and tailored? Was it significantly improved during the export/import process? Probably not. Chances are, the best practice that your department launched was a direct copy of the original.

Why wasn't the best practice improved upon? Was it really because that specific best practice was in a state of perfection, rendering improvement impossible? Did your department lack the competence to customize it, tailor it, or improve it through the adoption process?

No, none of the above questions provide solid explanation as to why the best practice was not enhanced. Most likely, the best practice was not perfect. It could have been improved, and your department was capable of improving it during the adoption process. But that didn't happen. Belief in best practices results in a "cut and paste" mentality.

So, what would have been the outcome had your department believed in better practices? The initial version of the initiative would still be considered the starting point—the point of reference. But, prior to launch, there would have been questions, challenges, and conflict resulting in refinement, improvement, and enhancement. Why? Because your department believed that this program wasn't the best way; it was simply a better way than your previous way.

If you embrace better practices, you will be more likely to spot untapped potential, because you are looking for it. A belief in better practices allows for more adjustments and faster course-corrections than a belief in best practices.

This might seem like semantics. It's not; words matter. If you force yourself to embrace better practices instead of best practices, you will force yourself to ask questions that lead to improvement and maximize potential. And as a conscious leader, that's really what you want—to be able to create more impact tomorrow than you can today.

Woven tightly within the myth of best practices is another myth of conventional leadership, which brings us to the following sub-principle:

Sub-principle #1:
Embrace Failure, but Challenge Faults

"It may be all right to be content with what you have; never with what you are."
- B.C. Forbes

Both ends of this sub-principle warrant significant exploration. There are some powerful myths of conventional leadership that need to be debunked to fully comprehend and leverage this concept. A series of faulty beliefs have been widely accepted as truth. However, if you can debunk those myths and change your beliefs, you will enable yourself to benefit from a tremendously powerful principle.

Let's start with a simple definition of terms. We won't draw any conclusions based on these definitions, but we want to establish a common framework to ensure alignment as we continue:

- **Failure:** External in nature; Substandard, inferior performance that does not meet expectations.
- **Faults:** Internal in nature; Imperfect character that is flawed, blemished, or deficient.

How do failure and faults relate to our fundamental model (Belief ➜ Behavior ➜ Outcome)? Failures primarily occur at the outcome level of the model. They are tangible and highly visible. You will notice a failure. A failure is a "point-in-time" event; it doesn't persist indefinitely. Once you have failed, that moment is over.

Note that we consider failure as primarily relating to outcomes, not behaviors. It is true that a failed outcome is the result of an inadequate behavior. However, rarely will you notice—or be affected—by a failed behavior not tied to an outcome. For example, if a sales representative communicates abrasively with customers, the behavior is not typically considered to be a failure; it might be ignored. However, when the angered customer converts business to your competitor, the outcome is no longer ignored; it is classified as failure.

Faults, however, occur most often at the belief level. They are intangible and invisible. Unlike a failure, a fault can persist indefinitely, and it will unless it is proactively changed. A fault doesn't have a start and stop moment.

We will continue to explore this relationship between failure and faults throughout the chapter. These definitions are sufficient to launch our discussion. Let's begin by examining failure.

Failing to Believe

What do you believe about failure? This is a hard question to answer for a couple of reasons. First, it is very broad and vague. It depends largely on circumstances and situational context. Second, there is a good chance that you just don't know the answer. Why?

Mixed messages have been sent regarding failure. Conventional leadership claims failure is a necessary part of leadership. But your own experience with conventional leaders and their reaction to failure invalidates that claim; it leads you to question how they define "a necessary part." Although you hear conventional leaders say that they embrace failure, that's not what you see. You see conventional leaders who sometimes tolerate— and often penalize—failure.

Conventional leadership's flexible stance on failure has been consistently ambiguous; but a reflection upon better practices and best practices will provide some additional clarity.

If you discover a best practice, you have figured out the answer and gotten it "right." If you discover a better practice, you acknowledge that tomorrow, someone else will displace your idea with a better one. This means the better practice you just discovered will eventually be considered "wrong." What's another word for "wrong"? How about "failure"? This is yet another reason why conventional leadership prefers best practices to better practices.

Here is disturbing insight: think about your two most recent failures—specifically, failures at work. How do you feel when recall those failures? The feelings were probably unpleasant. But, what if "unpleasant" is not really the right word, as it doesn't really capture the intensity of those feelings? What if there's more? If the feeling contains dread, fear, or a sense of embarrassment, then perhaps you have bought into a myth.

Despite its verbal assertions to the contrary, conventional leadership does not believe that failure is a necessary part of leadership. Instead, it believes a myth that failure should be avoided if at all possible. If avoidance is impossible, then failure should only be tolerated.

This myth is deeply embedded into conventional leadership's thinking, despite being absent from their speaking. It has subtly infected the way we view almost everything, including people, process, and performance. And when given a foothold, this myth— this inaccurate belief about failure—has the power to cripple your ability to generate impact.

It's not enough to tolerate failure. You tolerate that which you do not accept. And not only must you accept failure, but in order to generate impact and transformational change, you must embrace it!

Identity Crisis

"Never confuse a single defeat with a final defeat."
    - F. Scott Fitzgerald

Conventional leadership is afraid of failure. It's not the "guy *watching* a horror movie, sitting in a movie theater while eating popcorn" type of fear. It's the "guy *in* a horror movie, running for his life while being chased" type of fear. And it all goes back to the original model, "Belief ➜ Behavior ➜ Outcome."

The conscious leader is aware of the distinction and separation between who he is, what he does, and what he produces. He is defined by his beliefs, not his outcomes. As the conventional leader is unaware of beliefs, he is defined by his outcomes. He cannot separate who he is from what he produces. Here is a different way of expressing this truth:

- **Conventional Leader:** "Who I am" is defined by "what I produce"
- **Conscious Leader:** "Who I am" is not defined by "what I produce"

Who you are is defined by your beliefs. As the conventional leader is not aware of beliefs, he isn't aware of this dynamic. The conventional leader believes that outcomes define who he is. However, just because the conventional leader isn't aware of these beliefs regarding the source of his identity doesn't mean he isn't impacted by them. Beliefs, either consciously or unconsciously, drive behaviors which influence outcomes.

External outcomes define the conventional leader. Internal beliefs define the conscious leader. The conscious leader controls what he believes, and thus controls who he is. Although behaviors influence outcomes, behaviors don't control outcomes. Tragically, the conventional leader can't control his perception of himself.

Failure is external—a substandard, inferior outcome. Do you want to be defined as substandard and inferior? Neither does the conventional leader. Failure is a personal indictment on the conventional leader. This isn't true; this outcome is based on a myth. However, it is the perceived reality of the conventional leader.

"External" and "internal" are somewhat relative terms. They are used to define and describe each other. In the absence of an "internal" (he isn't conscious of it), the "external" expands and becomes the default setting for everything. For the conventional leader, there is no distinction between the outcome (external) and who he is as a person (internal). So when failure occurs, "inferior" and "substandard" become terms that describe who he is, not what he does.

The conscious leader has no reason to fear or avoid failure. Failure is not an attack on his person, but a description of a result. Fueled by his beliefs, and his awareness of them, he is capable of distinguishing the "internal" and the "external." He can distinguish between who he is from what he does and what he produces. Thus, the conscious leader can experience failure, and confidently describe the external event as "inferior" without that definition becoming an indefinite critique on him personally. In some cases, the inferior outcome was ultimately driven by an inferior belief, but the conscious leader knows that he has the power to mold his beliefs to more accurately reflect the truth.

Standard Deviation

"The things we fear most in organizations—fluctuations, disturbances, imbalances—are the primary sources of creativity."
- Margaret Wheatley

When you challenge the status quo, or innovate in a non-conventional method, there are only a couple of potential outcomes. Sometimes you will succeed. Often, however, you will fail. The degree of failure may vary; failures come in all shapes and sizes. But if you deviate from normalcy with enough frequency, failure is inevitable.

The hallmark of a leader is to create meaningful change, regardless of the pending failure. Change will often result in failure. If the change is good, then the failure will be limited to the temporary perception of those who crave normalcy. If the change is bad, then the failure won't be merely perceived, it will be real. Sometimes, the change will be good but the timing will be bad, which results in temporary failure but ultimate success. However, you should be conscious of the fact that you cannot consistently generate meaningful change and not experience failure.

In fact, the level of failure experienced by a leader can be proportionate to the level of impact generated. The more change you attempt to create, the more often you will experience legitimate failure. A truly great conscious leader will fail many times as a result of continually creating change.

Impact requires change; change is a result of deviation; and deviation will result in failure. Thus, failure is required for impact; they are inseparable.

Conventional leadership doesn't believe in the correlation between failure and impact. In fact, it considers the entire relationship to be myth. In reality, the myth is the relationship between conventional leadership and impact—it is pure fiction. The conscious leader believes that failure is not just a result of transformational leadership, it is a prerequisite—an ingredient—of transformational leadership. We last visited the idea of ingredients in our discussion about knowledge and wisdom. Just as knowledge is an ingredient of wisdom, failure is an ingredient of impact.

Quantity or Quality

The recipe for wisdom also calls for failure. Failure serves as a critical catalyst for the learning process. Failure is fundamental in the conversion of knowledge into wisdom. Just as bread won't rise without yeast, the 5i's process won't work without failure.

Wisdom is the application of knowledge, and failure is a technique of application. The wise leader will learn from both his failures, as well as the failures of others, to avoid repeating a mistake. If you are afraid of failure, you won't reflect on it; instead you will tolerate, shun, ignore, or avoid it. Without reflection on failure, wisdom is unattainable.

Embracing failure requires confidence. The confidence, and humility, of a conscious leader means that he has no problem admitting (both to himself and others), "I was wrong." The cockiness which characterizes most conventional leaders makes this admission not only more difficult, but also more infrequent.

Remember, conventional leadership verbally claims that failure is part of leadership. But, have you heard the words "I was wrong" from your leader this month? This quarter? Ever? This should be sufficient evidence to officially classify the supposed relationship between conventional leadership and failure as a myth. You must debunk that myth. You can't learn from failure if you are running from it. Conscious leaders embrace failure; they believe it to be a great teacher.

Recently, there was a behavioral science experiment conducted that further validated this concept. The experiment, conducted over a single, eight-hour day, involved the creation of clay pots. The participants were divided into two groups, and each individual was given a potter's wheel and clay. Group one was the "quality" group. They were instructed to build one, single, clay pot—the perfect clay pot. They had complete liberty to create it in any manner they desired. They were each to work on that one pot throughout the course of the day. At the end of the eight hours, each member of group one was expected to have completed their attempt at perfection and turn in that single one pot.

Group two was the "quantity" group. Each member of the group was instructed to create one-hundred-pounds worth of clay pots. They were expected to build the pots at a pace which allowed them to use all hundred pounds of clay within the eight hours. When they completed one pot, they would put it off to the side, grab some new clay, and start on the next pot.

Once the day was over, and all of the participants had left, the researchers compared the perfect pot produced by each member of the "quality" group with the final pot produced by each member of the "quantity" group. Which group do you think produced better pots? Group two—the "quantity" group! On average, the quality of the final pot made by each member of the "quantity" group was, ironically, much higher than the pots made by the "quality" group. Why?

The "quantity" group had a much better teacher than the "quality" group—*failure*. The repeated failures throughout the day actually taught them how to build better pots. They had no choice but to embrace that failure, as they didn't have enough time to perfect each pot. But, learning from their mistakes, each subsequent pot continued to get better and better. The "quality" group never failed—they only made one "perfect" pot. But by avoiding failure, they never grew.

Although we will never know with certainty (as the researchers never polled the participants on this topic), we would be willing to bet that the "quality" group believed in best practices, while the "quantity" group believed in better practices.

Expensive Training

Now that we have discussed what a conscious leader believes about failure, let's see how he behaves when it actually happens. We will see not only how Todd deals with failure, but also how he has progressed and developed as a conscious leader.

Todd is conducting a debriefing session with Jeff, an account manager, who is one of his direct reports. Jeff had a track record of solid performance—including breaking sales records in his promotion of dry erase markers. He also had some initial success with the launch of StarGate. His success streak was impressive and unbroken—until now.

TODD: So Jeff, let's talk about what's going on out there. You've been killing it with the dry erase marker program! I didn't know it was possible to sell that many markers. There is no way to produce results like that without some serious selling skills. You've got a ton of potential.
JEFF: Thanks!
TODD: But we have to shift gears, and this one isn't as pleasant. What in the world is going on with StarGate? Somehow, while trying to integrate our web-portal, you not only lost one account, but you almost lost two! So now we are $2 million in the hole and fighting to keep from going down by $4 million. What happened?

Todd is using the coaching sandwich with Jeff. He opened with sincere praise and is now moving to critique.

JEFF: I honestly don't know. I presented the web-portal in the same fashion to these two accounts as I have been to all the others. The others loved the portal, and we were able to integrate Acme into their business models. When I presented StarGate to these two customers, however, they had the most visceral negative reaction that I have ever seen in a sales call. I was honestly a little afraid.
TODD: So let me ask you a question: What was different about these two accounts? Your other customers loved StarGate!
JEFF: I wish I knew.
TODD: Come over here. I want to show you something [Jeff walks over to his computer screen]. I have pulled up the websites of these two companies, and they both contain a lot of information.

Look at each one's vision and mission statements. Look at the way they describe their business models. What do you observe that they have in common?

JEFF (hesitantly): I don't know. They seem very different. The only thing that really stands out to me is this term, "full-service." They both mention the importance of being "full-service" frequently.

TODD: Okay, good. So what does "full-service" mean?

JEFF: I don't know.

TODD: If an organization wants to be "full-service," it means that it is pursuing the idea of complete, vertical integration; they want to be a one-stop shop. They want to research, develop, produce, market, sell, and ship their own products. They plan to derive their competitive advantage from the efficiencies gained by complete ownership of all the links within the business chain. I know that's a lot; does it make sense?

JEFF: It does, but truthfully, I still don't really understand why they got so mad. They both have been big participants in our dry erase marker program. And they don't make those markers, we do.

TODD: Right! I'm really glad you picked that up. That insight brings up a great point. For the moment, our dry erase program represents a unique offering to these customers. Because it is a novel idea and a new product, it doesn't compete with their business models; it actually complements them. They might be able to develop and manufacture all of the typical and standard products on the market, but Acme dry erase markers aren't standard products. Right now, the only way they can get those markers is through us. This might not be their ideal situation, but they know they can make money on Acme markers.

JEFF: Okay, that makes sense to me.

TODD: So what do you think was going through their minds when you presented StarGate to them? Specifically, as you presented the integration features of the portal?

JEFF: Yeah, they must have thought I was clueless. StarGate made no sense for their business. But, now that I think about it, they probably thought that I was insulting them and their business model.

TODD: That's the best-case scenario. The worst-case scenario is that they thought you were either trying to compete with them or trying to sabotage their business by undoing their competitive advantage.

JEFF: And so that explains why they were mad. No wonder—I would have been ticked off as well. It's like I declared war on my customers.

Todd's transformation into a conscious leader is evident. Remember that Todd, at this point in the journey, has seven direct reports. And he is very busy. Yet, he takes the time to coach Jeff. Todd is explaining new business principles to Jeff by asking him questions (instead of just telling him the answers). Although Jeff was wrong, and his mistake cost Acme, and Todd, millions of dollars, Todd isn't focused on making a point; he is focused on making a difference.

TODD: What'd you learn from this? And what will you do differently in the future?

JEFF: Well, I now understand vertical integration. And I definitely will make sure that I don't present StarGate to customers who want to be "full-service."

TODD: There's more, Jeff. Vertical integration is nothing more than a single checker. Think broader, like a chess player. Think several moves ahead. What's the big-picture learning here?

JEFF: Okay, I see. I need to understand my customers better. Not just about vertical integration, but about their desired outcomes. I need to gather as much information as possible before I meet with them.

TODD: That's good, but that's still only part of it. You must then apply that knowledge and change your interactions with them. We will probably never get that business back.

JEFF: Not good...

TODD: I had to tell Julie yesterday. As you might imagine, she was furious. She demanded a full explanation and an action plan—

not a happy camper—but fortunately the other three accounts—including PaperClips—are doing well. Their performance should cover this setback.

JEFF: So, does this mean you are going to fire me?

TODD: Fire you!?! Why would I do that? I just spent somewhere between $2 and $4 million dollars teaching you to think differently about your customers and their business. I need to get a positive ROI from that investment...

Todd, believing that people are valuable and that the quality of Acme's performance is linked to the quality of its people, is still spending time developing Jeff. Although it was never implicitly stated, he has just finished walking Jeff through the 5i's process. Todd embraces the failure and uses it to facilitate Jeff's conversion of knowledge into wisdom. Not satisfied with Jeff playing checkers, Todd wants him to play chess. Although Todd embraced failure, he is about to challenge Jeff in a big way about something else:

JEFF: Really? So you're not mad? You're okay with everything?

TODD: I didn't say that. I'm not mad that you didn't understand the implications of a vertically integrated business model. I do expect better performance from you in the future as you apply these learnings. We all fall down, and you need to get back up. I am very concerned, however, about something bigger. This incident is indicative of a deeper issue with you that I have seen developing over the last six months.

JEFF: What's that?

TODD: As I said earlier, you have been very successful. Unfortunately, your success is making you arrogant and complacent. You could have asked others for their input and advice before going to see these accounts. Based on their size, you should have. But you thought you knew everything. This isn't the first negative outcome resulting from your attitude, but it is the most severe. And it's not okay. Your attitude must change, and you need to change it.

JEFF (silent for a moment): You're right. My attitude has drifted, and it has hurt my performance. It'd be great if it got back to where it was six months ago. I just need to snap out of this.

TODD: That's a start, but still not good enough. Arrogance and complacency have no place on my team, or in this department. Your attitude is not to be left up to chance and circumstances. You are responsible for changing it. You need to show a little humility and get back to the fundamentals—doing homework on your accounts before you go see them and talking to different stakeholders before you make a sales call. If you don't, I can promise you that this will happen again. Arrogance and complacency are not traits of high performers, and this is a high-performance team. Okay?

JEFF: Okay. I got it. That's a tough pill to swallow, but I understand. And I'll make the change.

TODD: Jeff, wait a minute. There is more. Do you know why I am jumping on you so hard about this?

JEFF: No, why?

TODD: Because I see something you don't. You have no idea how good you could be, but I do. You are already seen as a leader of this team, especially by the younger members. They look up to you, and they imitate you. Your complacency will become their complacency. And then you will hurt their careers as well as your own. You have a responsibility to them. Right now your past success has you running on cruise control, which is not acceptable. You're better than this. You have the potential to be a great salesperson and a leader within this organization. You have potential to make a tremendous impact within this organization. But you're not there yet. You must make some internal changes or your will never realize that potential.

Unfortunately, this probably doesn't happen very often in your organization, but it would be great if it did. The potential impact that can be generated by legendary leaders like Todd is limitless.

Todd finishes the interaction with Jeff by utilizing the lower portion of the coaching sandwich. He provides Jeff with some positive reinforcement, casting a vision for Jeff's potential future. Todd is making a significant difference in Jeff's life, and you can bet that prior to his next sales call, Jeff will do his homework.

Todd's approach to Jeff's failure, however, was the complete opposite of his reaction to Jeff's faults. And this leads us into the second half of the "Embrace failure but challenge faults" sub-principle:

Zero-Tolerance Policy
"Our own self-love draws a thick veil between us and our faults."
    - Lord Chesterfield

Todd didn't just tolerate failure, he embraced it. But he neither embraced nor tolerated faults. He was relentless in his challenging of them. Jeff's recent failure was a result of flawed ideas that were creeping into Jeff's belief system. Todd had been increasingly aware of their prevalence, and this incident brought those faults to the surface. With increased clarity as to the nature of those faults, Todd challenged them immediately and aggressively. Todd openly accepted Jeff's failure, but he displayed zero tolerance for Jeff's faults.

Unlike failure, which occurs at a single point in time, a fault (flawed belief) persists indefinitely. If faults go unchecked and unchallenged, they will continue to produce failure again and again. This capacity to produce repeated failure is only one of the consequences of faults that make them so dangerous. The other is much more severe.

Unlike failure, faults are contagious. At first glance, this is counterintuitive. Failure is external, but it is not contagious. Faults are internal, but they are readily transmitted and highly infectious. A fault is like a virus or a disease. My blemished internal character and deficient belief system has a way of infecting your belief system. Once you have caught the disease, and your belief system is weakened, the fault will produce failure— repeated failure—in your life.

Although faults have the potential to be lethal, there is a cure. We can be healed. So what's the antidote for faults? Challenge. Challenge is the best medicine to cure faults.

Like all medicines, challenge can come in different strengths and dosages. One of the strongest forms of challenge—maximum strength challenge—is failure. A dose of failure, when properly applied, can remedy many faults. Failure was Todd's drug of choice when confronting Jeff's faults. Todd used Jeff's recent failure to challenge his faulty beliefs.

Faults, due to their internal and intangible nature, can be difficult to observe. They like to stay hidden. Often, failure will surface faults and reveal them. Sometimes, as in Jeff's case, failure is a visible symptom of an underlying disease. This isn't always true; failure is not always caused by faults. But in this story, Jeff's failure revealed a belief issue, and Todd used that failure to challenge the flawed belief and ultimately, cure him of the fault.

Your Story

All stories have protagonists, and readers will follow them throughout their journey. Some stories are good. In these stories, the protagonists are actually heroes or heroines. Readers relate with them and cheer for them as they embark on noble quests and thrilling adventures.

But some stories are legendary. Like good stories, legends have heroes or heroines, and you cheer for them as they defend good and fight evil. However, in a legendary story, at some point the hero or heroine always falls down; they fail. The villain is never defeated easily. At first, the villain appears to win as he knocks the hero or heroine down. But, they don't stay down; they get back up. And that is why we remember their story.

Don't just tolerate failure—embrace it. Learn and grow from it. Don't pursue best practices and pretend failure doesn't exist. Accept it as a prerequisite for driving change; welcome it as your companion as you create better practices.

Be careful not to confuse failure with faults. Embrace failure openly, but challenge faults relentlessly and ruthlessly. Avoid faults, as they can cripple your leadership, rendering it inconsequential and impotent, but leverage failure. It can exponentially strengthen your leadership.

When leveraged and embraced, failure can enable you to create transformational change previously considered impossible, and failure can enable you to generate impact forever considered legendary.

Mirror, Mirror on the Wall…Chapter 11

The Conscious Leader's Toolbox

1. **Exercise:** Stop using the phrase "best practices" in your daily vernacular. Replace it with "better practices." What kind of response do you get?

2. **Questions:** How do you react to failure? Is there a difference between your reaction to your personal failure and the failure of others?

3. **Questions:** Describe, in detail, your biggest failure in the last six months. What happened? How did you feel? How did you react? How did others around you react? How did they make you feel? What did you learn from that failure? Was it the result of a fault? If so, what was it? Are you cured?

4. **Questions:** Describe, in detail, one of your report's biggest failures in the last six months? How did you feel? How did you react? How did they react? How did your reaction make them feel? What did they learn from that failure? Was their failure a result of a fault? If so, have you challenged it?

5. **Questions:** Your reaction to the failure of others will reveal what you really believe about failures and faults. Based on your reactions documented in the previous questions, what do you really believe? Are you okay with that belief?

6. **Questions:** What was the your biggest new idea within the last two years? How did it deviate from the standard norms? Did it get implemented? Were there failures along the implementation process? How did you, and others, handle that failure?

7. **Ideal Experiences:** This is a tool to help you implement the concept of better practices. It will help you identify some areas where you excel. Once you identify why you were able to excel in those areas, look for ways for those strengths to transfer into other areas.

Ideal Experiences

Your Non-Work Best

- Think about a *non-work related* activity/accomplishment
  - It makes you proud
  - You played a significant role

- Describe the event :

- How do you feel as you describe it? Why?

- Why were you successful (list 3 specific strengths/abilities that allowed you to succeed):

- How did you use those strengths (and how did you feel as you were using them)?

- Why were you critical to the success of the activity?

- Were you surprised at your success? Why?

- What insights can you glean from that experience? Can you replicate it?

- Where else could you use those strengths? Could you use them at work?

- Other

Notes

CONSCIOUS
LEADERSHIP

Ideal Experiences

Your Work Best

- Think about a *work-related* activity/accomplishment
  - It makes you proud
  - You played a significant role

- Describe the event :

- How do you feel as you describe it? Why?

- Why were you successful (list 3 specific strengths/abilities that allowed you to succeed):

- How did you use those strengths (and how did you feel as you were using them)?

- Why were you critical to the success of the activity?

- Were you surprised at your success? Why?

- Where else could you use those strengths at work?

- What needs to happen in order to use those strengths more frequently?

- Other

Notes

CONSCIOUS
LEADERSHIP

Reflection Points

- I don't believe in best practices; I believe in better practices.
  - o Best practices
    - Looks for solutions
    - Accepts normalcy and status quo
    - Disproportionate and ineffective allocation of resources
    - Assumes environment is static—a photograph
  - o Better practices

Asks questions

Deviates from today's standard and status quo

Accounts for relative importance of improvement

Assumes environment is dynamic—a video

- Embrace failure, but challenge faults
  - o Failure
    - External; substandard, inferior performance
    - What you do/what you produce
      - Does not define who you are
    - Single point in time
    - Unavoidable by-product of innovation
    - Required for learning
    - A strong belief system mitigates fear of failure
    - Great teacher
    - Catalyst in the conversion of knowledge into wisdom
    - Requires confidence to admit that you were wrong
  - o Faults
    - Internal; imperfect character that is flawed, blemished, or deficient
    - Who you are
    - Can persist indefinitely
    - Will produce continual failure
    - Conventional leaders aren't aware of their existence
    - Contagious
    - Relentless and ruthless challenge can provide a cure
      - Failure is strong medicine
    - Zero-tolerance policy

CHAPTER 12

THE BRIDGE

"We should be taught not to wait for inspiration to start a thing. Action always generates inspiration. Inspiration seldom generates action."

> - Frank Tibolt

"Good ideas are not adopted automatically. They must be driven into practice with courageous patience."

> - Hyman Rickover

Using the framework created during the initial portion of this book, we have finished our exploration of each of the domains of conscious leadership—people, process, and performance. We have taken some jabs at conventional leadership, and we have introduced a new paradigm to view leadership. However, our journey isn't done just yet.

This book was designed to help you write your story by transforming who you are. The story of conscious leadership will be defined by those who tell it; its story will reflect your story. Most stories can be classified into one of the three following categories:

- **Comedy:** Within this category is the story of conventional leadership. Comprised of internal contradictions, unsolvable riddles, and false claims, its level of ridiculousness is often much easier to see from a distance than from a front-row seat. This doesn't mean that people aren't interested in observing conventional leadership from the front-row; in fact, as we discussed earlier, conventional leadership has inspired several comedic productions which have generated millions of dollars of revenue.

- **Legend:** We introduced this idea at the beginning of the book, and we have continued to explore it as we've moved forward. This is the ultimate goal of a conscious leader—to write a story so powerful and full of impact that is classified as legendary. Unlike myths—which are based in fiction and falsehood—legends are based in reality. This is the category where your story belongs. This is the type of story that you want to write and are capable of writing.

- **Tragedy:** No one wants to play the lead role in a tragedy. In ancient Greece, the birthplace of theater, tragedies followed a distinct and unique script. As you might expect, the story concluded with the protagonist undergoing immense suffering. Most of the time, this suffering was in some way self-inflicted—the result of poor decisions. What made Greek tragedy unique was that the audience, from their vantage point, had the ability to see the direction of the story better than the protagonist, who was living in the moment. Despite the desperate pleas of the audience, the protagonist proceeded down his chosen path which ultimately led to his destruction. The goal was to provide the audience with the opportunity to learn from the mistakes of the protagonist and avoid repeating them.

Tragedies are particularly jarring because they are avoidable. We wrote this chapter to help you keep your story from becoming a tragedy. Most tragedies have the potential to be legendary, but the protagonist makes decisions that predictably lead to his destruction.

The audience could see the path forward, but the protagonist couldn't. As your audience, we want to help you avoid some of those tragic decisions…or, more appropriately, those tragic indecisions. We consider it a tragedy if after finishing this book, nothing changes. If your leadership tomorrow looks the same as it did yesterday, we failed in our objective with this book.

Conscious leadership is founded on the "Belief ➜ Behavior ➜ Outcome" model. This chapter will help you tie everything together, not only introducing some new beliefs but also providing you with some behaviors so that you arrive at your desired outcome.

To accomplish this goal, the chapter will be broken down into the five classic "W"s" of reporting: who, what, when, where, and why. We will start with the "why."

<u>Why:</u>
I don't believe in inspiration;
I believe in impact.

We have been talking about this concept since page one: conscious leadership is about transformation and impact. As a leader, you want to make a difference. You want to leave your mark on the world and leave it a better place than you found it. If you didn't, you would never have picked up this book.

It's not that conventional leadership can't ever create some sort of impact. But it can't generate sustainable impact on a consistent basis; for you, intermittent, temporary change of questionable value is not good enough.

This brings us to yet another myth of conventional leadership—the inspiration myth. As it can't create the type of impact that you desire, conventional leadership shifts the focus to inspiration. It would have you believe that if you are inspired, you are making a difference. But the truth is, you aren't.

The role of inspiration is to create emotional energy, often by casting a vision of tomorrow and producing discontentment with today. Think back to the last time you read an inspirational book or listened to a motivational speaker. How did you feel? Probably pretty good. This emotional energy feels good, and it is useful. But it's incomplete; and that is the danger of the inspiration myth.

Conventional leadership would have you believe that when you are engulfed by emotional energy and glimpsing into your potential future, you are actually making progress towards that future. The truth is this: while inspiration gives the illusion of progress, it is not meaningful change.

There is a difference between *looking* ahead and *moving* ahead.

This difference links inspiration and impact. Inspiration is about feeling good about what you are going to do. Implementation is about doing it. Impact is the result of having done it.

Inspiration isn't enough. Anyone, anywhere, at anytime, can be inspired. Inspiration is easy, fun, and free. It requires no difficult decisions, necessary challenges, or ruthless self-assessments. The energy that inspiration creates by allowing you to peer into a different, more desirable future feels good and is of critical importance to leadership. But this energy lacks transformational power to create that future.

Don't misunderstand us—inspiration is a good thing. We aren't making the case to abolish inspiration. It plays a positive and necessary role in leadership, and it is one of the key ingredients in the creation of impact.

A leader should be inspirational. Hopefully, as you read this book, you have felt inspired to change some of your beliefs. However, there is a big step between today, where you feel inspired to see your beliefs change, and tomorrow, where you creating impact because they changed—a big step. This step is the difference between inspiration and impact.

What is this step? In one word—"implementation." Inspiration, when it is implemented, will lead to impact. Transformation requires implementation; implementation is the bridge between inspiration and impact.

The Missing Link

Inspired beliefs, if implemented through proper behavior, will lead to impact. Or, staying consistent with the model:

Belief ➜ Behavior ➜ Outcome

Inspired Beliefs ➜ Implemented Behaviors ➜ Impactful Outcomes

This might seem familiar. Does it remind you of the knowledge/application/wisdom axiom? It should. If we were introducing totally foreign and unrelated ideas at this point, you should be suspect. But the relationship between inspiration, implementation, and impact is different than previously introduced ideas. So what do you do with the concept of implementation? Let's start by asking a question: what do you believe about implementation?

This appears to be an obvious question with an obvious answer. But it isn't—thanks to another myth of conventional leadership. This myth is about the relative value of strategy and execution.

In our previous discussion regarding strategy, we concluded that despite the attention that conventional leaders place on strategic thinking, they are really playing checkers instead of chess. The conscious leader is much more strategic than a conventional leader. And now, because conventional leadership has accepted this myth as truth, a conscious leader is also much more proficient at execution than a conventional leader

Ironically, conventional leadership assigns execution significantly less value than strategy. It claims that developing a strategy is not only the difficult—and sexy—part of the equation, it is the only part of the equation that matters. If you can develop the right strategy, the tactics are easy...execution is secondary, right?

Wrong. The conscious leader doesn't believe this. Strategy is important—critically important. However, it is no more important than execution. This is why the Conscious Leader's Strategic Map contains both a vision statement (strategy) and a mission statement (execution). Frequently, a poorly designed, but well-executed plan will outperform a well-designed, strategic plan that is poorly executed.

Military history is full of such stories—stories about strategic plans that failed as a result of poor execution. For those of you familiar with some of the details of World War I, think about Winston Churchill and the Dardanelles. The strategy was sound—flank the enemy by enlarging the definition of the engagement zone. However, it failed as a result of poor execution. This is but one of many such examples.

Of course, the ideal combination is sound strategy and execution, the synthesis of vision and mission. But conventional leadership has led us to believe the execution myth: execution is secondary to strategy; strategy alone matters.

Belief in this myth has led to the widespread devaluation of execution. We behave in ways that demonstrate our acceptance of this myth, and the resulting outcome is pretty obvious. Today's leadership is incapable of creating impact, partly because it can't—or won't—execute the strategies that it develops.

But let's return to the original question: What do you believe about implementation?

Similar to vision and mission, the ideal combination is inspiration and implementation. Conventional leadership has focused all of its effort and energy on the first half of the equation—inspiration. And that is one of the reasons why conventional leadership isn't working. Please trust us when we say that we are not devaluing inspiration; no one wants to follow a leader void of inspiration. Inspiration has real value, but that value has been inflated.

Inspiration is a *nice*-to-have; implementation is a *need*-to-have. The conscious leader believes that implementation is critical, crucial, and essential for impact. In fact, the conscious leader believes that implementation is more critical than inspiration for impact. Inspiration comes and goes; the emotional energy it generates will wax and wane.

A belief does not require inspiration for implementation. In other words, you don't have to feel good to change a belief. But, a belief does have to be implemented to generate impact; you have to change a belief to change an outcome).

So, if you really believe that a belief must be implemented to create impact, how should you behave? Start by triaging. If implementation is the most important component of impact, then a few ideas that are well-implemented will generate more impact than many new ideas that are poorly executed. This is addition by subtraction; less is more. A broad view will inspire you with new ideas; a limited focus will allow you to implement those ideas.

This explains why the Conscious Leader's Strategic Map only allows you to focus on three to four beliefs and related behaviors at any single point in time. If you try to change everything; you end up changing nothing. Instead, only focus on a few things. To generate impact, select three to four beliefs identified in this book that really inspired you. Using your strategic map, lay out how you could implement these beliefs in your day-to-day life.

Then execute! Again and again and again. Two important caveats:
- Don't add anything else until you have made significant process in these areas. Stay focused until you have generated meaningful impact.
- Don't subtract anything even when (not if) you lose your inspiration. Stay focused regardless of whether or not you are feeling inspired.

Growth occurs not by watching, but by applying. Inspiration is about watching; implementation is about becoming. We can be inspired by watching the stories of others, but we really won't change and progress until we implement ourselves. Implementation is not as exciting as inspiration, but if impact is your destination, it is a road that must be traveled.

We are motivated by those who have implemented. When we focus on executing what we say we believe, we move from "talking the talk" to "walking the walk." And when others see us doing that, not only will they be inspired, they will know how to implement, increasing their potential for impact.

Decide or Desire

"There is no more miserable human being than the one in whom nothing is habitual but indecision."
   - William James

Implementation is fueled by decisions, not desires. Your application, not your intention, determines your outcome. This might be common knowledge, but it's not common sense, as it is conspicuous absent in the world of conventional leadership.

Webster's defines "desire" as "to wish or long for; crave; want." Desire, like inspiration, is actually a really good thing. Desire is born out of discontent. Not satisfied with today, you desire tomorrow to be different and better. Both conventional and conscious leaders have desires. Some desires are common; for example, everyone wants to be valued. Some desires are rare; only some people want to create transformational change within their world.

However, as powerful as desires might be, they don't produce impact. Decisions do.

Desires that are inspired should lead to decisions that are implemented. Just as wisdom is the application of knowledge, decisions are the application of desires. And just like conventional leadership is satisfied with knowledge, it is also satisfied with desires. Although decisions lead to impact, desires are much more...desirable. Why?

Desires don't compete with each other—decisions often do. You can desire many different things at the same time. Decisions are often mutually exclusive. For example, you can simultaneously desire to be the head coach of your nine-year-old son's baseball team and desire to be the vice-president of international business development at your company. Until we develop the transporter technology of Star Trek, a decision requires you to choose one or the other; you can't do both. You can't be the head coach of a baseball team when you are out of the country three weeks each month. And you can't develop international business without leaving your hometown.

The birth of a decision often results in the death of a desire.

If you agree to coach your son's baseball team, you will have to turn down the international job. It is very hard for anyone to kill their desires. It is painful and scary. And so the conventional leader doesn't—he avoids the decision because he is afraid to bury a desire. The conscious leader isn't immune to the pain of killing a desire, but he makes the decision anyway.

Desires don't require responsibility; decisions do. As soon as you make a decision, you are now, in some fashion, accountable for the outcome of that decision. But you will never be held accountable for a desire. To illustrate, you can desire to be a high-powered corporate lawyer with no consequences. But, when you decide to quit your current job, take out a loan, and go to that first class, you assume a whole host of new responsibilities.

True, decisions are scary and painful. But they are powerful—especially when leveraged appropriately. And they are part of the implementation process. You cannot implement if you cannot decide. If you can conquer the innate and natural fear of making decisions, you will be in the rank of elite leaders.

There is a chasm that separates inspiration and impact, and implementation is the bridge across that chasm. Decisions will fuel your implementation. Impact is our "why." Let's keep going to the next "W."

<u>Where:</u>
Evolution before Revolution

"In any moment of decision, the best thing you can do is the right thing. The worst thing you can do is nothing."
- Theodore Roosevelt

Revolution is exciting; it is almost synonymous with impact. Revolution always has been, and always will be, inspiring. We read stories about revolutions, and we want our story to fit into that genre. We desire our story to be a part of some sort of legendary revolution.

Consider the story of America. If you open a history book, it will transport you to the eighteenth century where you will watch the American Revolution unfold. The story line is epic. The heroes were nothing more than average colonists—mostly poor peasant farmers. The villain was the superpower of the day, the English empire. The plot? Untrained, under-armed, and out-numbered, the American colonists, burdened and oppressed, revolt against the mighty empire. Against all odds, they win and gain their freedom. And we tell their story today.

If you don't like history, grab any current business publication. What stories do you read about, again and again? What do the majority of case studies, offered as examples of excellence, have in common? They are revolutionary. You can read about Henry Ford's impact on the automobile industry through his innovative assembly line; or the ideas of Google that revolutionized the Internet; or the insights of Apple that transformed the way we experience music.

So, how do you start a revolution? Revolution starts with evolution, and evolution is right in front of you.

Education about Evolution

"Practice yourself, for heaven's sake, in little things, and then proceed to greater."
> - Epictetus

Evolution provides the answer to the "where" portion of our five "W's." Although it seems slow and boring, if you want to make an impact, and start a revolution, evolution is critically necessary.

Revolution is comprised of a one-time event that is large, transformational, and highly visible. Evolution is composed of many sequential events that represent small, sometimes invisible changes. Although the transformation of revolution might be in the distance, the next steps of evolution is right in front of you.

Evolution is concerned with the "next" thing, while revolution is concerned with the "big" thing. But often, the "big" thing is only made possible through the collective sum of multiple "next" things. These "next" things are critical to the "big" thing. Once the sum of these "next" things reaches critical mass, revolution explodes. This seems intuitive, so what is the myth that we need to debunk?

The myth of conventional leadership is that you can experience revolution without evolution. The truth is that before you experience revolution, you must experience evolution.

If you buy into this myth, you will ignore all of the "next" things right in front of you in your search to find the "big" thing. But the tragedy is that in doing so, you will render yourself incapable of ever sparking the "big" thing that you so desperately desire. Why does conventional leadership snub evolution?

We already addressed the fact that evolution is neither exciting nor glamorous. However, it is worth noting that evolution is difficult—perhaps more difficult than revolution. Within the context of revolution (often a short time period), you will fail at most once or twice. The price will be high, but it will be paid infrequently. Within the context of evolution (a much longer time period preceding revolution), you will fail often—perhaps daily. The price will be lower, but the frequency of payments (continuous) scares off most leaders.

In snubbing evolution, however, conventional leadership walks away from a significant source of power. Why is the "where" of evolution so powerful?

Evolution gives you control. You can decide the "next" things to pursue. Although alone, you might not be able to control the outcome of the Revolutionary War, you can control whether or not you will use your farmland to host militia training exercises this spring. You might not be able to trigger the "big" thing off in the distance just yet, but you there is no doubt that you can ignite the "next" thing right in front of you. In doing so, you are one step closer to revolution.

Evolution is where desires are converted into decisions. Having been inspired by a revolutionary vision, evolution is where you can implement the subsequent phases of your mission. If you control the "next" thing, then you will ready when the opportunity for the "big" thing presents itself. You don't have to wait for the "next" thing; it is always right in front of you. Don't skip ignore it.

Evolution should provide you with some criteria to guide your initial selection of beliefs within your Conscious Leader's Strategic Map. Your selection of ideas should be based on what you can implement where you are right now. Begin the internal process of transformation from where you stand today; impact is possible from any location.

For example, if Todd just got promoted, he isn't going to attempt to implement the "Important, not Urgent" principle immediately with regard to business decisions. Why? It isn't his "next" thing. In his new role, he will be at stage one of the Adult Learning Model, Unconscious Incompetence. He is going to have to diagnose some problems, embrace some failure, and develop wisdom before he will be able to distinguish the difference between important and urgent in his new role.

As a conscious leader, you want to create revolution. This is an appropriate and commendable, desire. Conscious leadership is about transformational change. However, evolution always precedes revolution. Expedite your revolution by implementing that which is right in front of you—those smaller, invisible, and vital decisions classified as evolution.

Implementation is the only bridge crossing the chasm that separates inspiration from impact. There is no other path. Your implementation is fueled by your decisions and is guided by evolution. "Where" is your next step? It is right in front of you.

Let's review the 5 "W's" so far:
- "Why": Impact (which requires Implementation)
- "Where": Evolution before Revolution

We now move to the "When."

When:
"How Often?" not "How Much?"

"The drops of rain make a hole in the stone, not by violence, but by oft falling."
   - Lucretius

Time magnifies the power of impact. The impact of a stream, magnified by time, is powerful enough to carve through a mountain. The impact of waves gently lapping up against a beach, magnified by time, is powerful enough to smooth away jagged edges of rocks. The power of decisions, when made continuously, increases exponentially.

This principle isn't just true in nature. The magnifying effect of time can be seen in other areas of our life. With regard to money, we refer to this magnification principle as "compounding."

Consider your bank account. If the current interest rate is 5% and you make a one-time-only deposit of $100.00, then at the end of the first year you will have earned $5.00 interest. You now have $105.00 in your account. During the second year, you will earn interest not just on the original $100.00, but also on the $5.00 in interest you gained last year. The total interest that you gain in year two will be $5.25, giving you a total of $110.25. If you don't deposit any more money ever again, at the end of 20 years you will have over $265.00. Your $100.00 became $265.00. What happened? Time magnified the impact of your initial deposit.

What if you don't have $100.00 today? Although you can't do the "big" thing and deposit $100.00, you decide to do the "next" thing and deposit $10.00 today. But, instead of making a one-time-only deposit, you make frequent deposits. You make that "next" deposit of just $10.00 every year for the next 20 years. At the end of year twenty, you will have over $347.00. Your $10.00 per year became $347.00. What happened? Time magnified the impact of your consistent deposits—exponentially.

Impact requires implementation; powerful impact requires *consistent* implementation.

This leads us to another myth that needs to be debunked—the metric myth. The metric myth of conventional leadership would have you believe that it is the size of your deposits that matter when calculating your ultimate return or impact. It tells you that if you can't make a big deposit, don't make one at all, because it won't matter.

Conventional leadership measures the wrong metric. It's about frequency, not size. It isn't the size of your deposit that determines your return on investment; it is the frequency by which you make those deposits.

The journey towards impact resembles a marathon, not a sprint. We learn about this principle as children. Remember the story of the tortoise and the hare? The tortoise won the race, not because of his great speed, but because of his continual, forward motion. This principle also applies to the physical world. If you want to get into shape, you don't run 20 miles once per month. Over the course of the month, you run a couple of miles a day, a few times per week. If you want to lose weight, you don't deprive yourself of all food for the next 48 hours. You reduce your caloric intake on a daily basis.

If you can leverage this magnifying effect of time, you can increase the power of your impact. So "when" should you implement? Start implementing something right now. And do it again tomorrow. And again the next day.

Your impact will be determined by your ability to successfully implement. And your implementation will be determined by your degree of consistency. Don't try to do everything today, but make sure you do something on a continual basis. Leverage time to magnify the degree of your impact, as impact results from not the size, but the frequency, of your deposits.

There is a chasm that separates impact from inspiration, and implementation is your bridge. Implementation is fueled by decisions. The direction of its next step is guided by evolution; its pace is set by consistency. As long as you are constantly and continuously moving forward, don't become concerned about your speed. Just don't stop moving.

Let's review the 5 "W's" so far:
- "Why": Impact (which requires Implementation)
- "Where": Evolution before Revolution
- "When": "How Often?" not "How Much"

And that brings us to the next of the five "W's," the "Who."

Who:
Me, not Them…We, not They

"A man, as a general rule, owes very little to what he is born with—a man is what he makes of himself."

    - Alexander Graham Bell

This concept is easy to understand, but it is difficult to apply. This principle is often quoted as truth, but it is rarely actually believed. But if you can accept this belief as truth, and implement accordingly, then you will be in an elite class of leaders who truly have the potential to generate significant impact.

To illustrate the challenge, and the power, of this principle, let us start by asking you a question. Think about the financial meltdown of 2007. We all are still feeling its pain. Many people lost their savings; many others lost their jobs. So here is the question: Who was responsible for the financial crisis in 2007? The banks? The politicians? The investors? If not them, who?

Before you answer, let's make this concept a little more personal. Think about this specific work situation. If you aren't experiencing it right now, you have experienced it at some point. You are currently aggravated with your department. There is no innovation, and the working environment is terrible. Your department creates no value, and is managed through fear. So here is a different version of the same question: Who is responsible for the current struggles in your department? Senior management? Your boss? Your employees? If not them, who?

Now, let's make this concept very personal. Again, if you aren't experiencing this right now, you have at some point. You are frustrated by the lack of impact you are generating. You aren't making as much of a difference as you should be, as you could be, or as you want to be. You find yourself just going through the motions, living in routine. You aren't creating transformational change. So here is the final version of same question: Who is responsible for your lack of impact? Your company? Your boss? Your co-workers? Your team? Your circumstances? If not them, who?

"Who" is *you*.

We aren't trying to oversimplify or minimize the difficulty of any of these situations; this book is designed for the real world. The real world has lots of real issues and lots of real problems. These complicated problems (the financial crisis, the work environment, your impact) all have multiple causes and inputs.

Although simplified and condensed, these examples expose another common myth of conventional leadership—the fault myth. The fault myth says that in order to solve a problem, you should start with those most at fault, which is always "them." As a conscious leader, you need to debunk the fault myth and accept this principle as truth: significant impact and transformational change always starts with "me."

The power of your impact will be determined by *your* ability to change, not your ability to change *others*.

This principle can be extrapolated to teams. The most powerful teams are composed of individuals who each embrace this principle. This fosters trust within the team. As the individuals on the team begin to merge and function as a single unit, something transformational happens—the team begins to collectively embrace accountability. A team that collectively accepts responsibility for its performance is truly a high-performing team.

Let's revisit our initial three scenarios. We are not debating nor evaluating the role that the banks, investors, and politicians played in the financial crisis. But we are suggesting that if you want to create an impact, the starting point will be to look in the mirror and assess your level of financial responsibility and discipline. Then, after you have changed yourself, you will be ready to address the issues caused by "them."

The same principle applies to the work environment within your department. Undoubtedly, some of the problems and culture issues stem from your boss and senior management. But do any of them stem from you? Have you ever thrown management under the bus to make yourself look good? Have you ever blamed your boss for an issue that you didn't want to confront? Again, impact begins with a focus on "me," not "them." Once you have executed a plan to change yourself, then you will be in a place to deal with the issues caused by "them."

Finally, let's discuss your frustration regarding your current level of impact. There might be very real circumstances, and perhaps people, currently hindering your efforts to generate transformational change. You might work for a manager who fears failure and constantly does what is fair instead of what is right. Or maybe you have reason to doubt the motives of your colleagues, and you are just trying to stay alive. We are in no way downplaying the significance—or the reality—of those circumstances. But a conscious leader looks inward before he looks outward. The power of your external challenge is proportional to the degree of your internal change.

You need to be changed before you challenge others to change.

There is no chauffer service in the journey towards impact. There is no passenger seat—you are the only driver that can navigate the bridge of implementation. While those that have arrived might act as beacons for others, each leader is responsible for his own journey.

Let's review the 5 "W's" so far:
- "Why": Impact (which requires Implementation)
- "Where": Evolution before Revolution
- "When": "How Often?" not "How Much"
- "Why": Me, not Them…and We, not They

This brings us to the last of the five "W's," the "What."

What:
Your Story

You already have the "what." The "what" includes all of the beliefs that we have introduced you to throughout the people, process, and performance domains. It also includes the leadership framework which we discussed over the first four chapters. All of those beliefs—those individual "why's"—now become the collective "what."

You've been given the "what." The question to you is, "What now?"

What are you going to do with all of that information? Having been inspired, what now? Right now, you might be inspired. You have the raw ingredients, but there is still a chasm in front of you separating inspiration from impact. Implementation is the only bridge that crosses that chasm.

Your behavior indicates what you really believe. The source of what you do is who you are. This book has introduced you to different beliefs; now it's time for you to absorb them and implement some different behaviors. There is no reason you can't cross that bridge.

You can create impact, but you must convert your desires into decisions. You can create a revolution, but only if you go through an evolution first. You can leverage the power of time, but you have to be consistent in your deposits. You can create meaningful change the world outside of you, but only after you have meaningfully changed the world inside you.

You have read this story. Now, it's time to write your story.

Mirror, Mirror on the Wall…Chapter 12

The Conscious Leader's Toolbox

1. **Exercise:** Revisit your Conscious Leader's Strategic Map from Chapter 4. What are the 3 or 4 beliefs, and related behaviors, that you want to implement? Complete the map, filling in any remaining "beliefs" and "behaviors."

2. **Questions:** Examine the beliefs/behaviors that you chose to implement. Why did you choose these particular beliefs/behaviors? Is there correlation with your "My Leadership Journey" from Chapter 2? What is the impact that you hope to generate from implementing these beliefs? What change do you want to create? Why does that inspire you?

3. **Questions:** What does excellent execution and implementation look like? Have you shown your strategic map to your partner? How can he hold you accountable?

4. **Questions:** What difficult decisions do you need to make? Do you have any desires that are mutually exclusive? Do any of those desires need to die? What is keeping you from making the right decision?

5. **Questions:** Are these beliefs/behaviors that you want to change right in front of you? Can you start immediately?

6. **Questions:** What does consistency look like for the implementation of these beliefs? What is the right level of frequency by which you should implement? What would cause you to stop?

7. **Questions:** What real circumstances will make implementation difficult? Who, or what, might you be tempted to blame? Why?

8. **Exercise:** Look at your "tomorrow" statement. Do you need to revise it at all? What do you want things to look like three weeks from now? What about three months from now?

9. **Questions:** What was the last "big" thing that you achieved at work? Make a list of all of the "next" things that you had to accomplish before the "big" thing could happen. What is your next "big" thing? What "next" things do you need to accomplish?

10. **Questions:** Over the past five years, at what point were you most inspired? Why? What, specifically, inspired you? How much of your inspiration was fueled by someone else's implementation?

11. **Questions:** Do you have a hero or a mentor? Does he/she inspire you? Why? What is his/her story? What are the gaps between your story and his/her story?

12. **Strategic Map Review:** Following is another copy of The Conscious Leader's Strategic Map. As this is a living document, you will make multiple revisions to it. You can download this template from the Conscious Leader's Toolbox on our website, www.debunkingtheleadershipmyth.com.

Strategic Map
Acme Office Supply

B TOMORROW
#2 in market share within 24 months; fully integrated into our retailers' business models as a preferred partner who provides recognized value

C D VISION/MISSION
Vision: Foundational to your business
Mission: Provide our customers all the necessary tools to run better businesses

TODAY

A
#3 supplier in market share in a crowded market; viewed as a supplier of low-end, inexpensive, commodity-like goods

E CSF #1: Escape the commodity price war	E CSF #2: Integration of business model with customers	E CSF #3: Create brand perception/equity as innovative	E CSF #4: Develop lasting competitive advantage

F Program #1 — G Outsource all non-core competencies — G Outsource

F Program #2 — G Redesign R&D, Supply Chain to increase value added to retail partners

F Program #3 — G Product Launch — G Launch 27 new products this year, enter 3 new product categories next year

F Program #4 — G Identify/exit low margin product lines — G Identify/exit low margin product lines

Notes:

CONSCIOUS LEADERSHIP

Strategic Map

TOMORROW

VISION/MISSION

Vision:

Mission:

TODAY

Notes:

CONSCIOUS LEADERSHIP

Reflection Points

- Three basic types of stories
  - o Comedy (the current state for most conventional leaders)
  - o Legend (the goal for a conscious leader)
  - o Tragedy (return to normal after exposure to impact)
- Why: I don't believe in inspiration, I believe in impact.
  - o Chasm between impact and inspiration
    - Implementation is the bridge
  - o Inspiration is about looking ahead, implementation is about moving ahead
    - Inspiration is easier than implementation
    - Creates emotional energy but cannot create change alone
  - o Conventional leadership devalues execution
  - o The level at which you implement will be the level at which you impact
  - o Implementation is about your decisions, not desires
    - The birth of a decision is often the death of a desire
- Where: Evolution before Revolution
  - o Revolution is exciting and inspiring
    - Revolution is a worthy goal for a conscious leader
  - o Evolution always precedes revolution
    - Focus on the "next" thing, not the "big" thing
    - Evolution gives you control
    - A series of small, invisible steps
- When: "How Often," not "How Much"
  - o Time magnifies the impact of our decisions - exponentially
  - o Compound Interest
  - o Your impact will be determined by frequency, not the size, of your deposits
  - o Consistency is powerful
- Who: Me, not Them...We, not They
  - o External forces are real and can affect my level of impact
  - o The "blame game" is tempting
    - Look inside before you look outside
    - Change yourself before you challenge others
  - o Your level of impact is determined by your ability to change

- What: What Now?
  - You have information and inspiration
    - Impact requires implementation
  - Write your story

CHAPTER 13
THE NEXT CHAPTER

"Change your thoughts, and you change your world."
> - Norman Vincent Peale

"Somewhere ages and ages hence:
Two roads diverged in a wood, and I—
I took the one less traveled by,
And that has made all the difference."
> - Robert Frost

In 1916, Robert Frost published the poem, "The Road not Taken," which concludes with the above lines.

If you were to conduct a thorough audit of all the conventional leadership books currently available, you would find those lines quoted many times. In fact, it is estimated—albeit not confirmed—that upwards of 10% of those books would contain these lines penned by Frost. Unfortunately, if you are reading about conventional leadership, it doesn't matter which road you take; you won't make a difference.

As long as you operate as a conventional leader, regardless of the road you choose, it will lead you right back to the very place you are today. Despite its promises, conventional leadership cannot induce real, meaningful change. Why not? Impact requires changing who you are, not just what you do. Transformational change is belief change. Conventional leadership can't even recognize beliefs—how can it possibly change them?

Unaware of beliefs, conventional leadership is unable to consistently generate sustainable impact; it can only maintain normalcy and foster the status quo. That's not good enough for you anymore. You picked up this book, and you are finishing it, because you need real, meaningful change that makes a real, meaningful difference. You want transformational change that creates impact.

If you choose to embark on the journey of conscious leadership, you will find your horizons expanded and your borders enlarged. The power of belief change will amplify your potential. You will be able to generate impact beyond what you currently imagine possible, making a significant difference in both your life and the lives of others.

Are we making large promises? Yes. But your experience validates these claims. Reflect on the leaders who made the biggest difference in your life. Think about the impact that their story had on your story. What did all of these individuals share in common? They were all conscious leaders. They may not have described themselves as such; but regardless of the terminology, their core beliefs, and their awareness of those beliefs, revealed their true identity. The leaders who have had the most impact on your story are those whose leadership most resembles conscious leadership.

Now it's your turn. As a conscious leader, let your story impact the lives of others. Conscious leadership enables you to generate this transformational change. It isn't just another dressed-up version of the same old thing—conventional leadership with slight alterations. Conscious leadership is fundamentally different than conventional leadership, and you can be fundamentally different than conventional leaders.

Conscious leadership isn't a singular event; nor is it a moment-in-time event. It is a paradigm shift. It changes the way you approach leadership as well as the way you write your story. It is about transforming who you are, not altering what you do.

Although conscious leadership isn't a singular event, the decision to embrace this new paradigm is. You can desire impact all day long, but if you want to experience impact, then you must make decisions. You must decide to take the next step.

The road divides. And you must make a decision.

The Story of Truth

"People readily believe what they want to believe."
> - Julius Caesar

To effectively debunk the myths of conventional leadership, we spent a good portion of this book challenging beliefs. Some of these beliefs might have been your beliefs. We observed Julie and Todd's reactions when their beliefs were challenged. You might have experienced similar reactions; we definitely did. Challenge tends to take each of us through some sort of self-discovery process, and it is important we interpret that process correctly.

What does this self-discovery look like? When we encounter a new truth, how do we process it? Arthur Schopenhauer, a German philosopher in the nineteenth century, claimed that upon discovery, a new truth underwent a three-stage process:

- It is ridiculed.
- It is violently opposed.
- It is accepted as being self-evident.

As we stated earlier in this book, our goal was to intentionally challenge your beliefs. It is the only way to create transformational change, and it is the only way to generate impact. Undoubtedly, some of the beliefs that we challenged were both deeply rooted and highly emotional. Unlearning those beliefs will probably cause some pain.

If you never felt jolted or angry while reading this book, then we failed to challenge effectively, and unfortunately, we probably didn't generate much impact. However, if the challenges provoked reactions resembling the stages described above (especially stage two anger), you should be excited. The jolt or anger is a sign that you are somewhere along the journey of processing a new truth.

If you complete the journey and accept the new truth as self-evident, you will find yourself in the company of other legendary leaders. You will also find yourself in the minority, as only the minority of leaders chooses this road.

The *minority* of leaders generate the *majority* of impact.

Only the minority bridges the gap between inspiration and impact. Rejecting Unconscious Competence, they move backward (which is really forward) in the Adult Learning Model, reaching Conscious Competence. Only the minority has the humility, self-awareness, and confidence required to complete the difficult work of unlearning. Only the minority has the courage to embrace conflict and challenge the status quo. But, it is only the minority of leaders who is capable of generating impact. It is only through the leadership of this minority that history is written, and the world is transformed. What about the majority?

The majority of leaders, when faced with the pain of unlearning, moves in a different direction. They wander down the other road—the well-traveled road. The majority is inspired and feels good about the information received. The majority changes what they do. They experience slight behavior modification, but over time, regress back to what is normal and familiar. Lacking real change at the belief level, they are unable to transform who they are. Eventually, habit overpowers intention, and the majority slowly drifts back to Unconscious Competence. The majority finds the journey of truth to be too difficult. Merging with the crowd, they join the ranks of other conventional leaders. Incapable of generating real impact, the leadership of the majority doesn't matter.

Do you want to be in the minority or the majority?

The Infamous Pro/Con List

Although we have consciously challenged conventional leadership throughout this book, we aren't required to purge ourselves of all conventional tools and devices. We don't want to throw the baby out with the bathwater. One such tool that we don't want to discard is the conventional Pro/Con list. When faced with options, it can provide some clarity. Below are lists that highlight the pros/cons—not the summaries—for both conventional leadership and conscious leadership:

Conventional Leadership	
Pro	**Con**
You already know how to do it	You already know how to do it
Everyone else is doing it	Everyone else is doing it
You won't rock the boat	You won't rock the boat
It works – to a limited extent	It works – to a limited extent
Outcomes are easier than beliefs	Outcomes are easier than beliefs
Comfortable/Familiar/Easy	Comfortable/Familiar/Easy
You don't have to change	You don't have to change
Predictable, normal results	Predictable, normal results

We did not make a typo when compiling the Pro/Con list for conventional leadership. The very attributes which are its pro's also comprise its con's. Conventional leadership is all about normal. If you prefer normal and predictable, if you want to do what everyone else is doing, if you are satisfied with the status quo and the current standards, then these attributes should all be considered pro's. If the thought of ordinary and normalcy disappoints and frustrates you, if you want to create transformational change in the lives of others, and if you are not satisfied with your current level of impact, then these attributes are all con's.

Here is the Pro/Con list for conscious leadership:

Conscious Leadership	
Pro	**Con**
Untapped potential	Challenging, difficult, demanding
Unknown capacity	Requires ruthless self-assessment
New journey	Must abandon the familiar (habits)
Real growth and development	Will rock the boat, you will be challenged
Sustainable internal change	Will make you uncomfortable at times
Meaningful relationships with others	Will make others uncomfortable at times
Your success will inspire others	You must change
Consistent, significant impact	Unpredictable, unknown results

Maybe this exercise was helpful; maybe not. Nothing captured in these lists should be a complete surprise; however sometimes it is helpful to write it all down on one sheet of paper.

One word of caution: note the final lines on both of these lists. While the final outcome of conventional leadership is predictable, normal and known, the final outcome of conscious leadership is unpredictable and unknown. These unpredictable and unknown might initially seem daunting, but we would encourage you to embrace them instead of fearing them. By its very nature, transformational change must be both unpredictable and unknown. If an outcome is fully predictable and known, it isn't impactful; it's just normal.

Normal isn't what you really want. As a little kid, you dreamed of being an astronaut, a musician, a professional athlete, or a military commander. None of those professions are typical; they are all unique and exciting. As a kid, you didn't dream that your story would be coring and inconsequential; most kids don't. We "learn" that as we grow up. As a child, you wanted your story to be legendary.

And deep inside, you still do, or you wouldn't be reading this book. Your frustration with the status quo of conventional leadership is proof of your true desires. You want more than conventional leadership is currently offering. Your increasing level of frustration and discontentment with the current state of normal is evidence that you don't want to be a conventional leader. You never did.

But somewhere during your journey, through subtleties and half-truths, myths and fables, conventional leadership confused you. You were tempted to believe the myths of normalcy, routine, and complacency. You raced to climb your ladder, never questioning if it's on the correct building. It's not too late; the journey towards impact can begin right now, and you can start debunking those myths today.

Or you can continue to pursue the status quo, ensuring that the outcomes of tomorrow mirror the outcomes of today. With your leadership rendered powerless by myths and fables, you will lack the ability to consistently generate impact. If you don't debunk those myths, you will never realize your full potential as a leader. It is this unrealized potential that makes this story a tragedy. Instead of creating meaningful change, you can confidently take your place in the middle of the bell curve among the other conventional leaders of history. There, in the 50th percentile, as the epitome of average, you can be the champion of normal and the guardian of the predictable.

However, if you have read this far, most likely you don't define yourself as ordinary, and you probably aren't okay with normal.

The Semi-Conscious Leader

"No great man lives in vain. The history of the world is but the biography of great men."
   - Thomas Carlyle

Before you decide to become a conscious leader, you need to know this: There is no such thing as a semi-conscious leader. The choice to pursue conscious leadership is a binary, polarizing decision. Either you are in, or you are out; there is no middle ground. If you can't—or won't—fully engage and commit to this journey, then, being truthful, we encourage you not to embark at all. You will just get frustrated, and you will frustrate others. Why?

The semi-conscious leader won't get a return on his investment. Consider the original model: "Belief ➜ Behavior ➜ Outcome." The potential to generate impact multiplies as the focus shifts from right to left. But as the size of the return increases, so does the required investment. It is much easier to change what you do than it is to change who you are.

Conscious leadership requires significant amounts of both time and energy. Incrementally improving outcomes is easy. Temporarily adjusting behaviors requires more effort. Impactfully molding beliefs is extremely costly.

Be patient. You won't become a conscious leader overnight, and you can't transform who you are in a week. You can't make the move from Unconscious Competence to Conscious Competence, debunk a host of myths, unlearn old beliefs (charged with emotion), and accept new beliefs within the confines of a 30-day action plan. Implementation and internalization of these new beliefs requires consistent deposits over a long period of time. This is why the decision to become a conscious leader is binary.

You can't try to "time the market" if your goal is to transform who you are. Conscious leadership only yields a positive return on investment (ROI) for the minority—leaders who are long-term investors.

However, assuming you have been qualified you as a long-term investor, what is your initial move? The first and most critical step is the identification of currently held beliefs. Conscious leaders continue to repeat this practice periodically throughout their journey. As we have said earlier, this requires both reflection and introspection. If you didn't complete the exercises from the Conscious Leader's Toolbox at the end of Chapter 2 (My Leadership Journey and the Leadership Philosophy), we encourage you to do that now. It is impossible to realize the vision for conscious leadership without developing your mission for how to get there.

So how do you know what you really believe? It's not that complicated. Look at what you really do. Your behaviors reflect your beliefs. Your actions are determined by your thoughts. Who you are manifests in what you do.

Thus, your first step towards conscious leadership is to look for contradictions between what you say that you believe and what you see that you do. You need to identify inconsistencies between your expressed (verbal) beliefs and your experiential (physical) behaviors. How would your behaviors change if you really believed what you said you believed?

Belief identification is often painful because you won't always like what you find. But when you find inconsistencies between what you say and what you do, don't excuse them; examine them. Then challenge them and change them. If you rationalize those faulty beliefs, you will never be able to repair them.

One Myth Away...

Conscious leadership is about impact, not perfection. This is good news, but it's also bad news.

Here is the bad news: just because you were a conscious leader yesterday doesn't mean that you are a conscious leader today, nor does it guarantee that you will be a conscious leader tomorrow. Who you are can change.

Here is the good news: just because you were a conventional leader yesterday doesn't mean that you have to be one today. Conscious leadership is about transformational change; you can change who you are

This is one of the rare similarities we find between conventional leaders and conscious leaders. They both are only one myth away from changing the power of their impact and transforming who they are. For both types of leaders, the remit is the same: *be conscious of your beliefs.*

All conscious leaders, at some point in time, have believed a myth, accepting it as truth. While it might lessen your impact, it doesn't necessarily disqualify you from being a conscious leader. You just need to identify your beliefs through challenge, expose and debunk the myth, and accept a new truth. Through implementation, you will regain your previous level of impact.

Conscious leaders are not perfect. Who you are is not determined by *if* you fall, but by your reaction *after* you fall.

Conscious leadership demands a premium price but provides a valuable ROI. The currency of both the investment and the yield is the same: transformational change. Changing who you are is a high price and a valuable reward. Is it worth it? It depends on the type of story you want to write.

This is where the road divides. And *now* is when you must make a decision.

Your Story

"Never underestimate the power of a small group of dedicated individuals to change the world. Indeed, it is the only thing that ever has."
 - Margaret Mead

One thing is certain: you know how the story of conventional leadership ends. We all do; we have read it before. It's a normal story.

It stars an unremarkable protagonist. He travels a well-trodden, brightly lit, familiar road towards a fairly common destination. On arrival, he is greeted by a large crowd. Startled by the size of the crowd, he initially feels threatened. However, seeing that they are pretty nice and generally normal, he relaxes. Later, he learns from another traveler (whose name he can't recall) that this location is quite ordinary and commonplace. The protagonist smiles to himself, knowing that he will quickly blend in.

But, your story could be different. It has the potential to be exciting, challenging, and impactful. It could even be legendary, told and re-told by future generations. Your story could fill the pages of history books and be retold around campfires.

As a conscious leader, you write your own unique story. The ending is unknown, and the story isn't typical. In fact, it's *never* been written before.

All leaders write a story. The stories you remember are those of legendary impact. Although these stories are vastly different, they do share one commonality: all of the authors were legendary leaders. A story's impact is determined by the *author*, not the *audience*. Only legendary leaders are capable of writing transformational stories. You will determine the impact of your story.

Be conscious of the story that you are writing, because you only get to write it once. Write it well.

Mirror, Mirror on the Wall...Chapter 13

The Conscious Leader's Toolbox

1. **Questions:** Think about a new concept that you accepted as truth over the past 6 months. How closely did your experience resemble the 3 stages of truth (ridicule, violent opposition, acceptance as self-evident)?

2. **Questions:** Do you really believe that people can change? Can you change? What makes change difficult? What would make change easier? If you could change one thing about yourself right now, what would it be? How can you go about creating that change?

3. **Questions:** Do you tend to think of perfection as a requirement for leadership? Why or why not?

4. **Questions:** Consider the promises of conscious leadership. Which one resonated with you the most? Why?

5. **Challenge:** We have talked the talk, and now we will walk the walk. Visit our website—www.debunkingtheleadershipmyth.com—and give us feedback:
   - What should we <u>start</u> doing?
   - What should we <u>stop</u> doing?
   - What should we <u>continue</u> doing?
   - What did we do really well?
   - What can we do better?

6. **Your Story:** Every leader has a story. Visit the Conscious Leader's Toolbox on our website—www.debunkingtheleadershipmyth.com—and download tools to help you write your story with impact.

Reflection Points

- The road divides, and you must make a decision
- Three stages of truth:
  - o It is ridiculed
  - o It is violently opposed
  - o It is accepted as being self-evident
- Pro/Con list of conscious leadership

Conscious Leadership	
Pro	**Con**
Untapped potential	Challenging, difficult, demanding
Unknown capacity	Requires ruthless self-assessment
New journey	Must abandon the familiar (habits)
Real growth and development	Will rock the boat, you will be challenged
Sustainable internal change	Will make you uncomfortable at times
Meaningful relationships with others	Will make others uncomfortable at times
Your success will inspire others	You must change
Consistent, significant impact	Unpredictable, unknown results

- The ROI of conscious leadership
  - o Expression of value in terms of cost expended
  - o Requires long-term investors
- People can change, even at the belief level
- How you behave reveals what you believe
- Conscious leadership is about impact, not perfection
- All leaders write a story
  - o Normal story or impactful story
  - o Be conscious of your story
  - o Write it well

ACKNOWLEDGEMENTS

The message communicated in "Debunking the Leadership Myth: The Story of Conscious Leadership" represents a unique synthesis of material originating from many disparate sources. These sources include:

- Formal Education
- Experience
- Historical literature
- Observation
- Books/Articles on leadership theory
- Lectures
- Mentors

Although it would be impossible to include an exhaustive list of these sources, we want to specifically acknowledge the following:

The Arbinger Institute. Leadership and Self-Deception: Getting Out of the Box. Berrett-Koehler Publishers. 2010. Second Edition.

Gardner, Howard. Leading Minds: An Anatomy of Leadership. USA: Basic Books. 2011. Second Edition.

Heifetz, Ron. Leadership without Easy Answers. Harvard University Press. 1998. First Edition.

Kotter, John: "What Leaders Really Do." Harvard Business Review; Dec, 2011. Product #: R0111F.

Kouzes, James and Posner, Barry. <u>The Leadership Challenge.</u> Jossey-Bass. 2003. Third Edition.

Maxwell, John. <u>Leadership Gold: Lessons I've Learned from a Lifetime of Leading.</u> Thomas Neslon. 2008. First Edition.

Stanley, Andy. "Andy Stanley Leadership Podcast." Northpoint Community Church. 2011.

Stanley, Andy. <u>The Next Generation Leader.</u> Multnomah Books. 2003, First Edition.

ABOUT THE AUTHORS

Ryan:

Ryan attended Duke University where he received a B.A. in Sociology and a certificate in Marketing. He played baseball for the Blue Devils, and as the team captain, he led the ACC in innings pitched during his junior year. After a brief stint with semi-pro baseball, he founded a non-profit organization for students at Wake Forest University in Winston-Salem, NC. In addition, he coached a high-school baseball team to finish as the North Carolina state runner-up.

In 2008, he received his MBA with a concentration in accounting from The University of Texas at Dallas. He has also received a certificate in Operations Strategy from the Massachusetts Institute of Technology and has received leadership training from The Wharton School of Business.

Ryan has worked in the private sector in a variety of roles and industries. He has held positions in sales, sales leadership, training, and operations. He currently lives in Wayne, PA with his wife Lindsay and their son, Chase.

Jake:

Jake Caines has a broad commercial background spanning multiple industries, specializing in marketing and sales leadership roles. As a lifelong student of leadership, Jake has a passion for providing strategic direction, coaching and mentoring.

Jake's other passion is college football and he is a proud alumnus of the University of Georgia where he received his BBA in Marketing. He has also received an Executive Certificate in Strategy and Innovation from the Massachusetts Institute of Technology.

Jake currently resides in Cumming, GA with his wife Molly and their daughter Zoe.

THE STORY OF CONSCIOUS LEADERSHIP

All leaders write a story.

You are familiar with the legendary stories of leadership: Churchill, Lincoln, Thatcher, Gandhi, and so on. You know of these stories because of the tremendous impact generated by the leaders who wrote them. Leadership that generates legendary impact results in legendary stories. But when we examine today's leadership and the tales of current leaders, we quickly discover that they bear no resemblance to these great stories.

What happened? Plagiarism. The story of leadership has been replaced by a myth, and this myth has devalued and diminished leadership such that it bares only the faintest resemblance to its former self.

Conscious leadership restores leadership to its intended state, where it is once again capable of creating meaningful change and significant impact. One by one, conscious leadership debunks the myths that shackle current leadership.

Conscious leadership isn't another training manual dedicated to telling leaders *what* they should *do*. Instead, it is a transformational mirror showing leaders *who* they could *become*.

What you do flows from who you are. We don't need to learn about better leadership; we need to develop better leaders.

The story of leadership will be determined by the leaders who write it. Legendary stories can only be written by legendary leaders.

What type of story will you write?

www.debunkingtheleadershipmyth.com

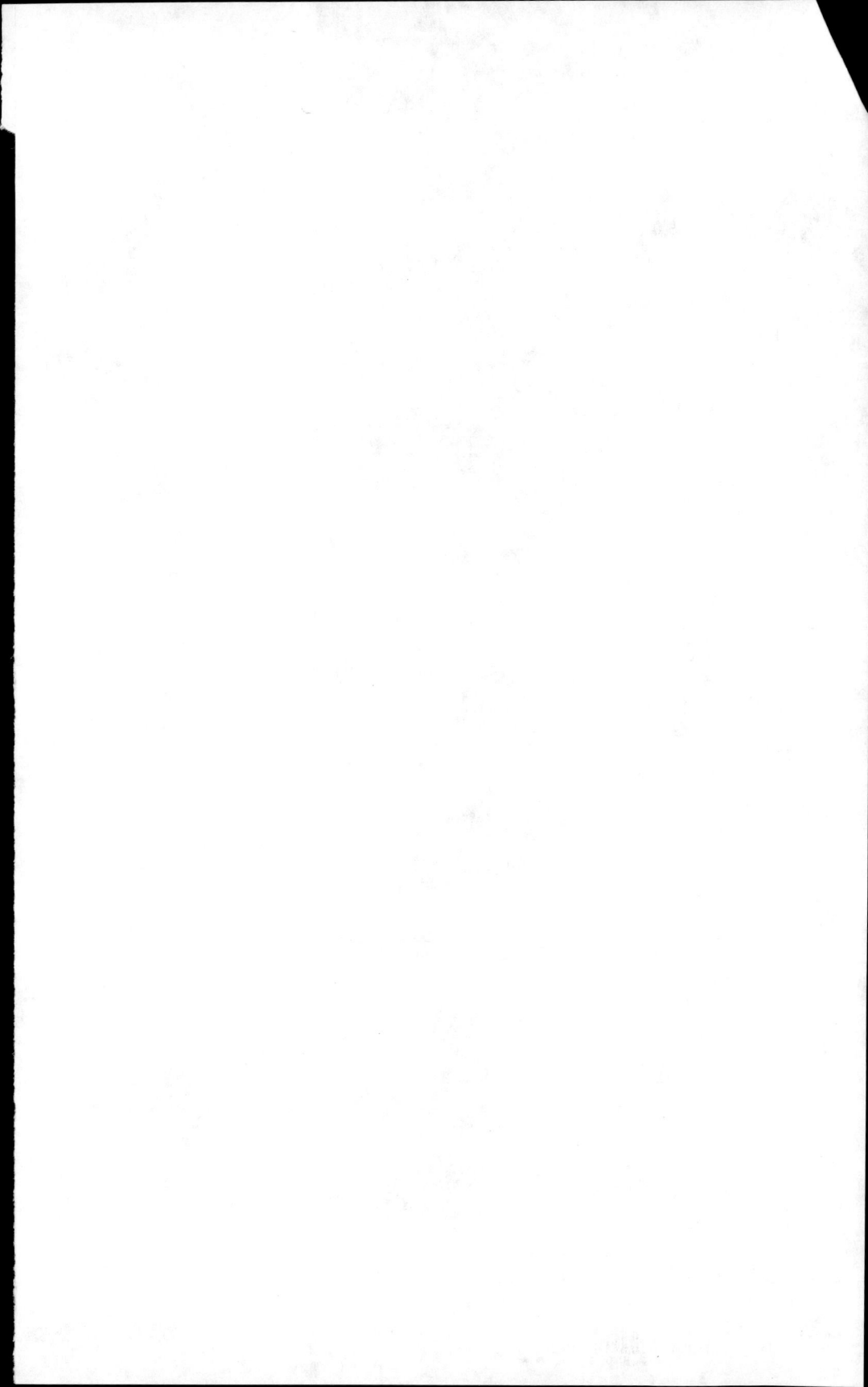

www.ingramcontent.com/pod-product-compliance
Lightning Source LLC
Chambersburg PA
CBHW071625270326
41928CB00010B/1787